How to Do
Everything™

Pages, Keynote & Numbers
for OS X and iOS

About the Author

Dwight Spivey (Mobile, AL) has been a bona fide Macophile for 18 years. He's the author of *How to Do Everything: Mac OS X Mountain Lion* (McGraw-Hill, 2012), *OS X Mavericks Portable Genius* (Wiley, 2013), and many more books on the Mac, iPhone, and Microsoft Office. His technology experience is extensive, consisting of OS X, iOS, Linux, and Windows operating systems in general, desktop publishing software, laser printers and drivers, color and color management, and networking.

About the Technical Editor

Joshua Fleetwood has been taking things apart since he learned to crawl. As he acquired better and better motor skills, he even learned to put them back together occasionally. While actually a superhero, he daylights as a mild-mannered computer technician and photographer in Austin, TX.

How to Do
Everything™

Pages, Keynote & Numbers
for OS X and iOS

Dwight Spivey

New York Chicago San Francisco
Athens London Madrid Mexico City
Milan New Delhi Singapore Sydney Toronto

Library of Congress Cataloging-in-Publication Data

Spivey, Dwight, author.
   How to do everything. Pages, keynote & numbers for OS X and iOS / Dwight Spivey.
     pages   cm
   ISBN 978-0-07-183570-1 (paperback)
   1. Mac OS.   2. iOS (Electronic resource)   3. Operating systems (Computers)
I. Title.   II. Title: Pages, keynote & numbers for OS X and iOS.
   QA76.774.M64S65   2014
   005.4'32—dc23   2014020130

McGraw-Hill Education books are available at special quantity discounts to use as premiums and sales promotions, or for use in corporate training programs. To contact a representative, please visit the Contact Us pages at www.mhprofessional.com.

How to Do Everything™: Pages, Keynote & Numbers for OS X and iOS

1 2 3 4 5 6 7 8 9 0 DOC DOC 1 0 9 8 7 6 5 4

ISBN   978-0-07-183570-1
MHID   0-07-183570-9

Sponsoring Editor	**Technical Editor**	**Production Supervisor**
Roger Stewart	Joshua Fleetwood	George Anderson
Editorial Supervisor	**Copy Editor**	**Composition**
Janet Walden	Bill McManus	Cenveo Publisher Services
Project Manager	**Proofreader**	**Illustration**
Tania Andrabi,	Susie Elkind	Cenveo Publisher Services
Cenveo® Publisher Services	**Indexer**	**Art Director, Cover**
Acquisitions Coordinator	Karin Arrigoni	Jeff Weeks
Amanda Russell		**Cover Designer**
		Jeff Weeks

For Mamaw, Papaw, Mom, Aunt Linda, Uncle Gary, and Uncle Randy

Contents at a Glance

Contents

Acknowledgments

Roger Stewart, you have been too good to me, my friend. Thanks for yet another opportunity to work with and for you.

Thank you so much, wonderful agent of mine, Carole Jelen.

Thanks to Amanda Russell and Tania Andrabi for taking turns driving this bus and keeping it on the road.

Joshua Fleetwood, thank you kindly for taking a break from your superhero duties to help with the technical editing. Did you ever find your missing cape?

Much appreciation to Bill McManus and Janet Walden for their editing prowess as well.

Finally, I sincerely thank all who have had a hand in bringing this book from my MacBook Pro to bookshelves everywhere!

Introduction

Congratulations! You're about to discover how much simpler being productive is when Apple leads the way! Word processing, presentations, and spreadsheets are approached in a refreshing way with Apple's iWork suite, which consists of Pages, Keynote, and Numbers, and this book will be your guide to getting up and running with them.

Why This Book?

Almost anyone who's touched a computer in the last couple of decades has created a document with a word processing application. Many of those people have also sweated over loads of data with a spreadsheet application, or have put together slides to display in front of audiences (large or small) using a presentation application. Many different applications have been offered to help users handle these three tasks—some of which do so very well, and others not so much—but all have seemed to make each of the tasks more difficult than they needed to be.

Apple to the rescue! This book is intended to introduce you to Apple's way of performing these tasks, which is (of course) as intuitive and fun as computer geeks can possibly make them. If you've ever worked with documents, presentations, or spreadsheets, you owe it to yourself to check out the iWork suite before going back to the old standbys.

How Is This Book Organized?

I've divided this book into four parts to help you, dear reader, navigate between the topics that interest you at any particular time.

Part I covers what each app in the iWork suite can help you accomplish, and gives you a brief overview of features that are common to each of them. It also helps you understand what iCloud is and how it is used in conjunction with iWork.

Part II gives you the inside scoop for Pages, Apple's answer to the word processing world. Creating and sharing documents, adding and editing text, placing images and shapes, and commenting and highlighting items are just some of the items discussed.

Part III handles the task of explaining how to build slide presentations with Keynote. You'll learn how to choose a template for your presentation, manage and insert multimedia into slides, play your presentations for an audience, and much more.

And finally, Part IV guides you through the sometimes daunting task of working with spreadsheets using Numbers. Importing and exporting spreadsheets into various supported formats, printing spreadsheets, building formulas into your cells, displaying information using charts, and many more options are covered here.

You can read the chapters in any order you like, but I strongly suggest reading Chapter 1 first because it covers some of the barest of basics, which are referred to in later chapters.

It's my sincere hope that you'll find the iWork suite to be as productive and fun as I do, and that this book is more than an introduction, but a doorway to working better, simpler, and smarter.

PART I

Introducing Productivity, the Apple Way

1

A Brief Overview of Apple's Productivity Software

HOW TO...

- Understand Apple's way of being productive
- Learn what Pages, Keynote, and Numbers can do for you
- Discover common features of each app based on platform
- Navigate compatibility and other potential problems
- Find further help

By now, the world knows that Apple's way of doing things is often the best way. When you think of Apple and their products, you think of simplicity, form *and* function, and unparalleled user-friendliness. You already know that when it comes to creativity, Apple is hands down the best in the computing biz at providing an experience that nurtures the creative mind.

What about the productive side of us Mac users? For years, another giant in the computing world has held sway when it comes to being productive on the Mac, in terms of word processing, creating presentations, and building spreadsheets. Certainly, Apple could turn its collective software genius toward creating a better way to perform these tasks—an Apple way, as it were—right? The answer to that question, dear reader, is a resounding "yes!," and in this chapter, you'll get a bird's-eye view of this "Apple way."

Why Be Productive the Apple Way?

Apple has always been seen as the "anti-Microsoft," so when they first introduced their suite of productivity apps, iWork, some were put off by the notion. Hardcore Microsoft Office users simply snickered at the idea of using Apple software to conquer their productivity needs, while others kicked the tires but didn't take to it, wishing to continue doing things the way they always had. However, as Apple began including the iWork apps (Pages, Keynote, and Numbers) with every Mac purchased, more and more folks began to not only use them, but prefer them. The interfaces of the apps were so much more intuitive than those from Microsoft, and if you could use one of them proficiently, you could very quickly adapt to using the others.

Another interesting thing happened that opened the door for the iWork apps to new users: Apple created versions of them for their insanely popular iPad. As the iPad began to gain popularity with businesses, so too did Apple's suite of productivity apps. You see, even as of this writing, Microsoft has yet to produce an iPad-ready version of their Office suite of apps, leaving the field wide open for Apple. Even though compatibility between the OS X (Mac) and iOS (iPad) versions of Pages, Keynote, and Numbers left much to be desired, some compatibility was better than none at all.

In 2013, Apple introduced new versions of their iWork apps, and this time compatibility between the OS X and iOS versions was of paramount concern. Apple now offers not only near-identical versions for the Mac, iPad, and iPhone in terms of functionality, but a web-based version of them as well (through Apple's iCloud), further extending the iWork apps to non-Apple computer users. Suddenly, Joe could begin a document on his Mac at home, edit it on his iPad while taking the train to the office, and, once in the office, further revise the document after logging in to his iCloud account via a web browser on his Windows-based work PC. In effect, Apple has now completed the productivity circle, making their way of productivity the simplest and most intuitive on the market.

Is Apple's way of handling productivity the best way for you? There's only one way to find out—try it! Since Apple is literally giving away their iWork suite with every Mac, iPad, and iPhone purchased on or after October 1, 2013, there's no good financial reason not to dip your toes in the water, if not take the plunge entirely. It's my hope that this book will be your go-to guide for getting to know this wonderful set of apps, and that you'll soon be spreading the good news about the Apple way of doing things.

For more information on getting the iWork suite of apps for free, please visit www.apple.com/creativity-apps/mac/up-to-date/.

Referencing Microsoft Office Applications

Dear Reader: Since many of you are very likely familiar with Microsoft's Office suite of applications, I'll frequently be making comparisons to some of the applications contained within it (specifically Word, PowerPoint, and Excel), in order to give you a bit of a reference point as to what the apps in Apple's iWork can do in relation to what you're used to. Those of you who are not familiar with Microsoft Office (lucky!) will still be able to follow along quite nicely, as I'm assuming that this is a first foray into productivity apps for some of you. What's that? Oh! You're quite welcome!

Where to Get the iWork Apps

All three iWork apps (Pages, Keynote, and Numbers) can be downloaded from the App Store. The App Store is available on the Mac in OS X and on iPads and iPhones running iOS.

In OS X, click the Apple menu in the upper left corner of your screen and select App Store. Once in the App Store, type **iWork** or the name of the app in the search field in the upper right corner of the App Store window and press RETURN to find the apps. Select the app to install it on your Mac.

In iOS, find the App Store icon and tap it (where it's found is entirely up to where you've placed it on your device). Once in the App Store, type **iWork** or the name of the app in the search field found in the upper right corner of the screen and tap Search on the onscreen keyboard. Tap the name of the app and install it to use it on your iPad or iPhone.

What Does Pages Do?

Pages is Apple's entry into the world of word processors. Word processing applications have been around for a long time, and almost everyone who's used a computer since the 1980s has used a word processing application at some point. These applications allow you to put your thoughts into words, the white square on your computer's screen acting as digital paper to your keyboard's digital ink. Word processors have varied from the most basic to the quite feature-rich, and Pages definitely falls into the latter category, as does Microsoft's Word. However, Pages separates itself from the rest of the word processor pack by virtue of its elegance, ease of use, and simple yet powerful approach to performing tasks that seem like pure drudgery on others of its kin. You'll come to see that these features aren't unique to Pages in the iWork suite, as Keynote and Numbers boast the same beautiful interface and intuitiveness.

Pages is much more than a word processor, though. Pages is very capable of page layout, enabling you to incorporate images, graphics, and creatively use fonts and colors to build beautiful documents, such as brochures and fliers. While Pages isn't meant to replace true heavy-duty page layout apps like Adobe's InDesign or Quark's QuarkXPress, it is quite capable of producing gorgeous output in its own right.

Here are just a few of the things you can do with Pages at your command:

- Easily drop images and other graphics into your documents. You can even align them simply and accurately with little effort, giving your documents a super-appealing look and feel.
- Share your documents with others easily and quickly, whether they (or you) are on a Mac, using an iPad or iPhone, or on the Web using a non-Mac computer (unfortunately, sometimes it happens) and iCloud.

Image courtesy of Apple Inc.

- Import documents created by folks who use Microsoft Word. You can also export your documents into Word format.
- Get off to a fast start when creating documents using the beautiful templates that come with Pages.
- Change the look and feel of an entire document in an instant using Pages' preset styling options.
- Type a document. Yep, if you want it that simple, you got it.
- Utilize built-in coaching tips, which help guide you in the right direction when you're in the middle of a fever-pitched word processing session.
- Edit documents and make comments with uncanny ease.
- Write the next bestselling ebook and become an Internet sensation! (In case you're wondering, Pages can indeed export your entire document in ePub format, which is the default ebook format.)

Check out Chapter 3 to get started with Pages. Yes, you have permission to skip ahead if you wish.

What Does Keynote Do?

Keynote is to Microsoft PowerPoint what Pages is to Word: Apple's (fantastic) answer to creating knockout presentations. For years PowerPoint has been the de facto standard of presentation-creation applications, but Keynote has caught the eye of many a presentation-giver since its release. Keynote first began as software used by Apple co-founder Steve Jobs to build his world-famous Macworld Expo keynote address presentations, and eventually made it to the masses in January of 2003.

As part of the iWork suite of apps, Keynote handles its tasks with the same elegance, simplicity, and power as its word processor and spreadsheet cousins. If you've created presentations with PowerPoint, you'll be pleasantly and quickly at home with Keynote.

Here are a few of the things you can do with Keynote:

- PowerPoint-compatible presentations can easily be imported and exported.
- The included themes designed by Apple can help you kick-start your presentation, or start from scratch and build your own impressive "preso" (cool business lingo for *presentation*).
- The format panel puts all the tools you'll need to build your presentation within easy reach, so you won't have to go menu hopping to make things just right.
- Like Pages, turning on Keynote's coaching tips gives you instruction and direction on the fly.
- Emphasis builds, which are slight—but attention-getting—animations, accentuate important objects in your presentations without taking away from your main message.
- The Presenter Display feature allows you simple and intuitive control over your presentation, with your audience being none-the-wiser.
- Interactive charts will wow even the most bored onlooker, and give your presentation that extra little SNAP that brings attention to your points.
- As with all things iWork, sharing a presentation with others is as simple as sending a link to it via Mail (OS X's and iOS's default email program), Facebook, Twitter, and/or Messages (Apple's messaging system, native to both OS X and iOS).

Chapter 6 is where we get rolling with our presentation of Keynote (get it?... presentation... Keynote...), so mosey on over if you want to get a jump-start learning the best presentation software out there.

What Does Numbers Do?

Ah, spreadsheets. How the world does love its spreadsheets. We use spreadsheets for everything from the company budget to the family grocery list, from lists of military supplies to lists of the world's greatest athletes and their accomplishments. Well, Numbers is what we've all wished the leading spreadsheet application (yes, I'm looking at you, Excel) was, and is powerful yet easy to use and understand. And let's not forget beautiful. Yes, your spreadsheets don't have to be simple, drab documents, but they certainly can be if simple and drab is your style (and there's nothing wrong with that, mind you).

So, just how does Numbers help you get the items in your life organized? Here are a few features to whet your appetite:

- Let's face it: Excel is the most widely used spreadsheet application around (for now), so the ability to work with it seamlessly is a must for those of us who have to work in corporate life. Luckily, like Pages and Keynote, Numbers is extremely adept at not only importing and working with Excel-formatted spreadsheets, but also creating them. Sharing spreadsheets with others is just as simple as it is with the other iWork apps, too.
- As I said, if you want simple and drab spreadsheets, you can certainly have them. But Numbers is also quite adept at turning your spreadsheets into near works of art with gorgeous charts and graphics built right in. Tables and other staples of spreadsheets can be customized to suit your tastes and needs with ease.
- Utilize one of more than 30 different templates to get you started.
- Numbers also benefits from having coaching tips built right in, giving you help as you go about the business of putting together a great spreadsheet.
- The functions browser is a wonderful tool for seeing the built-in mathematical functions offered to Numbers users. Use it to find the functions you want to use, as well as see examples of each.
- A neat function of Numbers is that when you select a group of cells, Numbers shows a list of quick calculations near the bottom of the screen. Simply pick the calculation you want to use (more on this great feature later).
- Animated charts help you spot fluctuations in your spreadsheets data. They also look great.
- iCloud integration allows you to view, create, share, and edit spreadsheets across multiple types of devices.

Image courtesy of Apple Inc.

We begin our exploration of Numbers in Chapter 9; feel free to jump on over if you feel the need.

Common Interface Features, Based on Platform

Apple has seen the wisdom of going multi-platform with iWork, and that is a very good thing for all involved. As mentioned, iCloud allows you to create, view, and edit a file on several different types of devices. Macs running OS X (Apple's operating system for their superb lineup of computers) and devices running iOS (such as iPads and iPhones) are afforded native versions of each of the iWork apps. Computers and devices running alternative operating systems with access to the Internet can also go to www.icloud.com, where they can use web versions of Pages, Keynote, and Numbers.

Each app has its own set of very unique features, of course, but there are also other interface features that are common to every app, which helps keep the learning curve a little less curvy and the familiarity a little more familiar when moving from one app to the other. In this section, we'll take a look at the interface features common to all the apps, but we'll divide them based on the platform the apps are running in. This way, you'll know where items are before you even need them.

Please note that in the following sections I'll just briefly introduce what each feature does; I'll go into much more detail for most features in later chapters.

OS X

OS X (in case you're unfamiliar, the X is the Roman numeral, not the letter) is the best computer operating system on the planet, hands down; if you don't believe it, just ask me. I've used the latest and greatest versions of each operating system for years, and there is simply no experience like OS X. Every Mac on the planet comes preloaded with OS X, so if you've got a Mac, rest assured that you've got OS X.

The iWork apps are most at home on OS X, and that's where you'll find they are at their most robust. While the iOS and iCloud versions of each app are feature-rich, you won't find everything in them that you'll find in the OS X versions—yet!

Figure 1-1 shows a typical toolbar containing features common to each of the iWork apps (common features are highlighted). Table 1-1 lists the features and provides a brief explanation of each.

FIGURE 1-1   Highlighted items are features common to each of the iWork apps in OS X.

TABLE 1-1   Features Common to Pages, Keynote, and Numbers in OS X

Feature	Description
View	Click to show items like the ruler, comments, word count, find and replace, or thumbnails.
Zoom	Zoom in or out of the document by using the selections in the pop-up button.
Table	Click to choose a table style from the pop-up menu.
Chart	Click to choose a chart style from the pop-up menu.
Text	Allows you to modify the characteristics of your document's text.
Shape	Click to choose a shape from the pop-up menu.
Media	Use this button to insert photos, music, or movies from your Mac's collection of multimedia.
Comment	Click to place a comment box at the area of the insertion point (cursor).
Share	This button lets you send a link to your document that others can access via iCloud, or you can send a copy directly to them through Mail, Messages, or AirDrop.
Tips	Click this button to initiate the onscreen help. These instructions can help get you around in your app and understand what certain features are capable of.
Format	Click to open the Format bar on the right side of the app's window. The Format bar allows you to make adjustments to elements in your document; what options appear depends entirely on what type of element you've selected.
Full screen	Click the two small arrows in the upper right corner of the toolbar to open your document in full screen mode.

iOS

In case you haven't guessed by now, in my humble opinion, if it has an Apple logo on it, then it has to be the best *whatever* (computer, mobile device, etc.) that it is. When you first turn on your iPad or iPhone, you will see an Apple logo. Since what you're seeing is the launch of iOS (Apple's operating system for its mobile devices), the Apple logo automatically brands iOS as being the best of its kind (again, in my humble opinion).

Apple recently revamped the iOS versions of the iWork suite of apps to better work with their OS X and iCloud compadres. Apple also wanted to make sure that when you move from app to app, you can quickly find your bearings through common interface features, enabling you to get around easily within each app.

Figure 1-2 displays the common features of the iOS versions of the iWork apps, and Table 1-2 gives a quick rundown of what they accomplish.

FIGURE 1-2   Common features of each iWork app, according to their iOS versions

TABLE 1-2   Features Common to Pages, Keynote, and Numbers in iOS

Feature	Description
Undo/Redo	Tap to undo the previous action, or hold and select Redo to restore the action.
Format inspector (paintbrush icon)	Tap to open the Format menu, which allows you to make adjustments to elements in your document. Available options depend on the type of element you've selected in your document.
Add (+ icon)	Tap to add items to your document. Elements to choose from include photos, tables, charts, and shapes. You can also adjust textual elements from this menu.
Tools (wrench icon)	Some options are specific to the app being used, but others, such as Settings, Set Password, and Print, are common to each app.
Share (square with upward-pointing arrow)	This button lets you instantly share your document with others via iCloud, Mail, iTunes, and other options. You can also choose to open the document in another app on your device.
Coaching tips (? icon)	Tap this button to initiate the onscreen help.

iCloud

iCloud is the new kid on the block when it comes to the iWork apps. As a matter of fact, as of this writing, the iWork apps are still considered to be in beta (as evidenced by the little yellow flag in the upper right corner of each one), which just means that Apple is still working on making them the best apps they can be. Don't let the beta tag fool you, though; these apps are still quite capable, especially for a web-based product.

Figure 1-3 shows the toolbar in Numbers, which is largely representative of what you'll see in Pages and Keynote for iCloud, in terms of features. Table 1-3, like its predecessors, tells you briefly what each feature is capable of handling for you.

FIGURE 1-3   Features common to the iCloud versions of each iWork app are highlighted.

TABLE 1-3   Features Common to Pages, Keynote, and Numbers in iCloud

Feature	Description
Format panel (not pictured in Figure 1-3)	The format panel can be found on the right side of the app's window. It allows you to make adjustments to elements in your document; the available options depend on what type of element you have selected.
Zoom button	Zoom in or out of the document by using the selections in the pop-up menu.
Undo/Redo	Select Undo to undo the previous action, or click Redo to restore the action.
Table	Click to choose a table style from the pop-up menu.
Text	Allows you to modify the characteristics of your document's text.
Shape	Click to choose a shape from the pop-up menu.
Image	Select and then click the Choose Image button to add an image from your computer.
Share	This button lets you instantly share your document with others via a web link.
Tools	Some options are specific to the app being used, but others, such as Download a Copy and Print, are common to each app.
Feedback	Click to send your feedback to Apple regarding the particular app you're working in.

Compatibility and Other Potential Issues

Of course, we all know what THE major question one has before using new software to do the jobs they're used to performing with other titles: "Is it compatible?"

Compatibility is rightly no small concern. You get this great new software that everyone's raving about, you go to open one of your mainstay documents, and—WHAM!—all of a sudden the text looks like something off of a 1940s vintage typewriter and the images make van Gogh's work look like that of a Realist. At this point, the blood begins to rapidly boil and thoughts of tossing your computer out the window are (temporarily) entertained.

To prevent this from happening to you (and possibly to your Mac and other innocent bystanders), Apple has provided quite a courtesy: a website that details each and every supported and unsupported feature when it comes to each iWork app and its kin in the world of Microsoft Office. And before you ask, yes, the list is limited to Microsoft Office. Other productivity suites are simply not in competition with the iWork apps on a broad scale, and as I've already stated, Microsoft Office is currently the alpha suite when it comes to productivity. Most businesses have used Microsoft Word, Excel, or PowerPoint at some time (and most of them always have), so in order for Apple to make any waves in the productivity suite universe, compatibility is of utmost concern. You can find the compatibility list, the top of which is shown in Figure 1-4, at www.apple.com/mac/pages/compatibility/; select the tab of each app to see its particular list.

FIGURE 1-4   Apple's website has a complete and up-to-date list of Microsoft Office compatibility issues.

Tip Pages is akin to Word, Keynote to PowerPoint, and Numbers plays nice with Excel. You can go right to the list you need by inserting the name of the appropriate app into the "pages" area of the link I provided. For example, instead of www.apple .com/mac/pages/compatibility/, you could type www.apple.com/mac/keynote/ compatibility/ and jump right to the PowerPoint to Keynote compatibility list. Bookmark the page if you plan to return to it frequently.

Where to Go for Help

Even the most seasoned of us needs help every now and again, so there's no shame to ask for it when necessary. There are multiple ways to get help with Pages, Keynote, and Numbers, and you're holding one of them in your hands. Apple graciously provides the other methods of acquiring help; they want you to know how to use their products so that you'll be more able and ready to share the good news of them with others in your sphere of influence.

Note You will need Internet access to get the help I speak of in the remainder of this chapter, with the exception of the onscreen coaching tips that are provided in-app.

Built-in Help

It should go without saying that I am writing this book in hopes that it will be your main source of instruction for all things iWork, but what if you don't have this book handy (the horror!)? Luckily, Apple has that issue (somewhat) squared away, too; they've included a handy help section and other tools in each version of the iWork apps, so you're never too far away from help when needed.

Getting Help in OS X

You can gain Apple's insight into their OS X versions of iWork by clicking the Tips button (looks like a yellow circle containing a ?) in the toolbar. When you click the Tips button, the coaching tips appear in the app's window, pointing out various landmarks and offering a description of them.

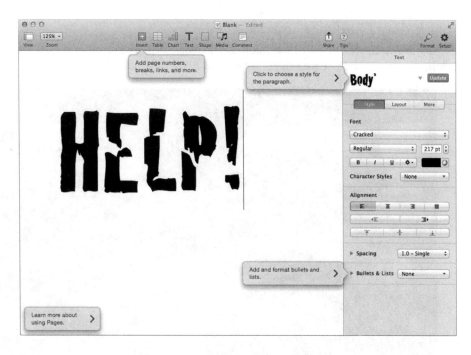

One particularly interesting coaching tip can be found in the lower left corner of the app window when tips are on: it's called "Learn more about using *App Name*" (*App Name* is, of course, the name of the app you're using). Click this tip to open the *App Name* Help window, and click the "visit *App Name* Help" link to open the app's Help manual in your default web browser. Use the menu on the left side of the screen to browse for the topics that interest you.

Finding Guidance in iOS

Once you're within an iOS version of an iWork app, you can tap the coaching tips icon in the upper right corner of the screen to turn on tips.

To access the full version of Help for the app in question, look to the lower left of the screen (with coaching tips turned on) and you'll see the "Learn more about using *App Name*" tip, just as in the OS X apps. Tap this tip to open the Help window for your app. From the Help window you can browse by topic or you can search for something particular by tapping the search icon (looks like a magnifying glass) and entering the search term in the field provided. Tap Done in the upper right of the Help window to return to your app.

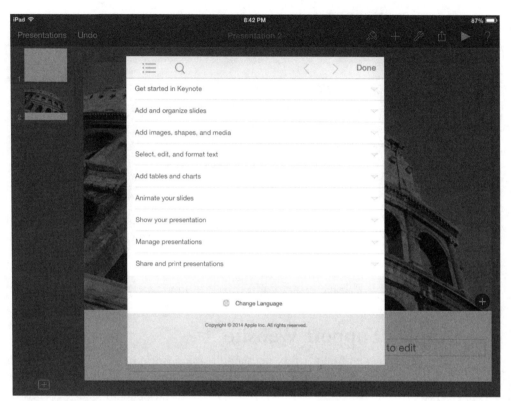

A Helping Hand Within iCloud

The iCloud apps may still be in beta, but don't think for a moment that Apple's forgotten to provide help here, too. As a matter of fact, the Help is quite robust for an app that's still considered to be in beta, but that's a good thing now, isn't it?

Unlike the OS X and iOS versions, Help can't be accessed directly within your working window; you'll need to get there from the main iCloud window. When you're working in a document within iCloud, iCloud opens a new browser window for it.

So, from the main iCloud window, click the coaching tips button (as in OS X, a yellow circle with ?) to turn tips on, then select Get Help from the coaching tips menu.

This action whisks you away to the Help window, where you're free to browse the topics (via the menu on the left) or search for something you need (the magnifying glass icon in the upper right).

Apple's Support Website

One more place to find a safety net when leaping from the iWork cliff is Apple's famous Support site. Apple is quite well known for providing excellent customer support, and their Support website is the first line of said support.

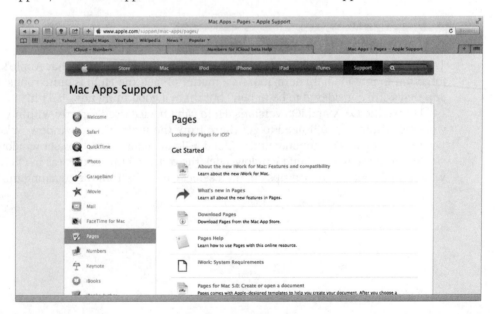

The main Support site can be reached by going to http://support.apple.com, but if you want to go directly to the support site for one of the iWork apps, just enter the following into your browser's URL (address) field:

Pages	OS X	www.apple.com/support/mac-apps/pages/
	iOS	www.apple.com/support/ios/pages/
Keynote	OS X	www.apple.com/support/mac-apps/keynote/
	iOS	www.apple.com/support/ios/keynote/
Numbers	OS X	www.apple.com/support/mac-apps/numbers/
	iOS	www.apple.com/support/ios/numbers/

These links don't just provide the standard Help; you can see the latest available software downloads, support articles pertaining to the particular app, links to the Support Communities for the app (online communities of other users where specific questions are posted and answered), and more!

Note Of course, if you're one who prefers to do things the old-fashioned way—speaking to real people—you can always call Apple's Tech Support at 800-275-2273, or visit your friendly neighborhood Apple Store.

Summary

You're now well versed in the "whys" of being productive the Apple way, and you've gotten your feet wet with each of the apps in their various configurations. We also dabbled a bit in how to get help beyond the little ditty you're currently reading from. At this point, we simply need to begin our exploration of iWork; it'll be a fun ride—promise!

2

What Is iCloud?

HOW TO...

- Understand what iCloud is
- Discover the different aspects of iCloud
- Set up an iCloud account

One would be forgiven if, upon hearing of iCloud for the first time, they began to wistfully imagine a place where angels can merrily listen to their iPods, make calls on their iPhones, and surf the Web on their Macs. As serene as this scene is, I must burst that bubble for you; however, iCloud may yet be the closest thing to digital heaven for many of us. Before I can explain iCloud, you need to understand another term first: *cloud computing*.

Cloud computing is best understood as the use of remote network servers that are utilized for managing, processing, and storing digital data. Typically, these servers are computers that are accessed via the Internet, but can also be within a company's local area network (LAN) or wide area network (WAN). Cloud computing gives you the ability to access your work from multiple devices (computers, tablets, smart phones, etc.) and multiple locations (usually anywhere you have an Internet connection). For example, if you download a song from Apple's iTunes Store, you can save that song to iCloud, where you can then access it on your Mac, your iPhone, or your iPad. The usefulness of such a concept is immediately recognizable, and the first time someone is successfully able to use this kind of service is likened to a kind of epiphany.

Image courtesy of Apple Inc.

iCloud is cloud computing done Apple's way, and it is a nifty service that offers the user many features and advantages. Want to know one of the best features (if not THE best) of iCloud, though?

It's free.

That's right—I used the four-letter "f" word: free.

Sounds kind of cool, huh? But what does iCloud have to do with helping you be productive? Well, if you read Chapter 1 you probably can take some educated guesses, but we'll delve a bit more into the reasons in this chapter.

This chapter isn't intended as an iCloud tutorial. I simply want to familiarize you with iCloud so that you know how to get started with it and understand what it's capable of, not only in regard to the suite of iWork apps, but to your overall Apple user experience.

A Quick Look at iCloud's Features

So, up to now you're thinking to yourself, "Self, this iCloud thingy sounds pretty good, but I wonder what all it does? It can't do too much, right? I mean, after all, it's free!" Well, curb your judgment and hang on to your keyboard! We're going on a ride into the iCloud!

Once you log in to iCloud (as described later in the chapter), you'll be presented with the Home screen, shown in Figure 2-1. From here, you can quickly navigate (or soar, if you prefer) to the individual features contained within iCloud.

Mail

Perhaps the most universally useful feature is iCloud's appropriately named email program, Mail. Mail in iCloud is very similar to Mail in OS X and iOS, and plays

FIGURE 2-1   iCloud's Home screen is where you get started after you log in.

extremely well with both. As a matter of fact, if you use your iCloud email account (more on how to get one later in this chapter) with all of your devices, everything you do in one version of it will automatically show up in other versions. For instance, if you add a folder to your account while logged in to Mail for iCloud, the same folder will appear in your OS X and iOS versions of Mail almost instantly.

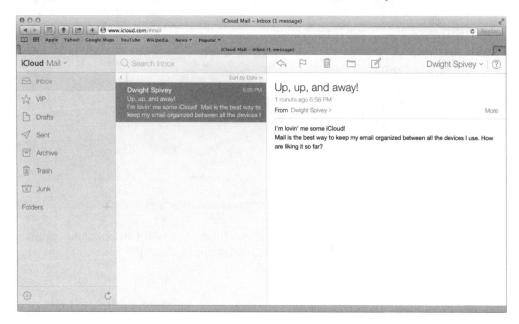

There are also no worries if you're a Windows PC user who utilizes Microsoft Outlook for your email program. Mail for iCloud will synchronize automatically with Microsoft Outlook 2007 or later.

 You must have OS X version 10.7.5 and higher on your Mac and iOS version 5 and higher on your iPad, iPhone, or iPod touch to properly use iCloud accounts with Mail.

Contacts

Now you won't have to worry about not having the address for Aunt Faye or the phone number for Uncle Gary when you're away from your Mac: you've got an iCloud account and you've synchronized all of your contacts across all of your devices!

Contacts for iCloud is your one-stop shop for all of your contacts. Once you set up an iCloud account, you can sync contacts from every device you use the account with. Contacts are then stored in iCloud, and from that time forward you'll have every contact you've ever created available to you, regardless of which device you happen to have handy. You can create new contacts, delete contacts, edit contacts, add contacts to groups, and more, and it will all instantly synchronize across platforms.

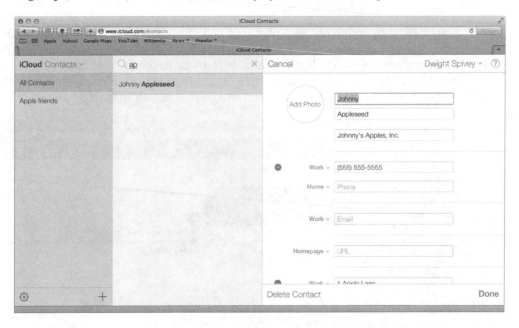

Again, PC users need not fret; if you have Microsoft Outlook 2007 or newer, your contacts will be synced with your iCloud account, as well.

Calendar

You're probably beginning to notice a pattern develop by now, having learned a bit about Contacts and Mail for iCloud. Both apps are as connected as both ends of a rope to your devices running OS X and iOS; making changes in one version of them immediately affects the other versions. Rest assured, this pattern continues throughout iCloud's offerings, and Calendar is (thankfully) no exception.

Calendar for iCloud works seamlessly with Calendar for OS X and Calendar for iOS. If you create an event in one of them, it is bound to show up in the others, as it should. You'll never have to worry about transferring your calendar from your phone to your computer again, or vice versa. iCloud handles all of that for you, and does it completely behind the scenes to boot. You can also easily share your iCloud calendars with others from within iCloud or your other supported devices.

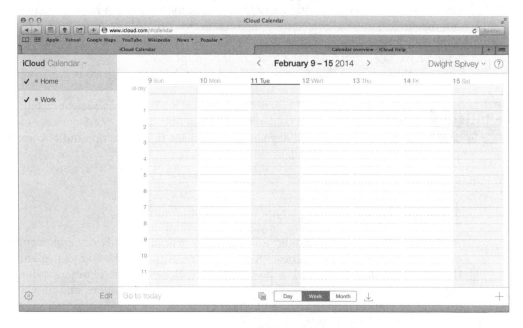

Once again, Microsoft Outlook 2007 and higher is supported with Calendar for iCloud for Windows PC users, so iCloud will sync your important dates just as it does for Mac users. All together now: "Thank you, Apple!"

Notes

We've all done it. From the deepest recesses of your mind springs a thought that, until now, no mortal human has ever conjured. You know this thought will change the world as we know it—for the better, mind you—but you're scared to near-death that you'll forget it before you get home. You scramble in your car's glove compartment for a scrap of paper and some kind of writing utensil, stumbling across an old envelope and one of your children's crayons. In a burst of energy and wonder, you scribble your paradigm-shifting idea onto the envelope and exhale a sigh of relief. You then place the envelope in a super-secret compartment of your briefcase and feel an overwhelming sense of peace, knowing your idea is safe until you arrive home.

You then promptly forget about your idea because someone in front of you almost runs your car off the road. Months later, you accidentally toss the idea into the trash when hastily cleaning out your briefcase before you have to catch your flight, consequently depriving humanity of what would have surely been the next step in our evolution as a species.

Please allow me to speak for the rest of humankind when I say "thanks—a lot," and with no small amount of sarcasm, I might add.

Now, imagine you were an iCloud user, and you had your trusty iPad or iPhone handy when this monumental thought struck home. You could have quickly whipped out the device, opened the Notes app, jotted down this Idea of Ideas, and it would have been instantly synced in iCloud. Within months, statues bearing your likeness would have been erected in the four corners of the world.

Yes, Notes can do that for you. Oh, and it can keep up with your grocery list, too.

 Caution Microsoft Outlook users, please be aware that while you can see your iCloud notes in Outlook, you should only edit them from a Mac, an iOS device, or within iCloud in a web browser. Any changes you make to them within Outlook won't be synchronized with iCloud.

Reminders

Remember the planners we older folks used to carry around? Every appointment we could schedule was listed in those planners, our entire months and year planned to the hilt. Reminders for iCloud is the digital equivalent of those planners. Whatever appointments or to-do lists you have can be loaded into Reminders, and they will show up on all of your Mac, Windows, and iOS devices.

 Note PC users rejoice: Reminders will synchronize with the Tasks app in Windows, assuming you have the iCloud control panel installed on your computer (more on that in a bit).

Find My iPhone

Find My iPhone is one great feature. Enabling this little bit of inspiration on your iPhone, iPad, Mac, or iPod touch allows you the ability to find it in the event that it's lost or stolen. One thing to remember, though: the device does actually have to be turned on in order for this feature to work.

Find My iPhone lets you

- Find the location of your Mac or iOS device on a map.
- Play a sound on your Mac or iOS device to help you locate it.
- Use Lost Mode to lock and track your iOS device or Mac.
- Remotely erase your information from the Mac or iOS device.

Another wonderful feature is Activation Lock, only available with iOS 7 or later. Activation Lock requires someone to enter your Apple ID and password before they can use your device.

For more information on Find My iPhone, please visit www.apple.com/icloud/ find-my-iphone.html.

This tool won't work for Windows-based computers, but Windows users can still use iCloud to track their iOS devices or Macs using the Find My iPhone for iCloud app in their favorite supported browser (Internet Explorer 9 or later, Firefox 22 or later, or Chrome 28 or later).

Now, if only Apple would come up with a Find My Keys app....

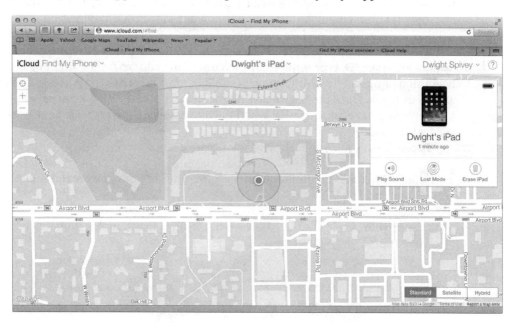

Pages, Keynote, and Numbers

The whole reason iCloud is mentioned in this book is, of course, because of its inclusion of the web-based versions of the iWork suite apps: Pages, Keynote, and Numbers. As I mentioned in Chapter 1, these apps are in beta as of this writing, but they are very functional and worth your time. Apple has also provided you an opportunity to weigh in with your opinion of each app, using the Feedback feature found in the toolbar of every document you work on in iCloud.

I'll be covering tasks that you can perform in the iCloud versions of these apps in the upcoming chapters. Don't worry if a feature you'd like to use in the iCloud versions isn't available yet; it may well be soon, as Apple is updating the iCloud, iOS, and Mac versions of these apps at a pretty good clip.

Begin Using iCloud

Now that you've got a good handle on just what iCloud can provide you in terms of functionality, allow me to show you how to get started with this gift of cloud computing goodness.

Creating an iCloud Account

To get started you'll need an iCloud account, also known as an Apple ID. An Apple ID is your key to unlocking all things Apple. You can use it to log in to iCloud, to purchase items on the Apple Store or iTunes Store, and more. You may already have an Apple ID from when you first purchased your Mac or iOS device, and if so, all you need to do is enable iCloud on your device.

If you don't have an Apple ID, though, let's put first things first and get one. To acquire an Apple ID, type **appleid.apple.com** (don't add "www." or anything else to the beginning of this address) into the URL field of your favorite web browser and press RETURN or ENTER. Once the page loads, all the links are there to help you get an Apple ID.

Once you have an Apple ID, you'll need to associate it with your devices so they sync with iCloud.

To associate your Apple ID with your Mac:

1. Click the Apple menu in the upper left corner of your screen and select System Preferences.
2. Once System Preferences opens, click the iCloud icon.
3. Enter your Apple ID and password in the appropriate fields, then click the Sign In button.

4. Decide whether to enable the options for using iCloud for mail, contacts, etc., and for Find My Mac, then click Next. If you're not sure, uncheck both options; you can revisit these options at a later time.

5. Check the box next to Documents & Data to use iCloud with Pages, Keynote, and Numbers. Click the Options button to the right of Documents & Data and check the boxes next to Keynote, Numbers, and Pages. All other options are up to you, but those options are outside the scope of this book, therefore I'm unable to advise you on them.

6. Close System Preferences when you finish setting up iCloud.

To associate your Apple ID with your iOS device:

1. Open the Settings app.

2. Select iCloud from the Settings menu on the left of the screen, enter your Apple ID and password in the appropriate fields, and tap Sign In.

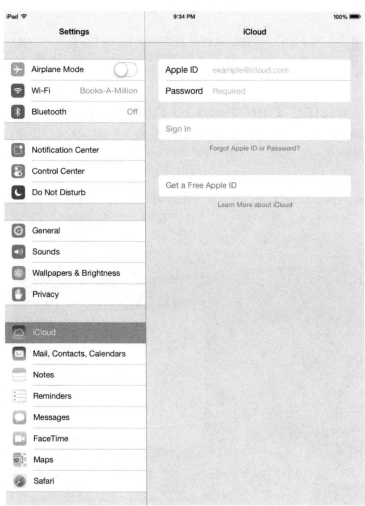

3. Once signed in, you'll be prompted whether to merge your data with iCloud. This is, of course, entirely up to you. If you're unsure, tap Don't Merge; you can always come back and change these settings later.

4. After deciding to merge your data or not, you'll be asked if iCloud can use the location of your iPad. Again, this is entirely up to you and outside the scope of this book. If you're not sure, tap Don't Allow and decide later.

5. You'll notice that lots of options, such as Mail, Contacts, and the like, are enabled. Yet again, all of those are beyond the scope of our little tome, so whether to enable or disable them is at your discretion. However, if you want to use iCloud with Pages, Keynote, and Numbers, you'll need to enable that feature. To do so, tap Documents & Data, and then tap the sliders next to Keynote, Numbers, and Pages to enable each of them.

You are now ready to roll as far as setting up your devices for the purposes of this book. Anything you do with Pages, Keynote, and Numbers on your Mac or iOS device will be synced automatically with iCloud.

For help with setting up your Windows-based PC, or even your Apple TV, with your iCloud account, please visit www.apple.com/icloud/setup.

Accessing Your iCloud Account

Now that you're set up with an Apple ID, or iCloud account, you can easily access iCloud via any supported web browser on a Mac or a Windows-based PC:

1. Open your browser.
2. Type **icloud.com** into the URL field and press RETURN or ENTER. If you have trouble, try adding "www." or "https://www." to the beginning of the address.

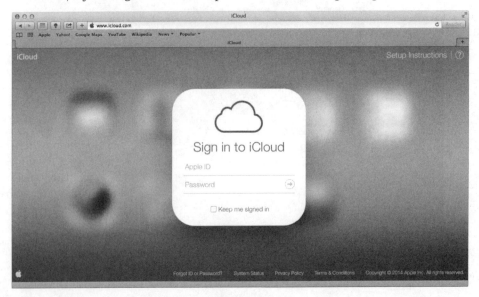

3. Type your Apple ID and password into the appropriate fields and press RETURN or ENTER.
4. Once the Home screen appears, click an app to use its features.

 Make sure you're able to access and fully utilize iCloud by understanding its system requirements. To see system requirements for your device, go to http://support .apple.com/kb/HT4759 from within your favorite web browser.

Summary

iCloud is the way of the future when it comes to managing, sharing, and using our digital information, and it's especially handy when it comes to being productive in the world of Apple. You're now set up to use iCloud and experience Pages, Keynote, and Numbers to their fullest extent. To learn more about iCloud itself, visit www .apple.com/icloud.

PART II

Word Processing and Page Layout, the Apple Way

3

Pages Basics

HOW TO...

- Navigate the interface of each version of Pages
- Set preferences to work the way you like to
- Work with your documents
- Add, edit, and format text
- Work with various parts of your document, including headers, footers, styles, and more

Well, you've heard quite a bit from me in the first two chapters about how great and marvelous the iWork suite of apps is, and now it's time for me to put up or shut up. In this chapter, I'll take our first venture into one of the apps, Pages, and you'll become more familiar with the Apple way of being productive.

Pages is more than a word processor: it's a way to make your text stand above the fray. Pages is deceptive in its simplicity, almost lulling you into a false sense of absence of power and functionality. Can Pages do anything and everything that someone would want a word processor to do? Well, honestly, no. But then again, no product on the market can promise that. While one word processor may have more functions, more functions doesn't necessarily translate to better usability. Also, what works for you may not work for me. As with everything, it comes down to a matter of need and taste. Some folks place more importance on having every possible tool available to them (even obscure ones they most likely will never use and probably have never used before) than on truly enjoying their user experience. Others would rather enjoy working with their apps and documents, while knowing that every last thing in the entire world that a word processor has ever been thought of as being able to do is simply not available, and most likely will not ever be necessary to them (or those they may share documents with).

I hope you fall into the latter camp, and will come to know Pages as not only a word processor, but a friend. A friend who helps you put together truly beautiful documents! It's never a bad thing for your creations to look better than everyone else's, unless they happen to be that of your spouse or boss (or worse, if they're both); you're on your own with that one, partner.

Getting Around in Pages

When a chef tries to work in a kitchen that's not his own, he needs to be shown where he can find the essential tools he needs to whip up something wonderful, and the same concept applies with an app you're not familiar with. Sure, you might know what all the little doodads and buttons are for Word's Ribbon feature, but you're not in Microsoft-land anymore. Let's kick off this chapter by exploring how to navigate Pages' interface so that you are better equipped to access its plethora of features.

Figure 3-1 affords a bird's-eye view of Pages from within OS X. This figure serves more as a map than a tutorial; we'll be going over how to use each of the landscape features as we go through this book, so no worries. You were given a brief explanation of many of these features in Chapter 1. As a reminder, other than Insert and Setup, all items in the Pages toolbar are also present in the Keynote and Numbers toolbars.

 The contents of the Format bar will change depending on the element you've selected in the document. If you select an image, image formatting options will appear; should you select text, text-related options show up, and so forth.

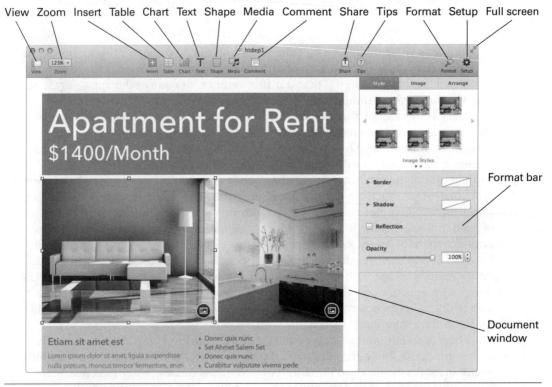

FIGURE 3-1 The layout of the land, as far as Pages in OS X goes, anyway

Figure 3-2 is a good representation of what the same document looks like when opened in Pages for iOS.

If you read Chapter 1, you already have a general knowledge of each of the toolbar features called out in Figure 3-2, except Documents, which I didn't cover because it's specific to Pages. If you tap Documents in the upper left corner, you'll be taken from the document you're presently working in to a list of documents you've previously worked with.

 Most screenshots I'll show throughout this book from iOS apps will be in landscape mode. I point this out only to put your mind at ease should you wonder why my screenshot might look slightly different from what you're seeing (aside from document content, of course) if you happen to be viewing your iOS device in portrait mode.

Figure 3-3 displays the same document again, but this time within iCloud's version of Pages. You'll note that the document and its contents remain the same throughout all versions. As a matter of fact, while writing this I had the document

FIGURE 3-2   The same document, as seen in iOS Pages

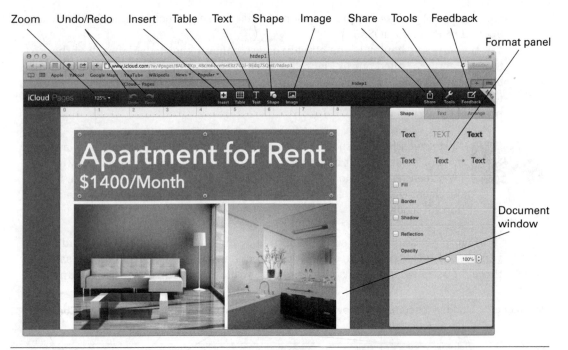

FIGURE 3-3 Pages documents look the same in iCloud as they do in iOS and OS X.

open in all three versions at the same time, and any changes I made within one version were automatically pushed to the others. I told you this was all pretty cool.

Setting Pages' Preferences

We all have our unique styles and ways we like to do things. As much as Apple would love for us to do everything the way they recommend, they at least give us some leeway as individual users for some of the options in Pages. These options are called preferences, and I'll show you how to set preferences within each version of Pages.

 If the same preference option is available within multiple versions of the app, you'll need to set the option in each version of the app in order for it to be consistent across platforms. Being logged in to iCloud doesn't mean you can set a preference in OS X, for example, and have the same preference changed automatically in iOS.

OS X Preferences

Let's look at preferences in OS X Pages first. To open the preferences, press ⌘-, or for those who are new to the Mac, press the COMMAND key and comma key simultaneously.

You could also click the Pages menu in the upper left of your screen (to the immediate right of the Apple menu) and select Preferences. Once the Preferences window is open, you have the option of selecting either the General tab or the Rulers tab.

The General tab of Pages' Preferences window is shown in Figure 3-4. From here, you can make several adjustments, such as:

- **For New Documents**   Select either Show Template Chooser or Use Template as the default action when you begin to create a new document. Selecting Show Template Chooser does just what it says, and selecting Use Template will automatically create a new document from a template you choose by clicking the Change Template button and selecting it from a location on your Mac.
- **Editing**   This section lets you set default actions for editing a document:
  - **Automatically detect lists**   Check this box to have Pages detect when you are typing a list. When a list is detected, Pages automatically formats it as such.
  - **Curves default to Bézier**   Check this box for curves to be Bézier curves by default, or leave it unchecked to use smooth curves.
  - **Show suggestions when editing table cells**   When this box is checked, Pages will offer advice to you based on information in other cells of the same column.

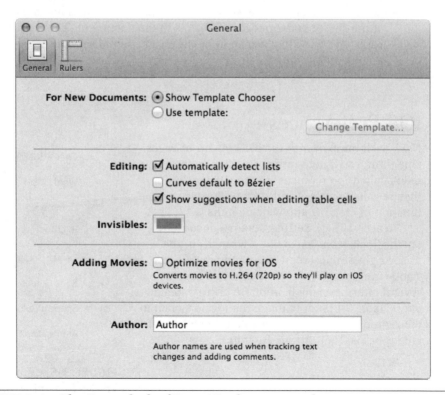

FIGURE 3-4   The General tab of Pages' Preferences window

- **Invisibles**   Every document contains invisible elements (such as line breaks) that don't appear in final output but can be helpful to see onscreen when working within the document, such as to format it. Click this box to set the default color for such elements when viewing them.
- **Adding Movies**   Check the Optimize Movies For iOS box when you want to add a movie to your document and it will be viewed by folks using iOS devices.
- **Author**   Add a name to use when tracking changes and making comments within a document.

The Rulers tab offers options for helping you decide where to place items within your document:

- **Ruler Units**
  - Click the pop-up menu to select a default unit of measurement.
  - Check the Show Size And Position When Moving Objects box to see an onscreen prompt that shows you exactly that.
  - Check the Enable Vertical Ruler For Documents With Body Text option to display a ruler on the left side of the document window when rulers are being shown.
- **Alignment Guides**
  - Click the box to select a default color for alignment guides.
  - Check the box to enable, or uncheck to disable, the options for showing guides at the center and/or edges of objects in the document. These guides make it easier to correctly place an item within the boundaries of the document and among other items in it.

iOS Preferences

Next, we'll jump over to the iOS version of Pages. One thing you'll note rather quickly: preferences aren't called "preferences" in the iOS version; they're called Settings, but they perform the same function of creating app-wide defaults.

To access these Settings, open a document, tap the Tools icon (looks like a wrench) in the upper right of the screen, and then tap Settings. The Settings menu, shown in Figure 3-5, gives us several offerings, which are more clearly spelled out in Table 3-1. Simply touch the toggle switch to the right of each option to enable it (toggle turns green) or disable it (toggle is white).

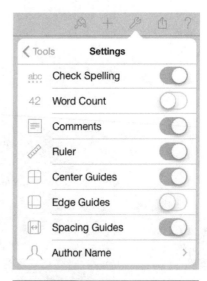

FIGURE 3-5   Preferences are known as Settings in Pages for iOS.

TABLE 3-1 Available Options in Settings for iOS Pages

Option	Description
Check Spelling	Enable to allow Pages to check your spelling as you type (more on this in Chapter 5).
Word Count	Enable to display a running count of words in your document at the bottom of the screen.
Comments	Enable to show comments in a document.
Ruler	Enable to show horizontal and vertical rulers in your document.
Center Guides	Enable in order to see guides when one item's center aligns with another item's center, or with the center of the page.
Edge Guides	Enable to see guides when an item's edges align with another item's edges.
Spacing Guides	Enable to see when three or more items are equally spaced apart on a line.
Author Name	Tap to enter a name into the available text field that will be used when tracking changes made to a document or when adding comments.

iCloud Preferences

As with its mobile cousin, Pages for iOS, Pages for iCloud also refers to its preferences as Settings. There is only a handful to cover, as shown in Figure 3-6, so let's get to it:

- **Show/Hide Format Panel** Select to show or hide the format panel on the right side of the screen.
- **Check Spelling** Select to enable or disable automatic spell checking.
- **Center Guides** Select to see guides when one item's center aligns with another item's center, or with the center of the page.
- **Edge Guides** Select to see guides when an item's edges align with another item's edges.
- **Spacing Guides** Select to see when three or more items are equally spaced apart within a line.
- **Set Password** Select to add a password for the document you're currently working in.

Changes made to Settings in Pages for iCloud only hold while the document is open, with the notable exception of Set Password. If you close the document and reopen it, you'll notice the Settings have reverted to their defaults.

FIGURE 3-6 Pages for iCloud offers several options for setting your defaults.

Working with Documents

Now that we've got the lay of the land in each of our versions of Pages, it's time to actually use this word processing wonder! Over the course of the next few pages, you'll learn how to tackle some of the most basic, but at the same time some of the most important, tasks in Pages. You'll thank me later.

Creating New Documents

It simply doesn't get more basic than creating new documents, and it's a cinch to do in all three versions.

To create a new document in Pages:

- **OS X** Choose File | New or press ⌘-N to open the Template Chooser. Select a template for your new document and click Choose in the lower right corner.
- **iOS** From within the Documents manager (if you're in a document already, simply tap Documents in the upper left corner to get to this screen), tap the Create Document icon to open the Template Chooser. Tap the template you want to use and it will open automatically.
- **iCloud** From within the iCloud Pages screen, click the Create Document icon to open the Template Chooser. Select the template you want to use, as illustrated in Figure 3-7, and click Choose in the upper right corner of the Template Chooser window to open it.

FIGURE 3-7   Opening the For Rent Flyer template in Pages for iCloud

Saving and Renaming Documents

Creating documents without saving them is typically a colossal waste of time, but hey, that's just one man's opinion, right? Well, for those readers who are of the same mindset, let's see how we go about saving our creations. While we're at it, we'll also take a look at how to rename documents.

- **OS X**   Press ⌘-s or choose File | Save to save a document. If this is the first time saving this document, the Save As window will open. Simply give the document a title, choose a location in which to keep it, and click the Save button. To rename a document, choose File | Rename, type the new name for your document (the document title in the middle of the window will be highlighted blue, in case you're wondering where your changes are appearing), and press RETURN; your document is now renamed.

If the location you want to keep the document in isn't in the pop-up menu, click the small square containing the downward arrow next to the Save As field to expand the window and your options.

- **iOS** Pages automatically saves your documents, but it doesn't give them a name other than "Blank" or "Blank 2," so you'll be more than a little glad for the ability to rename documents with ease. Open the Documents manager and tap the name of the document you want to rename. Enter the name of your document in the field provided in the Rename Document screen and tap Done on the keyboard.

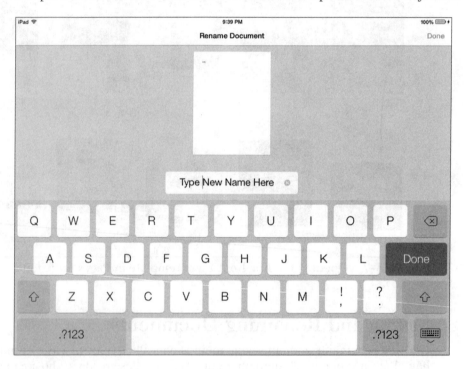

- **iCloud** Pages for iCloud automatically saves your documents, but like iOS you start off with names like "Blank." Thankfully, it's just as simple to rename the new document. Open the Documents manager, select the name of the document you want to rename, enter said name in the field provided, and press RETURN.

Opening Existing Documents

Creating new documents is a snap, and so is opening documents that already exist.

OS X

Opening documents that exist within iCloud or on your Mac itself is quite easy:

1. Press ⌘-o or choose File | Open.
2. Select iCloud or On My Mac in the upper left corner of the window, depending on where the document is located.

3. Click once on the document you want to open, and then click the Open button in the lower right corner of the window to open it. Of course, you can also double-click a document within the window to skip the last small step.

 Choose File | Open Recent to see a list of documents that you've recently opened in Pages. Just click the document in the list to open it.

iOS and iCloud

Opening an existing document is performed in the same way for both iOS and iCloud versions of Pages. Simply open the Documents manager and select the document you want to open (you'll need to double-click the document in iCloud).

Using Passwords and Locking Documents

Security is a pretty serious thing to some folks, and Pages affords those of us who want to keep our little secrets to ourselves the options to do just that. Using a password to prevent those who don't know it from changing a document is one option, and locking a document to prevent any tinkering with it at all is another.

Using Passwords

A password is a very secure way to protect your document from prying eyes and from others who might accidentally change its contents. Once a password is assigned to a document, no one can open it, much less change it, without knowing the password.

James Bond uses Pages as his default word processor, don't you know? Now, if we could only get M. on board...

 Both the OS X and iOS versions offer you a way to have Pages remember a document's password so that you don't have to enter it every time you open the document. If you want to truly be secure with your documents, using these options isn't the best idea (James Bond certainly doesn't).

To assign a password to a document:

- **OS X** Choose File | Set Password to open the password dialog. Enter the password in the Password and Verify fields, enter a hint in the Password Hint field if so desired (Apple recommends it, but I don't), and click the Set Password button.
- **iOS** Open the document, tap the Tools icon, and tap Set Password. Enter the password in the Password and Verify fields, enter a hint in the Password Hint field if so desired (Apple recommends it, but again, I don't), and tap the Go button on the onscreen keyboard (or Done in the upper right corner of the window).
- **iCloud** Open the document, select the Tools icon, and then click Set Password. Enter the password in the Password and Verify fields, enter a hint in the Password Hint field if you like (Apple recommends it, but still, I do not), and click the Set Password button.

To open a password-protected document, simply type the password when prompted. If you don't know the password, you're just out of luck, my friend.

Locking Documents

Locking prevents anyone from editing, renaming, moving, or deleting a document. Know, however, that locking a document is an option that's only available within the OS X version of Pages.

To lock a document:

1. Hold the mouse pointer over the title of the document (it must be open in Pages to be locked) until you see a small gray arrow next to it; click the gray arrow.
2. Select the Locked check box to lock the document. Click outside the window to return to the document. Whenever you try to change an element of the document, you will be reminded that it is locked.

 While locking is a good thing to do to prevent a document from being changed accidentally, it isn't nearly as secure as protecting a document with a password. You can still delete a document by ignoring the warnings given you by OS X if you try to do something so foolhardy, and you can easily unlock a document by simply unchecking the Locked box in the title bar.

Moving Documents to and from iCloud

Moving your documents to iCloud makes them available to yourself and others anywhere you (or they) can connect to the Internet with a computer or iOS device. Moving documents away from iCloud has the exact opposite effect, as you might gather. This nifty little trick is for the OS X version of Pages only, I'm afraid.

To move a document from your computer to iCloud, or vice versa:

1. Choose File | Move To.
2. Select a location from the pop-up menu. If you don't see the location you want in the menu, choose Other at the bottom of the menu to browse your hard drive.
3. Click the Move button. Your document will be physically moved, not copied, from its old location to the one you specified.

Sharing Documents with iCloud

If your mother was like mine, she always taught you to share, which is a good thing. Apple has taught Pages to share, as well, and it, too, is a good thing. Pages allows you to share a document with anyone by sending them a link to the document, which is located in iCloud.

 Be sure to password-protect your document before sharing it (as detailed earlier in this chapter) if you only want authorized users to make changes to it. If you just send a link to an unprotected document, anyone with access to the link can make whatever changes they see fit. Imagine the brouhaha had Bill Gates pasted little Windows Vista logos all over one of Steve Jobs' famous Macworld keynote speech slides. The horror...

As stated, when you share a document via iCloud, you are essentially sending a web link to the document's location within iCloud. Anyone with Pages (either on a Mac, an iOS device, or a Windows PC using iCloud) will be able to click the link and open (and edit) the document. Any changes they make will be saved to the document. This system can be either collaboration at its finest or calamity at its most calamitous; did you remember to password-protect your document?

By the way, the links can be sent through email, Messages, Twitter, Facebook, or any other method you can think of to get the link to your intended recipient.

OS X

To share a document via iCloud from OS X Pages:

1. Open the document you want to share. Protecting the document with a password is recommended.
2. Click the Share button in the toolbar.

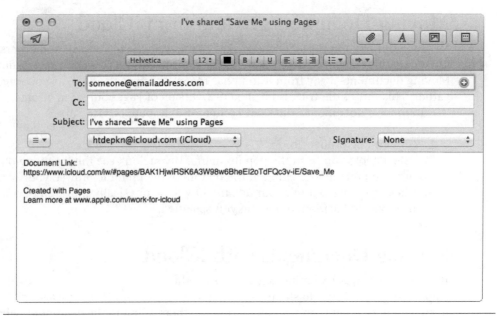

FIGURE 3-8 Sharing a document link from OS X's Mail app

3. Select the method you want to use to share the iCloud link to your document using the Share Link Via iCloud context menu. Figure 3-8 shows an email in which I am sharing a document via OS X's Mail app; notice the link in the email's text? This is the same link that will be sent using either of the other sharing methods, too.

Once the link is sent to the recipient, take a look at the Share icon in the toolbar. You'll notice it's changed from the white box with the upward arrow to a couple of oddly colored people. Those green goblins are simply showing you that the document is now being shared.

Click the Share button when in shared mode to do the following:

- Change the password for the document by using the Change Password button.
- Discontinue sharing of the document by clicking the Stop Sharing button.
- Send the link to someone else by clicking the Send Link button and selecting a method from the pop-up menu.
- Hold your mouse pointer over the link until you see a gray button called Copy Link, click the Copy Link button to copy the link to your Mac's clipboard, and then paste the link into any document or sharing mechanism you feel is appropriate.

iOS

To share a document via iCloud from iOS:

1. Open the document you want to share. Protecting the document with a password is recommended!
2. Tap the Share button in the toolbar.
3. Tap the Share Link Via iCloud option. Decide which method you want to use to share the iCloud link to your document. You'll notice that AirDrop is another method of sharing that can be utilized from an iOS device in order to share the link with other iOS devices.

 AirDrop sharing isn't currently supported for exchanging files from OS X to iOS devices or vice versa. Hopefully, this will change in the near future, but as of this writing it's unsupported.

You'll note that the Share icon has changed to our green guys, as it does in the OS X version of Pages. Tap the Share button when in shared mode to do the following:

- Change the password for the document by tapping Change Password.
- Discontinue sharing of the document by tapping Stop Sharing.
- Send the link to someone else by tapping Send Link and selecting a method from the pop-up menu.
- Tap the link to prompt a dark gray button called Copy, tap the Copy button to copy the link to your device's clipboard, and then paste the link into any document or sharing mechanism you like.

iCloud

To share a document via iCloud from within Pages for iCloud:

1. Open the document you want to share. Again, protecting the document with a password is recommended, if it isn't already.
2. Click the Share button in the toolbar, and then click the blue Share Document button.

3. A window opens that declares "This document is shared." From within this window, you can perform the following tasks:

      • Change the password for the document by using the Change Password button.
      • Discontinue sharing of the document by clicking the Stop Sharing button.
      • Send the link to someone else via iCloud's Mail app by clicking the Email Link button.
      • Click the link once to highlight it, press ⌘-C (Mac) or CONTROL-C (PC) to copy the link to your computer's clipboard, and then paste the link into any document or sharing mechanism you need to use.

To access the "This document is shared" window again, click the Share button in the toolbar (it's those green folks, again), and then click Settings.

Exporting and Importing Documents

Exporting and importing sounds like quite a cool occupation, but it has nothing to do with this book whatsoever in the context of shipping exotic goods, so I digress.

Exporting a document from Pages in one of our contexts means to save the file in a format other than the native one, which is .pages. The other context we'll be working with when talking about exporting is when transferring files from an iOS device to a computer through iTunes.

In most cases, importing documents is as simple as opening them when working with Pages. Importing documents also has a slightly different context in this book, and like exporting, it has to do with transferring files from iTunes onto your iOS device.

Exporting Files from Pages

Pages is a bit like a Swiss Army knife in that it can export files to multiple formats so they can be viewed and worked with in other apps.

OS X To export a document using Pages for OS X:

1. Open the document you want to export, if it's not open already.
2. Click the File menu and hold your mouse pointer over the Export To menu.

Export Your Document

| PDF | Word | Plain Text | ePub | Pages '09 |

☑ Require password to open [Change Password]

This document's password will be used for the Word file. To set a different password for the Word file, click Change Password.

▼ Advanced Options

Format: [.docx   ⬍]

(?)   [Cancel] [Next...]

FIGURE 3-9 Make selections according to the file format you are exporting to.

3. Select the format you want to export your file to.
4. When the Export Your Document window opens, make any selections you deem necessary according to the format you are exporting to, as shown in Figure 3-9.
5. Click Next.
6. Choose a location to save your new file, give it a new name if you like, and then click Export to complete the process.

Note File formats supported for export from Pages for OS X are PDF, Word, Plain Text, ePub, Pages '09, and ZIP. Formats supported by Pages for iCloud include PDF, Word, and Pages.

iCloud   There are two ways to export a document using Pages for iCloud: from within an open document and from within the Documents manager. We'll take a gander at both now.

To export from within an open document:

1. Choose Tools | Download A Copy.
2. Select the format you want to export your file to.
3. Once Pages finishes formatting the document, it will automatically download to your browser's default downloads folder.

To export from within the Documents manager:

1. Click one time on the document you want to export so that it's highlighted.
2. Click the Document And Sort Options button (looks like a gear) at the top of the window and select Download Document from the menu.
3. Click the format you want to export your file to.

4. Once Pages finishes formatting the document, it will automatically download to your browser's default downloads folder.

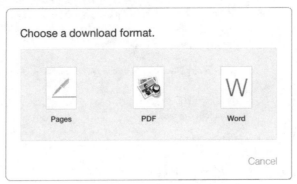

 This section of the chapter only deals with exporting files into non-native formats from the OS X and iCloud versions of Pages, because iOS doesn't support such a feature.

Importing Files into Pages

Non-native file formats supported by Pages include Pages '09, Word, PDF, ePub, and Plain Text. As noted earlier, importing a file into Pages is as simple as opening it, which for Pages in OS X is as simple a task as opening any other file:

1. Press ⌘-o or choose File | Open.
2. Select iCloud or On My Mac in the upper left corner of the window, depending on where the document is located.
3. Click once on the document you want to open, and then click the Open button in the lower right corner of the window to open it. You can also double-click a document within the window to open it.

However, you must actually get a file into Pages for iOS and Pages for iCloud before they can make the attempt to open them, and that leads to our discussion on transferring files using iTunes.

Transferring Files to and from Pages with iTunes

iTunes is everyone's favorite digital music and video store, jukebox, and tool for synchronizing our iOS devices with our computers, but it also has the ability to transfer files to and from Pages on said iOS devices. This little trick is especially handy when you don't use, or have access to, iCloud but still need to work on your documents via a computer.

To transfer files to Pages for iOS from iTunes:

1. Connect your iOS device to your computer and open iTunes on said computer.
2. Select your device in iTunes (it will show up in the upper right of the window) once it appears.
3. Select Apps in the toolbar at the top of the window and then scroll to the bottom of the window.
4. Click Pages in the Apps list under File Sharing.
5. Click the Add button in the lower right and then browse your computer for the file you want to transfer. Once found, select it and then click Add. The file will show up in the Pages Documents list.
6. Open Pages on your iOS device.
7. Go to the Documents manager and click the + in the upper left corner; select Copy From iTunes.
8. When the Copy From iTunes window opens, tap the name of the document you want to transfer into Pages on your iOS device. Once the transfer is complete, the document will appear in the Documents manager and can be opened with a simple tap.

To transfer files from Pages for iOS to iTunes:

1. Connect your iOS device to your computer and open iTunes on the computer (not the iOS device).
2. Select your device in iTunes (it will show up in the upper right of the window) once it appears.
3. Select Apps in the toolbar at the top of the window and then scroll to the bottom of the window.
4. Click Pages in the Apps list under File Sharing.
5. Open Pages on your iOS device and do one of the following:
   • If the document you want to transfer is not open, tap the Share button in the upper left of the screen (looks like a square containing an upward-pointing arrow) and select Send A Copy from the menu. Tap the document you want to transfer to highlight it.
   • If you are working in the document you want to transfer, tap the Share button in the upper right of the screen and select Send A Copy from the menu.
6. Tap the iTunes icon to open the Send To iTunes window.

7. Tap the file format you want to use for the document. Once the transfer is complete, the document will appear in the Pages Documents list in iTunes. Select the file, click the Save To button in the lower right, select a location in which to save the file on your computer, and click the Save To button.

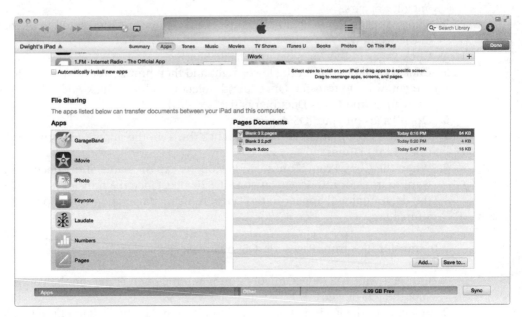

Printing Documents

Remember the dream that we once called "the paperless office?" Well, I think even the most die-hard digital nuts would agree that we're still quite a long way from that coming to pass. Honestly, I like a little paper in my office; it has the effect of keeping me from forgetting I still have work to do.

Printing documents from Pages is pretty straightforward, so let's get down to business, shall we?

OS X

To print documents from Pages for OS X:

1. Press ⌘-SHIFT-P or choose File | Page Setup to open the Page Setup sheet, and then do the following:
   a. Set the Format For menu to the printer you want to send your document to for printing.
   b. Select the desired Paper Size, Orientation, and Scale options, and then click OK.

2. Press ⌘-P or choose File | Print to open the Print dialog sheet, and then do the following:

   a. Select the printer you wish to send the print job to in the Printer pop-up menu.

   b. Make any other selections you deem necessary, such as the number of copies to print or whether to print two-sided (if your printer supports such a feature).

   c. Click the Print button in the lower right corner to send your job along to the printer.

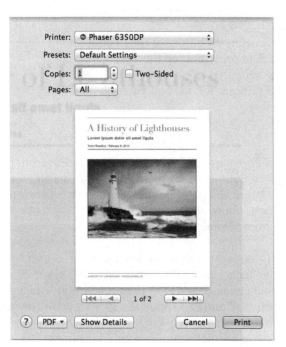

Tip If you don't see some of the options you need in the Print dialog sheet, it could be that they are hidden. Click the Show Details button in the lower left of the sheet to see a cornucopia of options not available in the standard dialog, including options specific to your printer. For more information on printing from OS X, I would suggest picking up a book that specializes in instruction of the OS.

iOS

Printing from Pages in iOS is even easier, since there's not much to tinker with in terms of options (it's pretty much print and be done with it).

Note You must have a printer set up to print with your iOS device already. Teaching you how to do this is outside the scope of this book, but you can find more information at http://support.apple.com/kb/HT4356.

To print from Pages in iOS:

1. Open the document you want to print.
2. Tap the Tools icon in the upper right and tap Print in the menu.
3. Tap Select Printer if the one you need isn't already selected. Browse the list of available printers and tap to select the one you wish to use.
4. Decide how many copies of the document you want to print and tap the + or – button correspondingly.
5. Tap the Print button to send your job on its merry way.

iCloud

Printing from Pages for iCloud is a wee bit different from printing from Pages for OS X or iOS based on the fact that Pages for iCloud can only print PDFs. Also, the PDFs generated by Pages will print directly from your browser or your computer's default PDF application, not straight from Pages itself.

To print from iCloud:

1. Open the document that you wish to print.
2. Click the Tools icon in the upper right and select Print.
3. Pages will generate a PDF of your document. Once the PDF is generated, click the Open PDF button to open the PDF in your browser or your default PDF application.
4. Print as you normally would from your browser or PDF app.

Working with Templates

Templates are Pages' way of lending a helping hand when it comes to creating new documents. They are basically documents of many varieties that have been prebuilt, so all you have to do is plug in your specific information, as opposed to starting from scratch.

You can either use the templates supplied by Apple or build your own templates, whichever floats your boat at any particular time.

Using Existing Templates

Each version of Pages is supplied with its own set of templates that you can use to jumpstart the creation of new documents. These templates exist in the Template Chooser, which can be accessed quite easily, and they are a cinch to begin working with. There are several categories of templates to browse through, so have at it.

To use a template, simply select it from the Template Chooser:

- **OS X**   Press ⌘-N or choose File | New to open the Template Chooser. Browse the templates, select one to open, and click Choose in the lower right.
- **iOS**   In the Documents manager, tap the Create Document icon to open the Template Chooser. Browse the templates, decide which to use, and tap it to open it.
- **iCloud**   In the Documents manager, click the Create Document icon to open the Template Chooser. Browse the templates, select the one you want to use, and click Choose to open it.

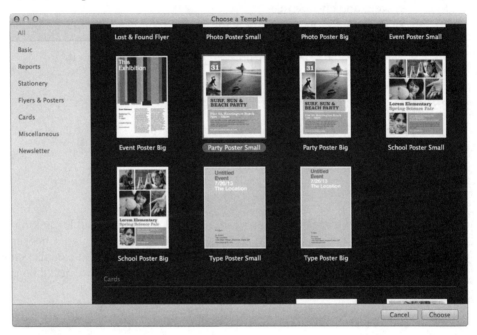

Templates are already populated by text, images, or both. These texts and images simply act as placeholders for the content you want to add to them. To add your own text, simply select the text box you want to work in and get to work. The same technique applies to graphics and images within the template; select the one you want to replace and select one of your own images. There will be much more coming up in this chapter when it comes to working with text, and more on using images in your documents in Chapter 4.

Creating Custom Templates

Believe it or not, Apple can't always dream up everything a user might need, so said user may just have to supply something for herself from time to time. Take templates, for example: the chances are pretty good that you might come up with a task that you need a template of your own design for. If that's the case, it's simple enough to create a template of your own making. Mind you, this will require the use of Pages for OS X; this feature isn't supported for iOS or iCloud.

To create your own template in Pages for OS X:

1. Create a document with all of the features you desire in your template (you'll learn more about how to do so as we progress through the book).
2. Choose File | Save As Template.
3. Do one of the following:
   - To create a template file to share with others or to use on iOS devices, click the Save button, give the template a name, select a location on your computer to save it to, or choose iCloud to make it available for your iOS devices as well, and click Save.
   - To instantly place your new template in the Pages for OS X Template Chooser, click the Add To Template Chooser button. The template will now appear in the Template Chooser where you can assign a name to it.

Adding Custom Templates to Pages for OS X and iOS

Custom templates are very simple to add and remove to and from both Pages for OS X and Pages for iOS.

OS X

Adding a custom template to Pages for OS X is as simple as double-clicking the file. Pages will ask you if you want to add the template to the Template Chooser; simply click the Add To Template Chooser button and you're done. You can also choose File | Open and open the template as you would any other document. You'll be prompted in the same way to add the template to the Template Chooser.

iOS

Adding a custom template to Pages for iOS can be done either through iCloud or iTunes.

- **Using iCloud** Once you save a template in iCloud from Pages for OS X, the template will appear in the Documents manager of Pages on your iOS devices. The icon for the template is easy to spot: it looks like a pen drawing on paper with a ruler at the bottom. Tap the template icon and Pages will ask if you want to add the template to the Template Chooser, as shown in Figure 3-10; tap Add to do so. The new template will appear at the bottom of the Template Chooser in the My Templates section and can now be used like any other template.

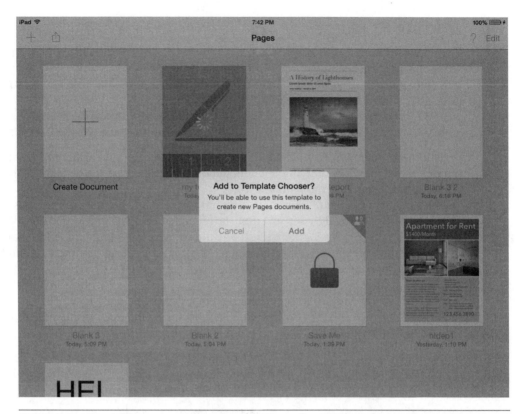

FIGURE 3-10   Add a custom template to Pages for iOS by tapping the Add button.

- **iTunes**   You can add a template to Pages for iOS in the same manner as you would add a document. Please see the earlier section "Transferring Files to and from Pages with iTunes." Once the template appears in the Documents manager, you can add it to the Template Chooser by tapping it as described in the previous bullet.

 Pages for iCloud doesn't yet support the import of custom templates, but you can create documents with them in Pages for OS X or iOS and edit those documents within Pages for iCloud.

T-E-X-T! Text, Text, Text!

Finally, we get down to the meat of it! You're actually going to start learning how to use Pages to build documents that you can use. By the way, (loudly) chanting the T-E-X-T cheer in the title of this section is an excellent way to get motivated for the tasks to come, but be careful, as some housemates and coworkers may be a bit unsettled by your sudden burst of energy.

Adding Text

Not many documents are worth a hoot if they don't have any text in them, so in a sense this part of the chapter is the most important, don't you think?

Adding text to anything on a computer or mobile device is pretty simple, so let's just knock this one out of the park.

OS X

Does it really get any easier? Open a new document in Pages for OS X and just start typing—that's it. By default, a new blank document greets you with a blinking cursor, practically begging you to tap on a few keys.

If you're using a template or a document that's already been formatted, just find the place you want to add your text and start banging away on the keyboard.

While it's all very basic, there's still one option we don't want to overlook, and that's the ability to confine text to a text box, instead of just leaving it to run amok on the whole of the document. To create a text box:

1. Click the Text button in the toolbar; its icon looks like a T.
2. Choose which type of text box you'd like to add to the document, and simply drag-and-drop it from the Text window into your document.

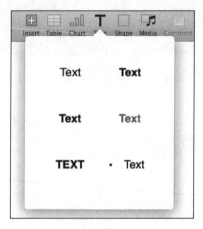

3. If you want to move the text box, simply click-and-hold the text and drag the box to the position you'd like it to be.

iOS

Adding text to iOS documents is easy, too.

If it's a new document, it doesn't get much easier. Like in OS X, as soon as the new document opens, the cursor is merrily blinking at you and you may commence typing, as the onscreen keyboard automatically opens, too. Should you lose the keyboard, simply tap inside the document to reopen it and start typing again.

To add a text box to a document in Pages for iOS:

1. Tap the + button in the upper right of the screen.
2. Tap the Text button, which amazingly enough looks like a T.
3. Determine which type of text you'd like in the text box, and then tap-and-drag it into the document. You can tap-and-drag the text box at any time to move it into a location more to your liking.

iCloud

It's no more complicated to add text to iCloud for Pages than it is in the other Pages versions. Again, a new document is ready and waiting for you to enter text the moment it opens.

Adding a text box is just as easy to do in iCloud, too, but with a very slight difference:

1. Click the Text button in the toolbar at the top of the window; yet again, it looks like a T.
2. This time the text box simply appears in the document; you don't get to drag-and-drop it into place like you can with OS X or iOS Pages. However, once the text box is in the document, you can go ahead and drag it to wherever your heart desires.

Choosing and Formatting Fonts

Fonts are just as instrumental as images when it comes to giving life to a document. Who wants to look at a page full of boring old Times New Roman (no offense meant to Times New Roman fans in the readership) when so many other lively choices exist?

Pages in all its incarnations is adept at selecting and formatting fonts to suit the style of whatever document you have in mind.

OS X

The Format bar is your pal in Pages for OS X, and that's never more evident than when working with text. The Text Format bar, shown in the illustration, pops up on the right side of the document window whenever you select text in the document.

To choose a font for your document, click the Font pop-up menu in the Format bar and select one from the list. The list is WYSIWYG (what you see is what you get), so you'll be able to determine what you want on-the-fly. Adjust the appearance of the font by changing its typeface, size, and color from within the Format bar, as well. Options for making the text bold, italic, or underlined are also available.

Click the gear icon to access advanced options such as baseline, ligatures, strikethrough, and the like.

The Alignment section of the Format bar allows you to align the text to the left side, center, or right side of your document, as well as justify the text (which aligns it to both the left and right margins).

Adjust spacing between the lines of text using the Spacing section. For more options, click the arrow next to Spacing.

iOS

The onscreen keyboard is a godsend for Pages users. It provides a toolbar that affords buttons to quickly format your text as you type. The toolbar is located at the top of the keyboard, as shown in Figure 3-11.

You can also use the format inspector to make changes to your text. Tap the format inspector icon (looks like a paintbrush) in the upper right of the screen when working with text to see the text format inspector, illustrated in Figure 3-12.

You may not have all the fonts available in Pages for iOS as you do for Pages in OS X if you've added fonts to your Mac, so you may want to keep that in mind when choosing them for your documents if they are to be used and edited across platforms.

iCloud

Changing the appearance of text in Pages for iCloud is nearly identical to doing so in Pages for OS X. Selecting text in the document will open the format panel, which affords the same functionality as the Format bar in OS X Pages, although font selection may be more limited.

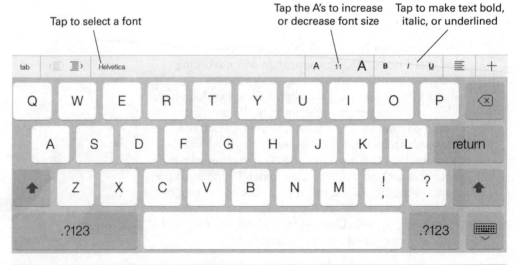

FIGURE 3-11   The keyboard toolbar allows you to make quick adjustments to text.

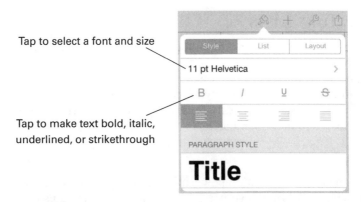

Tap to select a font and size

Tap to make text bold, italic, underlined, or strikethrough

FIGURE 3-12   The format inspector is also a convenient way to change the appearance of your text.

Using Paragraph Styles

Paragraph styles are preformatted sets of text attributes (such as a particular font, size, and color) that can be applied to sections of text, or even entire documents, at the click of a mouse (or tap of a finger). Every template uses paragraph styles for its different elements, and you can use them in new documents as well.

To use a paragraph style in Pages for OS X or iCloud:

1. Select the text you want to apply the style to.
2. Click the Paragraph Styles pop-up menu in the Format bar of OS X or format panel of iCloud.
3. Scroll through and select the style you want to use, and then click to apply it to the text.

You can create a new paragraph style based on the text selected in your document by clicking the + in the Paragraph Styles pop-up menu in Pages for OS X (not available in iOS or iCloud, though).

To use a paragraph style in iOS:

1. Select the text you want to apply the style to.
2. Tap the format inspector icon and then tap Style.
3. Scroll through and select the style you want to use, and then tap to apply it to the text.

Creating Lists

Lists, whether bulleted or numbered, are often very important elements used to help readers correctly understand a subject by organizing it better for them. Pages is quite the wiz with lists, as it is with most everything else. Pages can do much of list formatting all on its own by default, but, of course, you have full reign to turn off automatic lists (see "Setting Pages' Preferences" earlier in this chapter) and make adjustments to them manually.

OS X

Pages in OS X is a bit more powerful than its cousins when it comes to list creation, quite a bit more when it comes to iCloud, to be honest. Let's just dive right in, shall we?

To create a list in Pages for OS X:

1. Place the cursor where you want your list to begin.
2. Begin typing a bullet (press OPTION-8), a number, or a letter (numbers and letters must be followed immediately by a period), and then type the first item in the list.
3. Press RETURN, and Pages automatically kicks into list mode.
4. Continue to add items to your list by typing them out and pressing RETURN after each one.
5. To quit generating the list, press RETURN twice or press the DELETE key.

Nifty, huh? But that's not all! You can quickly change the hierarchy of a list by clicking-and-dragging items in the list left or right, or change the order by clicking-and-dragging an item up or down the list. When you start to click-and-drag an item, a blue arrow will appear and help you navigate to where it should go in your list.

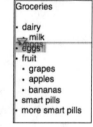

 You can get down to some serious customizing of your lists using the Bullets & Lists section of the Format bar. Select an item in your list and click the arrow next to Bullets & Lists to see a plethora of formatting options.

iOS

To create a list in Pages for iOS:

1. Tap where you want your list to begin in the document.
2. Begin typing a dash, a number, or a letter (numbers and letters must be followed immediately by a period), and then type the first item in the list.
3. Tap RETURN, and Pages automatically goes into list mode.
4. Continue to add items to your list by typing them out and tapping RETURN after each one. You can change the hierarchy of an item in the list by tapping the indent buttons in the keyboard toolbar (next to the TAB key).
5. To quit generating the list, tap RETURN twice.

As with Pages for OS X, you can easily change the hierarchy of a list by touching-and-dragging items in the list left or right, or change their order by touching-and-dragging an item up or down the list. When you start to click-and-drag an item, a blue arrow appears, along with blue alignment guides, to help with item placement.

iCloud

To create a list in Pages for iCloud:

1. Type the first item in your list and press RETURN. Repeat this step until all of your items are listed.
2. Select the text you want to include in your list.
3. Scroll near the bottom of the Text format pane to see the Bullets & Lists menu. Click the menu and select one of its styling options for your list.
4. You may continue to add items to your list by typing them out and pressing RETURN after each one. You can change the hierarchy of an item in the list by using the indent buttons at the bottom of the Text format pane.
5. To quit generating the list, choose None from the Bullets & List menu in the Text format pane.

Working with Special Characters

By "special characters" I don't mean the thirty-something-year-old fellow who you've seen bicycling down your street wearing a chicken costume and holding a Raggedy Ann doll. No, by "special characters" I mean the font characters that most of us don't have to use on a regular basis, such as and ©.

To utilize special characters in your Pages for OS X documents (this feature isn't supported in iOS or iCloud versions):

1. Place the cursor to the point in the document where you want to insert the special character.
2. Choose Edit | Special Characters to open the special characters window.
3. Select a category from the bottom of the window, and then click a character to insert it into your document.

Adjusting Text Flow

When typing text into a Pages document, the text flows automatically from one page or column to the next. Sometimes, though, it may be necessary to force text to flow differently from the default (for example, if a graphic on the page is in the way of the text). Pages for OS X and iOS allows you to easily change how text flows through your documents, but Pages for iCloud doesn't yet support this feature.

OS X

There are several ways to change the flow of text in Pages for OS X:

- **Line break**   Starts a new line in the same paragraph. Press SHIFT-RETURN to create a line break.
- **Page break**   Forces text in the next line to begin at the top of the next page. Click the Insert icon in the toolbar and select Page Break.
- **Add or remove text columns**   Select the text you want to add or remove columns for, and then click the Layout tab in the Text format bar. Add or decrease the number of columns using the pop-up menu, and then check the Equal Column Width check box if you want your columns to be uniform in size.
- **Column break**   Forces text to begin at the top of the next column. Click the Insert icon in the toolbar and select Column Break.
- **Pagination and breaks**   Click the More tab in the Text Format bar to see the four options under Paginations & Break:
  - **Keep lines on same page**   Makes all lines of a paragraph stay on the same page.
  - **Keep with next paragraph**   Keeps a paragraph on the same page as the one that follows it.
  - **Start paragraph on a new page**   Moves a paragraph to the top of the next page.
  - **Prevent widows and orphans**   Keeps the first or last line of a paragraph from being separated from the rest of the paragraph on the previous or next page.

iOS

Pages for iOS also sports a nice array of options for dealing with text flow:

- **Line break**   Starts a new line in the same paragraph. Tap where you want to place the break, tap + in the keyboard's toolbar (right side), and then tap Line Break.
- **Page break**   Forces text in the next line to begin at the top of the next page. Tap the place in the document that you want to insert the break, tap the + icon in the keyboard's toolbar, and then tap Page Break.
- **Add or remove text columns**   Select the text you want to add or remove columns for, tap the format inspector icon (paintbrush), and then tap Layout. Add or decrease the number of columns by tapping the + or − icons, respectively.

- **Column break**   Forces text to begin at the top of the next column. Tap where you want the current column to end, tap + in the keyboard's toolbar, and then tap Column Break.

Using Phonetic Guide Texts

Your Mac and iOS devices support international keyboards, which allow you to enter text using many different languages. Using any of the Japanese, Chinese, or Korean keyboards gives Pages the ability to add certain features to the text to help you or the reader to better understand it. One of these features is phonetic guides, which help you more easily pronounce the text. (Note that phonetic guides are not supported in Pages for iCloud as of this writing.)

 See OS X's built-in Help feature (from within the Finder, choose Help | Help Center) or visit Apple's OS X support site (www.apple.com/support/osx) for more information on how to use international keyboards and other languages with apps on your Mac.

OS X

To add phonetic guides to text in Pages for OS X:

1. Select the text that you want to apply the phonetic guide to, but be careful not to select any punctuation or breaks.
2. Choose Format | Phonetic Guide Text, or right-click (CONTROL-click) the selected text, and a phonetic guide displays.
3. Make any changes necessary by selecting the text you want to use. You can also enter your own text by typing in the text field provided.
4. Click outside of the phonetic guide to exit and apply the guide to the text.

It's easy to remove a phonetic guide, as well:

1. Click the phonetic guide you want to remove.
2. Click the Remove Phonetic Guide Text button.

iOS

To add phonetic guides to text in Pages for iOS:

1. Select the text that you want to apply the phonetic guide to, but be careful not to select any punctuation or breaks.
2. Tap Phonetics, and a phonetic guide displays with the text you selected in step 1.
3. Make any changes necessary by tapping Guide in the Phonetic Guide list and then selecting the text you want to use. You can also enter your own text by typing in the text field provided.
4. Tap outside of the phonetic guide to exit and apply the guide to the text.

You can easily remove a phonetic guide, too:

1. Tap the phonetic guide you want to remove.
2. Tap Guide in the Phonetic Guide list, and then tap Remove Guide.

 See the User Guide for your iOS device for information on enabling keyboards for other languages. When more than one language is enabled, a globe key will appear to the left of the spacebar; tap this globe to switch languages, or tap-and-hold to see the list of enabled languages (tap the one you want to use).

Using Bidirectional Text

Some languages, such as English, write from left to right on the page, while others, such as Hebrew and Arabic, write from right to left on the page. Pages for OS X and iOS (but not iCloud) includes support for both directions of text, or bidirectional text, to be more precise. Apple's gone global, y'all!

OS X

To utilize bidirectional text in Pages for OS X:

1. Select the text you want to change directions for, or click to place the cursor on the line in which you want to start changing the text direction.
2. Choose the language you want to use from the Input Source menu in Finder's menu bar (upper right of your computer screen).
3. Click the text direction button in the Text Format bar's Alignment section (looks like two arrows facing in opposite directions). If you don't see the button in the Alignment section, quit and relaunch Pages.

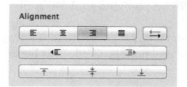

4. Type your text. The text will continue to enter into the document according to the direction chosen in the text direction button.
5. To change direction, simply click the text direction button. Be sure to select the correct language again from the Input Source menu.

iOS

To utilize bidirectional text in Pages for iOS:

1. Select the text you want to change directions for, or tap to place the cursor on the line in which you want to start changing the text direction.
2. Choose the language you want to use by tapping the globe button on the keyboard.
3. Tap the format inspector icon and tap Style.
4. Tap the text direction button, found to the right of the alignment buttons (looks like two arrows pointing in opposite directions).
5. Type your text. The text will continue to enter into the document according to the direction chosen in the text direction button.
6. To change direction, simply tap the text direction button again. Be sure to select the correct language again by tapping the globe icon on the keyboard.

Getting Your Documents *Just* Right

Next, you'll learn how to make the little adjustments—those "finer points"—that give documents that extra punch, help you organize your thoughts, and help your readers engage with your contents.

Setting Paper Size and Margins

You can change the paper size and margins for documents using Pages for OS X and iOS, but not Pages for iCloud (letter size is the only option as of this writing when creating a new document within Pages for iCloud).

OS X

Pages for OS X supports many standard paper sizes on its own, and also uses paper sizes supported by your installed printers. Setting paper sizes and margins is super simple using the Setup bar:

1. Open a document.
2. Click the Setup icon (looks like a gear) on the far right of the toolbar and click the Document tab.

3. Perform one or more of the following:
   - Change paper size by selecting a printer from the size pop-up menu (Any Printer is the default) and choosing a supported size from the size pop-up menu.
   - Change the page's orientation by selecting either the portrait icon or landscape icon.
   - Adjust margins by changing the values in the Document Margins section.

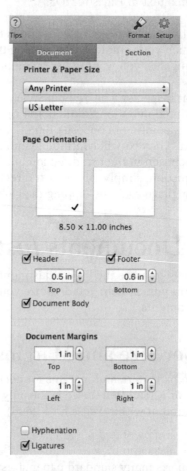

iOS

Pages for iOS only supports letter and A4 sizes, but you can easily change documents from one size to another and adjust margins to suit your needs.

To change paper size and margins in Pages for iOS:

1. Open a document.
2. Tap the Tools icon and tap Document Setup.

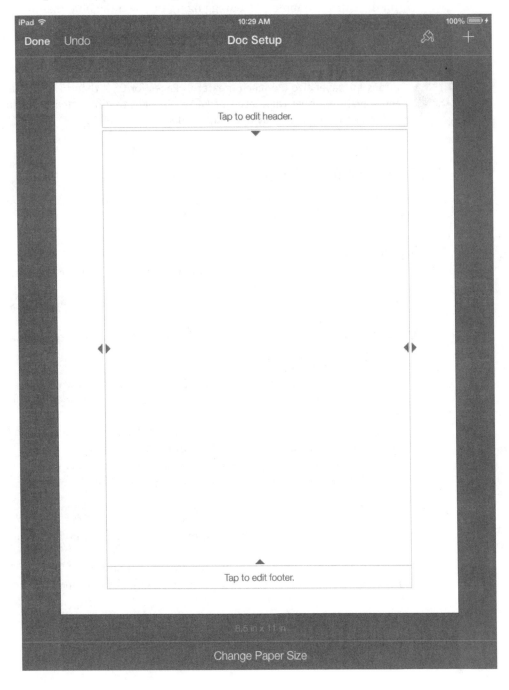

3. Perform one or more of the following:
   - Change the paper size by tapping the Change Paper Size option at the bottom of the screen, and then select either letter or A4.
   - Adjust margins by tapping-and-dragging left or right the blue margin arrows on the sides, or tapping-and-dragging up or down the blue margin arrows at the top and/or bottom.
4. Tap Undo to revert to the previous setting. Tap and hold the Undo and then tap Redo in the resulting menu to reapply a setting.

 Options for paper size are much greater in Pages for OS X than in iOS, so if you need something other than letter or A4, you'll want to either create the document in OS X or change it later by opening the document in OS X.

A Headers and Footers Primer

Headers and footers allow you to insert items, such as document titles, chapter titles, and page numbers, in the same locations on every page of your document.

OS X and iCloud

Adding a header or footer is handled the same way in both Pages for OS X and iCloud:

1. Hover your mouse pointer over the top or bottom areas of the page to see the header or footer blocks; there will be three blocks in both.
2. Click in either block to edit the header or footer; you can utilize as many blocks as you like.
3. Perform one or more of the following:
   - Add and format text in the header and footer blocks as you would any other text.
   - Click the Insert Page Number button to add page numbers to a header or footer block in Pages for OS X.
   - Click the Insert icon in the toolbar and select Page Count or Date & Time to add either to a header or footer block in Pages for OS X.
   - Click the Insert icon in the toolbar and select Page Number or Page Count to add either to a header or footer block in Pages for iCloud.

iOS

Adding headers and footers is a bit different in Pages for iOS, but no less simple:

1. Tap the Tools icon in the toolbar and tap Document Setup.
2. Tap either the header or footer section to see its blocks and open the keyboard.

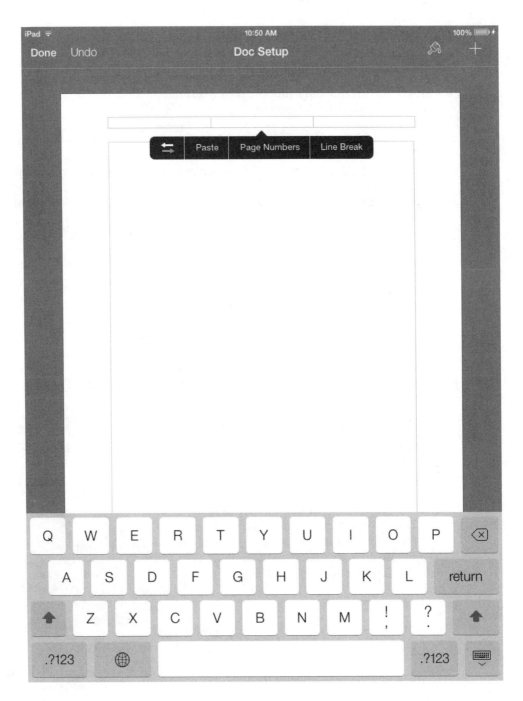

3. Tap in either of the three blocks to edit it. Perform one or more of the following:
   • Add and format text as you typically would.
   • Tap the Page Numbers option in the menu that appears when you tap a block to add page numbers to that particular block.

Organizing with Sections

Using sections is a really great way to divide your document into different parts, while maintaining the same or using different formatting in each one. Creating sections in a document is currently only supported in Pages for OS X.

To add sections to a document:

1. Click the place in the document at which you want the new section to begin.
2. Click Setup in the toolbar and choose the Section tab.
3. Click the Create A New Section pop-up menu (you may have to scroll down to see it) and choose an option from it.
4. If you want the new section to retain the formatting of the first section, do nothing. However, if you want it to have different formatting, use the Headers & Footers and Page Numbering options under the Section tab.

You can add as many sections as you like to a document. View the sections in your document by clicking View in the toolbar and selecting Show Page Thumbnails; sections are outlined in yellow.

Adding Background Colors and Borders

Pages for OS X allows you to add background colors and borders to pages or paragraphs in your document, but the iOS and iCloud versions don't as of this writing.

To add a background color:

1. Select the paragraph you want to add the background color to, or press ⌘-A to select the entire page and apply the color page-wide.
2. Click the Format inspector icon and click the Layout tab in the Text pane.
3. Click the arrow next to Borders & Rules.
4. Click the box next to Background Color to see a list of available colors, and click one to apply it. You can also click the color wheel to make your own color, if you're feeling especially sporty.

To add a border:

1. Select the paragraph you want to add the border to, or press ⌘-A to select the entire page and apply the border to it.
2. Click the Format inspector icon and click the Layout tab in the Text pane.

3. Click the arrow next to Borders & Rules.
4. Select a line type, color, and line thickness from the options available. You can also adjust the position and offset of the borders.

Viewing Formatting Marks

Formatting marks, also called invisibles, are hidden, nonprinting marks inserted on the page when you press RETURN or TAB or add elements such as line breaks and page breaks. They are useful to see sometimes, such as when you're trying to view the layout of your page, so we need a way to see them. Pages in OS X provides a direct way to see these marks, Pages in iOS has a rather indirect way of viewing them, and Pages for iCloud hasn't evolved that capability just yet.

To see formatting marks in Pages for OS X, choose View | Show Invisibles from the menu (not the View button in the toolbar), and to quit seeing them simply choose View | Hide Invisibles.

To see formatting marks in Pages for iOS:

1. Tap-and-hold anywhere in the document.
2. Tap Select All from the list. As long as everything is selected, you'll be able to view invisibles, but the moment you unselect everything, the invisibles go back into hiding. There's no way in iOS to continue showing formatting marks while working in the document.

Using Footnotes and Endnotes

Footnotes are notes that appear at the bottom of a page, and endnotes are notes that appear at the end of a document. You can add footnotes and endnotes to documents in Pages for OS X and iOS, but Pages for iCloud only supports the addition of footnotes.

 You can only use one type of note in a document; you can't combine footnotes and endnotes. If you change the type of one note, all other notes in the document are changed to the same type.

OS X

When you add a note to Pages in OS X, it's treated as a footnote by default, but you can easily convert it to an endnote after the fact (and all other notes will change as well).

To add a note:

1. Click the text in the document to which the note will refer.
2. Click the Insert button in the toolbar and select Footnote. The symbol for the note will appear next to the selected text, and the cursor will move to the bottom of the page.
3. Enter the text for your note.

To convert notes from footnote to endnote (or vice versa):

1. Click any note on the page; every note will be selected, as evidenced by the blue boxes that surround them.
2. Click the Format button in the toolbar.
3. Make modifications to your notes, such as their type, format, and numbering, by using the options in the Footnotes tab of the Format bar.

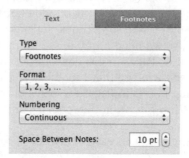

Quickly remove a note by placing your cursor directly to the right of the note's symbol in the document text and pressing the DELETE key. All other notes will be automatically reorganized to reflect the change.

iOS

Pages in iOS also treats your first note as a footnote by default. As with Pages for OS X, you can easily convert it to an endnote later.

To add a note:

1. Tap the text in the document to which the note will refer.
2. Tap + in the keyboard's toolbar and tap Footnote. The symbol for the note will appear next to the selected text, and the cursor will move to the bottom of the page.
3. Enter the text for your note.

To convert notes from footnote to endnote (or vice versa):

1. Tap any note on the page; every note will be selected, as evidenced by the blue boxes that surround them.
2. Tap the Format inspector icon and then tap Options.
3. Make modifications to your notes, such as their type, format, and numbering.

Quickly remove a note by placing your cursor directly to the right of the note's symbol in the document text and tapping the DELETE key. All other notes will be automatically reorganized to reflect the change.

iCloud

As mentioned earlier, Pages for iCloud gives you only one option when it comes to the type of note you can create: footnotes. However, it will retain endnotes you add to documents using OS X or iOS versions, so no worries of it reformatting your footnotes to endnotes.

To add a note:

1. Click the text in the document to which the note will refer. Be precise with cursor placement, or you might accidentally place the note in the middle of a word.
2. Click the Insert button in the toolbar and select Footnote. The symbol for the note will appear next to the selected text, and the cursor will move to the bottom of the page.
3. Enter the text for your note.

Remove a note by placing your cursor directly to the right of the note's symbol in the document text and pressing the DELETE key. All other notes will be automatically reorganized to reflect the change.

Fashioning a Table of Contents

Tables of contents are the bomb when it comes to finding a topic quickly in a document. Pages for OS X makes it surprisingly easy to add a table of contents that pertains to an entire document or a section/sections of it. Adding tables of contents isn't an option available to Pages for iOS or iCloud, but they will be retained when editing a document in one of them.

To add a table of contents to a document or section:

1. Place the cursor at the point in the document where you want the table of contents to be inserted.
2. Choose Insert | Table Of Contents from the menu (not the Insert button in the toolbar) and select one of the following:
   - **Document**   Creates a table of contents for the entire document
   - **Section**   Creates a table of contents for the section in which the cursor is placed
   - **To Next Occurrence**   Creates a table of contents for contents located between this table of contents and the next

3. Once your table of contents appears, click the Format button in the toolbar to see the Table of Contents pane. Check the box to the left of each element of your document from which Pages should pull information to fill your table of contents. If you want the page numbers of the elements to appear in the table of contents, check the box in the #'s column.

To remove a table of contents:

1. Select the table of contents so that you see its border.
2. Click just beneath the table of contents' border and begin to drag up until you see a heavy blue border surround it.
3. Press the DELETE key to delete the table of contents.

Summary

We've covered a huge portion of how to work with the basics of Pages in this chapter. Now, it's onward and upward into some of the more specialized (and fun) things we can do with our word processor compadre.

4

Dazzling Documents

HOW TO...

- Add images and other graphics to your documents
- Put audio and video to work for your Pages files
- Work with tables
- Place and edit charts

Now that you've familiarized yourself with the basics of building a word processing document in Pages, it's time to add some flare to this whole affair. Let me be clear: there's nothing wrong with a document consisting of text and only text, even if using a plain old font like Courier, so long as the content is worth the while. Having said that, though, everybody knows that you need images, shapes, and multimedia to spice up an otherwise great document! Graphics and media aren't there to just take up space (usually); they're included to provide information on their own accord. Colors used in a document can help convey the tone of the text. Images can save you a thousand words by clearly displaying the object of the document (for example, interior and exterior pictures of a home in a sales flyer). Multimedia, such as audio and video, can go even further by adding a sight and sound dimension far beyond that of text and pictures.

Tables and charts also help convey information in a document. They both take otherwise complex and overwhelming information and break it down into (hopefully) well-organized and manageable bite-sized morsels. A long and tedious list can be much easier to digest in table form, and loads of numbers benefit a reader much more when represented graphically.

Pages is wonderfully adept at adding all of these items to your documents, and does so in its typically simple and straightforward fashion, while not skimping on effectiveness. Let's get started dazzling up our documents!

Pictures Are Worth a Thousand Words: Objects and Media

The title of this section refers to "objects and media," but what the heck does that mean? Am I referring to cubes and journalists? That would be an emphatic "no" coming from your author, dear reader. Let's tackle those two terms before moving ahead, then.

When Pages refers to "objects," it means anything that you can place on a document. Images, graphics, and shapes all fall under the heading of "objects" (text boxes do too, technically speaking). Pages makes it easy to insert objects into your documents, and working with them once they are inline is a pleasure more than a chore, thanks to the attention to usability and functionality employed by Apple's team of iWork developers.

By "media," Pages means multimedia, aka audio and video. Media affords you yet another way to get your message across to its intended audience, to which anyone who's ever listened to iTunes or watched YouTube can testify.

In this section, I'll show you how to get objects and media into your documents, as well as how to manipulate them and maximize their impact.

Pepping Up Documents with Images

Whether it's a photo of a waterfall, a sunset, or a flower, or perhaps an unforgettable snapshot of your grandparents captured in the joy of an intimately sweet moment, an image is powerful, and no other form of media conveys a message and packs an emotional punch quite like images.

I'll go out on a limb and say that probably no other computer manufacturer understands this concept better than Apple, and Apple has made sure that users of iWork can use images in simple and powerful ways. Let's take a gander at how Pages can help you put the images you want into your documents.

Adding Images to a Document

Getting images into a document is just the first step when it comes to working with them, but it's the most important, of course. Remember that many of the templates that come with Pages include images already, but these are placeholders and are meant to be replaced with your own images.

OS X   There are four methods you can use to get images into your document when working in Pages for OS X:

- Drag an image from the Finder into your document and just drop it in.
- Pick Insert | Choose, browse your Mac for the image you need, and click Insert.
- Click the image button in the lower right corner of an image placeholder (the button looks like an illustration of a mountain and the sun) and select an image from your iPhoto or Aperture library, as shown in Figure 4-1.
- Click the Media button in the toolbar and choose an image from your iPhoto or Aperture library.

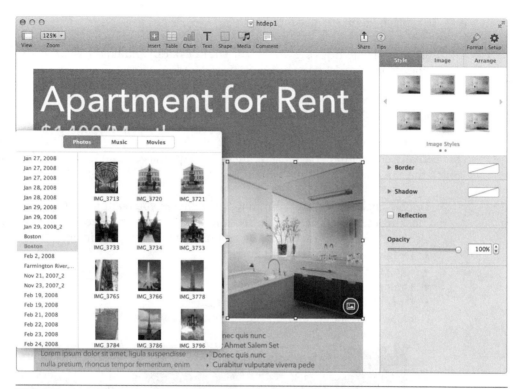

FIGURE 4-1   You can place an item from your iPhoto or Aperture library by clicking the image button in a placeholder.

iOS   Unlike the OS X version, Pages for iOS doesn't offer multiple options for getting images into a document, but you can indeed do so, and that's the goal now, isn't it?
   To add images in Pages for iOS:

1. Tap + in the toolbar or in an image placeholder (lower right corner).
2. Tap an image to select it; Pages only shows you images that are stored on your device.

iCloud   Pages for iCloud gives you a tiny bit more flexibility when adding images than does the iOS version, but not quite as much as the OS X version.
   Do one of the following to add an image to a document:

- Drag an image from the Finder (or your desktop if using a PC) and drop it in the document.
- Click the Image button in the toolbar, click the Choose Image button, browse your computer for the image you want, and click Choose.

To replace an image placeholder:

1. Drag an image from the Finder (or your desktop) and hold it over the image placeholder.
2. Once a blue outline appears around the placeholder, drop your image onto it.

Masking (Cropping) an Image

Masking an image is the act of hiding parts of it you don't want to be displayed, while not actually editing the image itself. Luckily for us, masking an image is done pretty much the same way in all three versions of Pages:

1. Double-click (or double-tap if in iOS) the image you want to mask to show the masking controls. The default mask is set to the original size of your image.
2. Use one or more of the following techniques to mask your image:
   - Drag the slider to resize the image.
   - Drag the image itself to reposition it within the mask window.
   - Drag the mask's border to move the mask.
   - Drag the mask's handles to resize it.
3. Click or tap Done when finished masking the image.

Removing Parts of an Image

There may come a time when you want only one element of an image to appear in your document, such as a person but not the environment surrounding them, or perhaps you'll decide there's a background color you'd like to remove from an image.

Both can be accomplished in Pages for OS X and iOS (sorry, iCloud users, but this isn't supported) by using the Instant Alpha tool.

 The Instant Alpha tool is powerful and pretty cool, but it can also be pretty tricky. I suggest you practice working with Instant Alpha if you think it's something you might utilize in the future, as it can take some getting used to.

OS X   To use Instant Alpha in Pages for OS X:

1. Click the image to select it.
2. Click Instant Alpha, found in the Format bar's Image pane.
3. Use the targeting tool (looks like a square containing cross hairs) to find the color you want to remove from the image.
4. Click to begin removing the selected color from your image. As you drag, you'll begin to remove more of the color (and those surrounding it). Hold down the OPTION key while dragging and all instances of the color will be removed from the image at once. Alternately, hold the SHIFT key while dragging and colors will be added back to your image.
5. Click Done when finished.

 If you need to be more precise with color removal, try zooming in on the image.

iOS   To use Instant Alpha in Pages for iOS:

1. Select the image.
2. Tap the Format inspector (paintbrush) icon in the toolbar.
3. Tap Image, and then tap Instant Alpha.
4. Touch-and-drag your finger over the area (or color) that you want to remove in the image. The more you drag, the more of the color, and those surrounding it, is removed, as shown in Figure 4-2.
5. Tap Done when finished.

Adjusting Color Levels in an Image

Pages for OS X offers a feature for images that the other two versions of Pages don't offer: the ability to adjust color levels in an image. To make color adjustments to an image in Pages for OS X:

1. Select the image.
2. Click the Image tab in the Format bar.
3. Make basic adjustments with the Exposure and/or Saturation sliders, or click Enhance to have Pages make automatic adjustments to the image.

FIGURE 4-2   The circle shows where your finger is dragging, and the % shows how much of the color you're removing.

4. For more advanced color features, click the slider button, which is highlighted with a dashed circle on the right side of Figure 4-3. Clicking this button opens the Adjust Image window, also shown in Figure 4-3, which offers up to 12 different options, including the ability to reset the image to its default color settings.

Time to Shape Up: Working with Shapes

"Shape up or ship out!"

No, I'm not criticizing you, dear reader; rather, I'm trying to motivate you to add some shapes to your documents in Pages to take them from the mundane to the interesting. Shapes don't simply have to be used for decoration, but can be helpful in telling your story through such tactics as adding text to a shape (for one example). Pages comes loaded with plenty of shapes already, but Apple also allows you to draw your own shapes (using the OS X version).

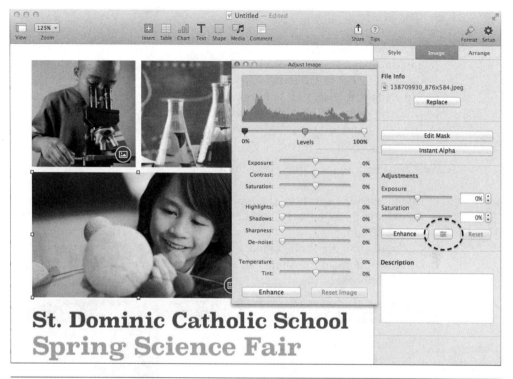

FIGURE 4-3   You can make advanced color adjustments to your images if needed.

Adding Shapes to Your Documents

You can add shapes to documents using all three versions of Pages, but of course there are slight differences in how this is accomplished within each one.

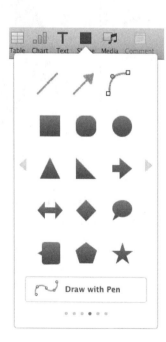

OS X   To add a shape using Pages for OS X:

1. Click the Shape button in the toolbar.
2. Select a shape from the pop-up menu by clicking it. If you don't see what you want at first, click the gray dots at the bottom of the menu or click the left and right arrows found on either side of the menu to scroll through all the options.
3. Click-and-drag the shape to place it anywhere within your document.
4. Click-and-drag the handles surrounding the shape to adjust its size.

iOS   To add a shape using Pages for iOS:

1. Tap the + button in the upper right.
2. Tap the Shape button (looks like a square) to see the available shapes. Swipe to the left or right to see more shapes in the menu.
3. Tap a shape to drop it in your document.
4. Drag the shape to the location you want it to occupy in your document.
5. Drag the handles to adjust the size of the shape.

iCloud   To add a shape using Pages for iCloud:

1. Click the Shape button in the toolbar. There is only one screen, unlike Pages for OS X and iOS, so don't bother trying to see more; you'll just wear out your mouse button.
2. Click-and-drag the shape to place it into position.
3. Use the options in the Shape tab of the format panel to change the color and other attributes of the shape.

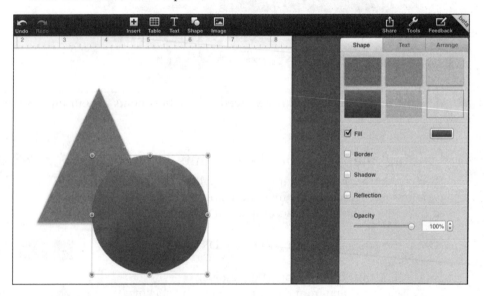

Adding Text to Shapes

Pages for OS X and iOS offer the neat feature of allowing you to add text inside of a shape; iCloud doesn't support this feature yet. This is similar to adding text to a text box, but instead of a square or rectangle (the shape of a text box), you are typing in whatever shape you choose from the Shape menu.

To add text to a shape using Pages for OS X or iOS:

1. Double-click the shape if in OS X; double-tap it if using iOS.

2. Once the cursor appears inside the shape, start typing. Should your text not fit the shape, you can simply pare it down or resize the shape by dragging its selection handles.

Editing a Shape's Curves

OS X's version of Pages allows a user to edit the actual curves of an image using sharp lines or curved lines, which can make for some really interesting shapes that you won't see in the default list. This is a great way to truly personalize your creations. And no, unfortunately, this isn't a supported feature in the iOS or iCloud versions.

To edit the curves of a shape using Pages for OS X:

1. Click to choose the shape in your document.
2. Choose Format | Shapes And Lines from the menu (not the Format button in the toolbar) and select Make Editable.
3. When the handles appear on the edges of your shape, you can begin editing the shape by dragging the handles to create whatever shape you desire (as shown in Figure 4-4). Double-click a handle to change the kind of line it produces:
   - A square handle lets you know the handle creates sharp (straight) lines.
   - A circle handle tells you the handle creates curved lines.
4. When you're finished editing the curves of your shape, simply click outside of it.

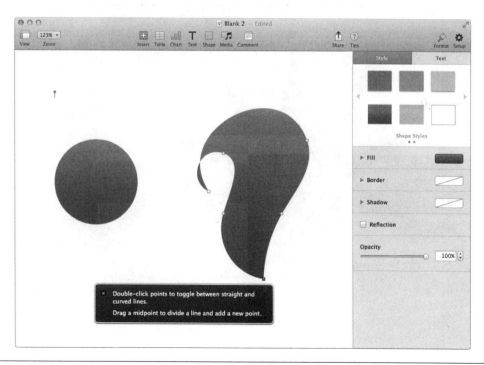

FIGURE 4-4   The shape on the right started as a copy of the red circle on the left, but I edited its curves to change it.

Hover your mouse over the edges of the shape when editing curves to see hidden handles that you can use to manipulate it.

Changing Attributes of Some Shapes

Some shapes in the OS X and iOS versions of Pages allow you to modify them. For example, the default star shape consists of five points, but you can modify the star to contain anywhere from 3 to 20 points. Other shapes that allow this kind of tinkering include the rounded-corner square, speech balloons, arrows, and the pentagon (no, not the office building in Arlington, Virginia).

To change a shape's attributes:

1. Select the shape.
2. Notice the handles: there's at least one, and possibly more, in particular that stand out due to the fact that they're green.
3. Drag the green handles up, down, and all around to discover the different ways in which you can toy with the shape's identity. Figure 4-5 shows two stars that started the same way, but the one on the left has been altered to include many more points than the default shape on the right.
4. Click (OS X) or tap (iOS) outside of a shape to stop editing the shape.

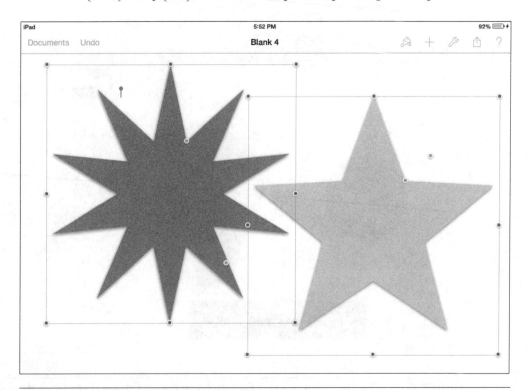

FIGURE 4-5 The star on the left has been modified quite a bit from its humble origins as a five-pointed shape.

Drawing Your Own Shapes

You're a creative kind of person, right? Heck, you don't need Apple to do everything for you; you can make your own shapes, thank you very much! Well, don't go getting your artistic hackles up too much—Apple understands you have a creative edge and offers you the chance (only in the OS X version of Pages, though) to draw your own custom shapes, using the Pen:

1. Click the Shape button in the toolbar and select Draw With Pen from the menu.
2. Click the area on the page where you want to begin your drawing. This action creates the first point on the screen, which is a red square.
3. Click another area on the screen to place the second point. This action will draw a straight line between the points. To create a curved line, click the area where the second point goes and begin dragging.
4. To finish creating your shape, click the first point made to close it, or press ESC to leave it open.

 I suggest you experiment a lot with the Pen to get a good grasp of it. Those of you familiar with drawing vector images in apps like Adobe's Illustrator will already have a leg up.

Multimedia Madness: Audio and Video

Incorporating audio and video adds a new dimension to documents. The result is not only just plain cool, it can also be useful, such as by making your documents more accessible to those who may be sight-impaired.

Once again, though, poor Pages for iCloud isn't allowed to play, but OS X and iOS do the job nicely. And while Pages for iOS cannot add audio to a document, it can alter the playback settings of an audio file already in a document.

OS X

Add audio or video to a document using Pages for OS X in one of two ways:

- Drag the audio or video file from the Finder directly into the document and drop it anywhere you darn well please.
- Click the Media button and select a file from either the Music tab or Movies tab.

Adjusting playback options is as simple as selecting the audio or video in the document and clicking the Audio tab or Movie tab (depending on which you're working with) in the Format bar. Options include

- **Controls**   Forward, Reverse, Play, and Volume are all available.
- **Edit Audio/Movie**   Trim the audio or movie to play only the parts you want. If you are using a movie, you will see a Poster Frame option, which allows you to select which frame of the video displays when the video isn't playing.
- **Repeat**   Select None to play the file only once, Loop to continuously play the file from beginning to end over and over, or Loop Back And Forth to have the file play forward and then backward over and over again.

If you want your movies to play on an iPad or iPhone, you'll need to go into Pages for OS X's preferences and enable the option to Optimize Movies For iOS.

iOS

To add a video using Pages for iOS:

1. Tap the + button in the upper right.
2. Tap the Media button (looks like a musical note).
3. Tap either Camera Roll or My Photo Stream, whichever contains the video you want to use.
4. Tap the video and then tap Use to place it in your document.

To adjust playback options of either an audio or video file in Pages for iOS:

1. Tap the audio or video to select it.
2. Tap the format inspector icon (paintbrush) and then tap the Movie tab (even if you selected an audio file).
3. Choose from the same playback options as those in Pages for OS X: None, Loop, or Loop Back And Forth.

Positioning Objects

The positioning and size of objects in a document is crucial to its overall look and feel, and thus is key when it comes to getting your message across to your audience in the manner intended.

Pages is a capable helpmate when it comes to positioning objects in your documents, regardless of which of its incarnations you're using at the moment.

OS X

Positioning objects in Pages for OS X can be accomplished in a number of ways:

- Position objects based on page coordinates:
  1. Click the object to select it.
  2. Click the Arrange tab in the Format bar.
  3. Enter x and y coordinates in the Position fields.

- Position objects on a vertical or horizontal axis:
  1. Click the object to select it.
  2. Click the Arrange tab in the Format bar.
  3. Click the Align pop-up menu and select an option.

- Position objects equally:
  1. Click three or more objects to select them.
  2. Click the Arrange tab in the Format bar.
  3. Click the Distribute pop-up menu and select an option: Evenly places even spacing between all the objects both vertically and horizontally, Horizontally only spaces them evenly on a horizontal axis, and Vertically spaces them evenly, only vertically (as advertised).

- Position objects one or more points at a time:
  1. Click the object to select it.
  2. Press an arrow key once to move one point at a time. Hold down the SHIFT key while pressing the arrow key to move ten points at a time.

iOS

Positioning objects in Pages for iOS can be just as fun.

Alignment guides are quite handy in iOS, as they allow you to get a better grasp of how items line up together visually on a touch screen. There are three types of alignment guides:

- **Center** Displays when the center of the selected object aligns with the center of another object or the center of the page
- **Edge** Displays when the edges of the selected object align with the edges of another object
- **Spacing** Displays when three or more items are spaced equally apart on a straight line

Turn on alignment guides by tapping the Tools icon, tapping Settings, and tapping the switches next to the guide types you want to enable (a green toggle indicates the guide type is enabled).

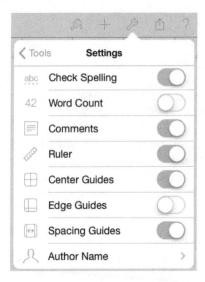

You can position objects one or more points at a time rather easily, too. Touch-and-hold an item with one finger, and then swipe anywhere else on the screen with another finger in the direction you want to move it. One of the cooler tricks is to move the item several points at a time when swiping with two or more fingers:

- 2 fingers = 10 points
- 3 fingers = 20 points
- 4 fingers = 30 points
- 5 fingers = 40 points

iCloud

Pages for iCloud gets in on the act of positioning objects, too. As in Pages for iOS, alignment guides are where it's at when it comes to positioning objects. The same three types of alignment guides are in effect here:

- **Center**   Displays when the center of the selected object aligns with the center of another object or the center of the page
- **Edge**   Displays when the edges of the selected object align with the edges of another object or the edges of the page
- **Spacing**   Displays when three or more items are spaced equally apart on a straight line

Turn on alignment guides by clicking Tools in the toolbar, hovering your pointer over Settings, and clicking each guide type you want to enable.

You can also position objects based on page coordinates in iCloud:

1. Click the object to select it.
2. Click the Arrange tab in the format panel.
3. Enter x and y coordinates in the Position fields.

Working Better Together: Grouping Objects

Grouping objects allows you to move them together at the same time. When you're building a document, knowing how to group objects is an absolute must. Imagine that you finally get all of your graphics positioned in just the right places on the page, only to remember you need to add one more item that throws everything else just slightly off kilter. If you've grouped the other items together, you'll need to move them only once; otherwise, you'll be moving them one at a time, and no one wants that headache.

Pages for OS X and iCloud both handle item grouping very similarly:

1. Select the items you want to group together:
   - In OS X, hold down the SHIFT key while selecting each item.
   - In iCloud, hold down the ⌘ key (Mac) or CONTROL key (PC) while selecting items.
2. Click the Arrange tab in the Format bar (OS X) or format panel (iCloud).
3. Click the Group button. Click the Ungroup button to undo the grouping.

Pages for iOS works a bit differently, but just as effectively:

Tip   To make Group available as an option in step 4 that follows, all objects you're selecting must be set to stay on the page by turning off the Move With Text option for them (tap the object, tap the Format inspector icon, tap the Arrange tab, tap Wrap, and then toggle the Move With Text switch to Off).

1. Touch-and-hold the first item.
2. Tap other items while continuing to hold the first.
3. Lift both fingers from the screen.
4. Tap Group in the menu to group the items (tap Ungroup to undo what you've done, should you need to at some point).

Putting It All on the Table

A table, a chair, a bowl of fruit and a violin; what else does a man need to be happy?
–Albert Einstein

I'm not certain if the kind of table our friend Einstein's referring to is the kind we'll be talking about in this chapter, but I'll bet his words ring true for some readers.

You see, tables in documents have helped folks organize their information for a very, very long time, and implementing and utilizing tables in Pages is simpler than in any other app.

Adding Tables to Your Documents

Before you can learn how to work within a table, you need to actually get one into a document. Pages is a champ at this little feat, regardless of version.

OS X

To add a table to a document in Pages for OS X:

1. Place the cursor where you'd like the table to appear in the document.
2. Click the Table icon in the toolbar.
3. Click to choose a table from the options, or drag one from the menu and drop it into the document. Click the left and right arrows in the menu to see different types.
4. Click a cell and begin typing to add content to it.
5. To move a table, click it to activate it, then click-and-drag the circle in its upper left corner.
6. Delete a table by clicking the circle in its upper left corner and then pressing the DELETE key.

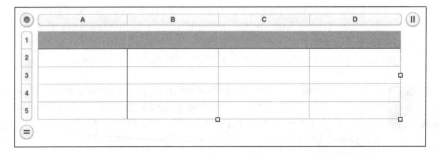

 If you can't move a table, it's probably set to move with the text in your document. To change this, select the table, click the Arrange tab in the Format bar, and select Stay On Page under the Object Placement section.

iOS

To add a table to a document in Pages for iOS:

1. Tap to place the cursor where you want the table to appear in the document.
2. Tap + in the toolbar and then tap the Table icon to see a menu of different tables.

3. Tap to select a table from the options, or drag one from the menu and drop it into the document. Swipe to the left or right to see different types.
4. Tap a cell and begin typing to add content to it.
5. To move a table, tap it to activate it, then tap-and-drag the circle in its upper left corner.
6. Delete a table by tapping it and then tapping Delete in the menu.

If you can't move a table, it's probably set to move with the text in your document. To change this, select the table, tap the Format inspector icon (paintbrush), tap the Arrange tab and then the Wrap option, and finally, tap to toggle the Move With Text switch to the Off position (to the left).

iCloud

To add a table to a document in Pages for iCloud:

1. Place the cursor where you'd like the table to reside in the document.
2. Click the Table icon in the toolbar.
3. Click to choose a table from the options.
4. Click a cell and begin typing to add content to it.
5. To move a table, click it to activate it, then click-and-drag the square in its upper left corner.
6. To delete a table, click its upper left corner to select it, and then press the DELETE key.

Adding and Adjusting Rows and Columns

Tables can be made to suit your needs, whatever they may be, and Pages is a capable partner when it comes to helping you include as much or as little as is necessary for your task.

Working with Rows and Columns in OS X

To add or remove the rows and columns of a table in Pages for OS X:

1. Click to select the table.
2. Do one of the following to add or remove rows or columns:
   - To add a column to the right side of the table or to add a row to the bottom of it, click the circle containing the two parallel lines and use the arrow to increase the number of columns or rows. Simply decrease the number to remove the rightmost column or bottommost row.

- Move the pointer over the column or row bar (lettered or numbered, respectively) of the column or row to which you want to make an addition. When you see a small gray arrow appear, click it to see a pop-up menu. Select to add a column before or after the one you're working with, or add a row above or below the one you're working with. To remove the column or row you're working with, simply select Delete Column or Delete Row.

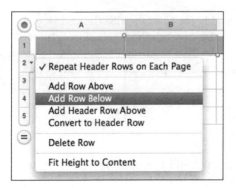
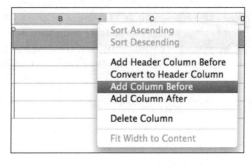

Working with Rows and Columns in iOS

To add or remove the rows and columns of a table in Pages for iOS:

1. Tap to select the table.
2. To add a column to the right side of the table or to add a row to the bottom of it, tap the circle containing the two parallel lines and use the arrow to increase the number of columns or rows. Simply decrease the number to remove the rightmost column or bottommost row.

Working with Rows and Columns in iCloud

To add or remove the rows and columns of a table in Pages for iCloud:

1. Click to select the table.
2. Do one of the following to add or remove columns and rows:
   - To add a column to the right of the table or to add a row to the bottom of it, click the handle to the right of the columns and/or the handle at the bottom of the rows. Use the resulting arrows to increase or decrease the number of columns and rows.
   - Move the pointer over the column or row bar (lettered or numbered, respectively) of the column or row to which you want to make an addition. When you see a small black arrow, click it to see a pop-up menu. Select to add a column before or after the one you're working with, or add a row above or below the one you're working with. To remove the column or row you're working with, simply select Delete Column or Delete Row.

Customizing Tables and Cells

Customizing a table or cell means dictating how data looks and operates within it. You can customize an entire table at once or one cell at a time, whichever strikes your fancy or the moment calls for.

There are *many* options available for customization, and playing around with them all is the only way to truly familiarize yourself with how they'll work for you. As is sometimes the case, the set of options available in each version of Pages varies a good bit. iCloud allows mostly basic options, iOS provides quite a wide array of options, and OS X offers a slew of great features.

OS X

To customize a table in Pages for OS X:

1. Select which part of the table you want to customize:
   - For the entire table, click the circle in the upper left corner of it.
   - For a single cell, click within that cell.
   - For multiple cells, click-and-drag to select the cells, or hold the ⌘ key while clicking the individual cells.
2. To make table-wide customizations, click the Table tab in the Format bar. Options available in the Table tab include
   - **Table Styles**   Change the entire look of a table using the predefined styles.
   - **Headers & Footer**   Increase or decrease the number of headers and footers, and enable the table's name (appears at the top of the table).
   - **Table Font Size**   Set the default font size for the table.
   - **Table Outline**   Determine whether to apply an outline to the table's outer boundaries, and what that outline should look like. You can also check the check box if you want to outline the table name.
   - **Grid Lines**   Apply boundary lines to the interior grids of your table.
   - **Alternating Row Color**   Alternate the color of the rows for easier viewing.
   - **Row & Column Size**   Set the default height of rows and width of columns.
   - **Resize rows to fit cell contents**   Performs as advertised.

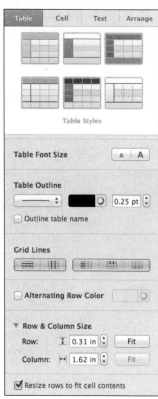

3. To make changes to single cells or groups of cells, click the Cell tab in the Format bar. Cell tab options are as follows:

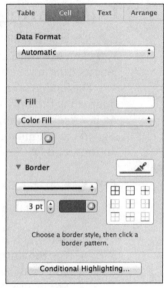

- **Data Format**   Determine how data in a cell appears and is used throughout the document based on what type of data it is. You can allow Pages to automatically format the data according to the type of data entered, or you can select the type of data a cell is to use. Data types are Number, Currency, Percentage, Fraction, Numeral System, Scientific, Text, Date & Time, and Duration.
- **Fill**   Adjust the color fill of the cell(s).
- **Border**   Adjust the color and style of the cell borders.
- **Conditional Highlighting**   Automatically highlight cells when they match the criteria you set for them.

4. To make changes to the text of a cell or table, click the Text tab in the Format bar. You're familiar with these options since they've been covered in Chapter 3.
5. To make changes to the arrangement of the table or selected cells within the rest of the document, use the options in the Arrange tab.

iOS

To customize a table in Pages for iOS:

1. Select which part of the table you want to customize:
   - For the entire table, tap the circle in its upper left corner.
   - For a single cell, tap within that cell.
   - For multiple cells, tap the first cell to see the blue outline showing the selected cell, including the blue dots in the upper left and lower right of it. Tap-and-drag the blue dots to select the desired cells.
2. To make table-wide customizations:
   a. Select the table as described in step 1.
   b. Tap the format inspector icon in the toolbar.
   c. Tap the Table, Headers, or Arrange tab in the Format bar and make the desired changes.
      - Items available in the Table tab include
        - **Table Styles**   Change the entire look of a table using the predefined styles.
        - **Table Options**   Enable or disable the Table Name, Table Outline, and Alternating Rows, as well as Grid Options such as Horizontal or Vertical Lines, Header Column Lines, and Header Row Lines. You can also make table-wide font settings from here.

- Items in the Headers tab allow you to increase or decrease the number of Header Rows, Header Columns, and Footer Rows.
- Items available in the Arrange tab include
    - **Move to Back/Front**   Allow you to position the table within the layers of the document.
    - **Wrap**   Determine how text in the document wraps around the table.
    - **Lock/Unlock**   Prevent or allow the table to be edited and/or moved.

3. To make changes to a single cell or a group of cells:
   a. Select the cell(s) as described in step 1.
   b. Tap the format inspector icon in the toolbar.
   c. Tap the Table, Headers, Cell, or Format tab in the Format bar and make desired changes:
      - Items available in the Table and Header tabs are the same as for table-wide changes, as described in step 2.
      - Items in the Cell tab allow you to adjust the look of the text within the cell, as well as its fills and borders.

- Items available in the Format tab let you determine how Pages formats the data in a cell (or cells) according to the type of data entered, or you can select the type of data a cell is to use. Data types are Number, Currency, Percentage, Text, Date & Time, and Duration.

iCloud

To customize a table in Pages for iCloud:

1. Select the table and then select the part of it you want to customize. When you move your pointer over a table, the cursor changes to look like a white cross. Click once on a cell to select it, or click-and-drag over multiple cells to select them.
2. To make table-wide customizations:
   a. Select the entire table as discussed in step 1.
   b. Click the Table tab in the format panel. Options available in the Table tab include
      - **Table Styles** Change the entire look of a table using the predefined styles.
      - **Headers & Footer** Increase or decrease the number of headers and footers.
      - **Table Options** Enable the table's name (appears at the top of the table).
3. To make customizations to a cell or cells:
   a. Select an individual cell or group of cells as discussed in step 1.
   b. Click the Cell tab in the format panel. Options available in the Cell tab include Font, Alignment, and Fill, all of which you're already familiar with. You will also see Merge Cells if you have selected more than one cell, but we'll discuss this in the upcoming section.
   c. Click the Data tab to select what type of data the cell(s) are formatted to handle. The options are Automatic, Number, Currency, Percentage, Date & Time, Fraction, Scientific, and Text.

Merging and Unmerging Cells

Merging cells allows you to combine the content of two or more cells, and unmerging them has the opposite effect.

Merging cells will cause the following to occur:

- Should only one of the selected cells contain content before the merger, the merged cell will keep the content and formatting of that cell.
- Should more than one of the cells have content, all of the content is kept, however it is all converted to text.
- If the top left cell (of those selected) contains a fill color, the merged cell keeps that color.

When you unmerge cells, the formatting of the previously merged cell is kept throughout the unmerged cells.

To merge cells:

1. Select the cells to be merged.
2. Follow the specific procedure for the Pages version you're working in:
   - **OS X** Choose Format | Table | Merge Cells (using the Format menu, not the Format button in the toolbar).
   - **iOS** Tap Merge in the pop-up menu.
   - **iCloud** Click the Cell tab in the format panel and click the Merge button at the bottom.

To unmerge cells:

1. Select the cells to be unmerged.
2. Follow the specific procedure for the Pages version you're working in:
   - **OS X**   Choose Format | Table | Unmerge Cells (using the Format menu, not the Format button in the toolbar).
   - **iOS**   Tap Unmerge in the pop-up menu.
   - **iCloud**   Click the Cell tab in the format panel and click the Unmerge button at the bottom.

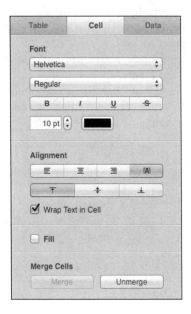

Formula Basics

If you use tables often, at some point you will find that you want to combine numbers from a column to get a total (for example, to show the total amount of groceries purchased in a monthly budget). Pages for OS X and iCloud are loaded to the gills with 250 predefined mathematical functions, which makes it simple for you to find the function you need to complete a formula for the cells in a table. You probably quickly observed that I didn't mention iOS, and yes, I'm sorry to inform you that insertion of formulas and functions within Pages for iOS is not something that's currently supported.

Tip   We'll cover the basics of using formulas and functions in this section, but to really get your hands dirty, you'll want to go to Apple's online resource for the topic. You can access the Formulas and Functions Help page at http://help.apple.com/ functions/mac/4.0/. There you'll find detailed descriptions and usage instructions for each of the supported functions in Pages, Keynote, and Numbers (as well as for Apple's iBooks Author app).

To enter your own mathematical formula into a cell:

1. Select the cell in which you want the result of the formula to display.
2. Press the = key on the keyboard to open the formula editor.
3. Create your formula:
   a. Select the first cell that you want to use for the first value in the formula (when you click it, the combined name of the column and the row appears, such as A2, B4, etc.), or manually enter a value.
   b. Enter the mathematical operator you need for your formula, such as + (add), - (subtract), * (multiply), or / (divide).
   c. Select the next cell that you want to use for the next value in the formula, or manually enter a value.
   d. Continue the process above until all the cells you need for your total are included in the formula.
4. Press the RETURN key or click the green check mark in the formula editor to complete the formula creation. Clicking the red × will cause you to lose the changes you've made.

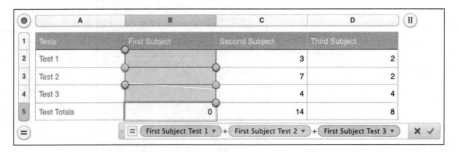

As mentioned, Pages comes preloaded with tons of different functions that you can cherry-pick and use at your discretion. Open the Functions panel in both the OS X and iCloud versions of Pages and you'll be treated to the sight of more functions than you can shake a stick at, as evidenced in Figure 4-6. Here's how to utilize the Functions panel:

1. Search for functions by entering their names in the search field, denoted by the magnifying glass, or...
   Select a type of function from the left side of the functions list, and then select a function from within that type to see its description (and several examples of how it is used in a formula) at the bottom of the panel.
2. Click the Insert Function button to place the function in your formula.

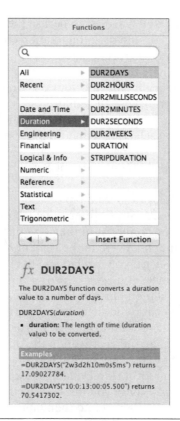

FIGURE 4-6   The Functions panel offers 250 functions to jazz up your formulas.

Chart Toppers

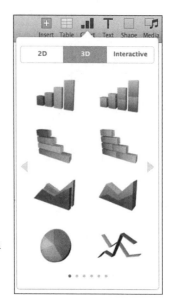

Charts are yet another way in which Pages helps you to share your findings, viewpoints, and so forth with the intended audience of your documented creations. Charts are beautiful and informative, and are easily implemented and manipulated within Pages for OS X and iOS (but not yet supported in the iCloud version).

Adding and Placing Charts

To add a chart to documents in the OS X version of Pages:

1. Click the Charts button in the toolbar.
2. Click either the 2D, 3D, or Interactive tab to select a chart type.
3. Choose a chart by clicking it in the pop-up menu or by dragging-and-dropping it into the document.

Click the right and left arrows to peruse the chart variations. If you select a 3D chart, you can click-and-drag the rotation controls in its center to rotate it to the angle you want to use (pretty cool, huh?).

4. Click the Edit Chart Data button to change the headings and data within the chart, and then begin entering your own information. Click the red dot in the upper left corner to close the editor.

5. Drag the chart anywhere you like to place it in the document.

6. Delete a chart by selecting it and pressing your keyboard's DELETE key.

To add a chart to documents in the iOS version of Pages:

1. Tap + in the toolbar and then tap the Charts tab in the menu.

2. Select either the 2D, 3D, or Interactive tab to choose a chart type.

3. Choose a chart by tapping it in the pop-up menu or by dragging-and-dropping it into the document. Swipe to the right or left to browse the chart versions. If you select a 3D chart, you can tap-and-drag the rotation controls in its center to rotate it to the angle you want to use (still pretty cool, huh?).

4. Tap the chart and then tap Edit Data in the menu to change the headings and data within the chart, and then enter your own data in the Editor Chart Data window. Should you want to change which data, rows or columns, is plotted as your data series, tap the gear icon in the upper left of the toolbar and tap the option you want to use. Regain the use of a full keyboard by toggling the switch next to the option for it. Tap Done in the upper right corner to close the editor.

5. Drag the chart anywhere you like to place it in the document.

6. Delete a chart by tapping it and then tapping Delete in the menu.

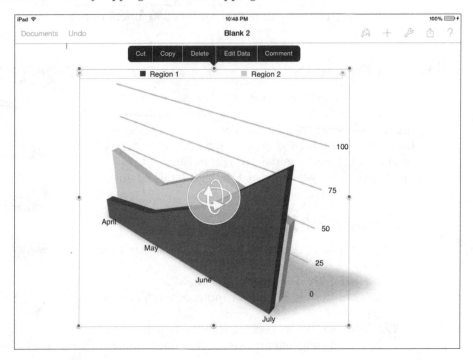

Adjusting a Chart's Appearance and Type

Sometimes we all need a good makeover, and Pages allows you to give a doozy of one to your charts, should you deem such measures be taken. Both supported versions, OS X and iOS, are quite adept at making changes to your chart and its contents.

OS X

To make changes to charts using Pages for OS X:

1. Select the chart to edit; this action opens the Charts format bar.
2. Make changes to your chart using options in the tabs available (the options under each tab vary greatly depending on the type of chart you're using):
   - **Chart**   Make changes to items such as the overall style, fonts, colors, shadows, and the like. You can also change the type of chart you're using, which may render some of your changes null and void if they're not supported for the new chart type you select.
   - **Axis**   Change the type of scale for your axis, enable value labels, edit gridlines, and more.
   - **Series**   Edit the way your data series is displayed in the chart.
   - **Arrange**   Make targeted changes to your chart's location in the document.

iOS

To make changes to charts using Pages in iOS:

1. Select the chart to edit.
2. Tap the Format inspector icon in the toolbar (looks like a paintbrush).
3. Make changes to your chart using options in the tabs available (the options under each tab vary widely based on the type of chart you're using):
   - **Chart**   Make changes to items such as the overall style, fonts, colors, shadows, and more. You can also change the type of chart you're using, which may render some of your changes null and void if they're not supported for the new chart type you choose.
   - **X Axis and Y Axis**   Change the type of scale for your axis, enable value labels, edit gridlines, and more.
   - **Series**   Edit the way your data series is displayed in the chart.
   - **Arrange**   Change the order of the chart in regard to other elements in your document by moving it forward or backward, and determine how to wrap text around the chart.

Summary

You've spiffed up your documents quite a bit in this chapter, using images, charts, tables, and whatnot. You're ready to create and share documents with the best word processing gurus around (or you're getting there, at least). In Chapter 5, you'll see how to edit your documents to give them that little extra polish.

5

Tidying Up Pages Documents

HOW TO...

- Track changes when editing a document
- Find and replace text
- Check spelling and use autocorrect
- Use the built-in reference tools
- Make comments and add highlights to text

As the title of the chapter indicates, it's time to wrap things up in regards to Pages. Don't fret, though: we've still a bit more to cover before turning the lights out on this topic.

Adding text to a document and spicing it up with a few images and graphics is only part of document creation. Now comes the fun of editing, proofreading, and generally trying to make sure you've got all of your ducks in a row before making your document available for mass consumption. The last thing one wants when disseminating a document is to have an unruly *anas platyrhynchos* bring the entire show to a screeching halt. So let's jump right in to see how to make your documents ready for the spotlight!

Tracking Changes

A document that's being created for others to see is often subjected to heavy editing, whether said editing is performed by the individual who crafted the document or by many other interested parties, such as copy editors, technical editors, and the like (you all know who you are).

While getting input from several sources is great and can certainly make for a more polished final product, if you don't know who is saying what in the editorial comments, it can make things a bit unnerving, not to mention all manner of higgledy-piggledy.

Pages helps you sift through the mountain of editing info through the feature of tracking changes, which simply means that it can display changes and comments made by your document's other benefactors in an orderly fashion. When you enable Track Changes, the text that's changed appears in a color that's different from the text in the rest of the document, and a change bar is visible in the document's margin.

 Pages for OS X and iOS are quite adept at tracking changes, but at present the iCloud version isn't quite prepared for this task.

Enabling and Disabling Track Changes

To enable Track Changes in OS X, choose Edit | Track Changes. The review toolbar now appears at the top of the page, as you can see in Figure 5-1. You can completely turn off tracking by clicking the action menu (looks like a gear) and choosing Turn Off Tracking. You can also temporarily stop change tracking (instead of completely turning it off) by toggling the Tracking switch to Paused.

FIGURE 5-1   The review toolbar appears at the top of a document when Track Changes is on.

To enable Track Changes in iOS, tap the Tools icon (the wrench) in the toolbar, tap Change Tracking, and then toggle the Tracking switch to On (green). Enter a name that Pages can use to identify you when prompted (this happens the first time you enable Track Changes). You can completely turn off tracking by simply toggling the Tracking switch to Off. You can also temporarily stop change tracking (instead of completely turning it off) by tapping the Tools icon, tapping Change Tracking, and toggling the Pause switch to On (green).

Viewing Tracked Changes

Pages allows you to select how you want to view tracked changes; choose from one of these three options:

- **Markup**   Any deleted items appear with a strikethrough and all new text appears in a different color than the rest of the document's text.
- **Markup Without Deletions**   Only text will appear onscreen, while deletions are hidden.
- **Final**   Your text appears in a normal fashion, with deletions hidden and new text blending in with unchanged text.

Change how tracked changes are viewed in OS X by clicking the action menu in the review toolbar and selecting one of the aforementioned options.

Change how tracked changes are viewed in iOS by tapping the Tools icon in the toolbar, tapping Change Tracking, and then tapping the option you want to use.

Accepting or Rejecting Changes

Who said that your editor's input was the final word in this little game of document creation? (I hope my benevolent editors will kindly ignore the preceding question...) Pages gives you the option of accepting a collaborator's suggestions or rejecting them outright.

Pages for OS X allows you to accept or reject a change to your document in one of the three following ways:

- Click the actions menu (gear icon) in the review toolbar and select Accept All Changes or Reject All Changes to make a single, sweeping choice.
- Choose a selection of text and click either Accept or Reject in the review toolbar to perform one or the other on changes made within the selected text.
- Move your pointer over changed text and select either Accept or Reject from the pop-up menu, illustrated in Figure 5-2.

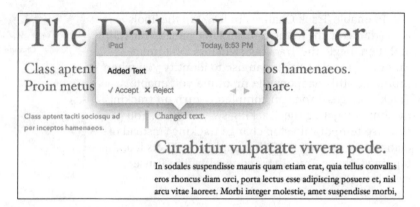

FIGURE 5-2 Click either Accept or Reject to perform that very action on changed text.

In much the same vein, Pages for iOS allows you to accept or reject a change to your document in one of three ways:

- Turn off change tracking in the document. When you perform this action, Pages will ask if you want to Accept All Changes or Reject All Changes; simply tap your choice.
- Choose a selection of text and tap either Accept or Reject in the pop-up menu.
- Tap anywhere on an instance of changed text and select either Accept or Reject from the pop-up menu.

Working with Comments and Highlights

Commenting text and making highlights to text are major parts of an editor's job, so naturally Pages makes it super simple to do both.

Making Comments and Highlights in OS X

To place comments or highlights in a document while working in Pages for OS X:

1. Click in the document anywhere that you want to add your comment or select the text you want to highlight.
2. Click Comment in the toolbar to open a comment window. To highlight selected text, click Highlight in the toolbar or choose Insert | Highlight from the menu (not the toolbar).
3. Enter your comments as desired (which isn't necessary, of course, if you simply want to highlight an item).

4. Click outside the comment window to make it disappear. The comment is still in the document, mind you, it's just safely out of sight until someone wants to view it again.

To work with a comment or highlight in a document in Pages for OS X:

- Hover your mouse pointer over the comment or highlight to see it.
- Click the commented/highlighted text or item to open the comment and leave it open (until you click outside of it to make it disappear again, that is).
- Dismiss the comment or highlight altogether by opening it and then clicking Delete in the lower left of the comment window.

Making Comments and Highlights in iOS

To place comments or highlights in a document while working in Pages for iOS:

1. Tap the document in the location or on the item that you want to add your comment to or select the text you want to highlight.
2. Tap Comment in the pop-up menu to open a comment window or tap Highlight to highlight the selected text.
3. Enter your comments if working with a comment window.
4. Tap outside the comment window to make it disappear.

To work with a comment or highlight in a document in Pages for iOS:

- Tap the commented text or item to open the comment.
- Remove a comment from the document by tapping it and then tapping Delete in the lower left of the comment window. Remove a highlight by tapping it and then tapping Remove Highlight in the pop-up menu.

Finding and Replacing Text

Pages can help you find text in a document quite easily and can even help you replace that text if need be. Thankfully, this is a task that can quickly be done from any of the three Pages versions.

OS X

To find text in a document using Pages for OS X:

1. Click the View button in the toolbar and select Show Find & Replace.
2. Type the word, character, or phrase you're looking for. Pages highlights matches for your search term as you type. Narrow your search results by using the Whole Words (find only the whole words you entered) and/or Match Case (find items

that exactly match the capitalization you enter) search tools. To use them, click the action menu (looks like a gear) on the left side of the Find & Replace window and click to select one or both options.

3. Click the right or left arrow to see the next or previous match, respectively.

 You can see a list of past searches, and also clear that list, by clicking the small gray arrow next to the magnifying glass in the search field of the Find & Replace window.

To find and replace text in a document using Pages for OS X:

1. Click the View button in the toolbar and select Show Find & Replace.
2. Click the action menu (gear icon) on the left side of the Find & Replace window and select Find & Replace from the menu.
3. Type the word, character, or phrase you're looking for in the first field. Pages highlights matches for your search term as you type. Narrow your search results by using one or both of the Whole Words and Match Case search tools.
4. Type the replacement text, character, or phrase in the second field. If you leave the second field blank, the text in the first field will be deleted.

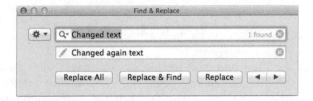

5. Use the buttons at the bottom of the Find & Replace window to perform an action on the found text:
   - **Replace All**   Replaces every match at once.
   - **Replace & Find**   Replaces the first match and moves on to the next.
   - **Replace**   Replaces the first match and does not move to the next.
   - **Arrows**   Click the left or right arrow to move to the previous or next match, respectively, without replacing anything.

iOS

To find text in a document using Pages for iOS:

1. Tap the Tools icon (wrench) in the toolbar and then tap Find.
2. Type the word, character, or phrase you're looking for in the search field that appears directly above the keyboard. Pages highlights matches for your search term as you type. Narrow your search results by using the Whole Words (find only the whole words you entered) and/or Match Case (find items that exactly match the capitalization you enter) search tools. To use them, tap the action menu (looks like a gear) on the left side of the search window and toggle the switches to enable one or both options.
3. Tap the right or left arrow to see the next or previous match, respectively.

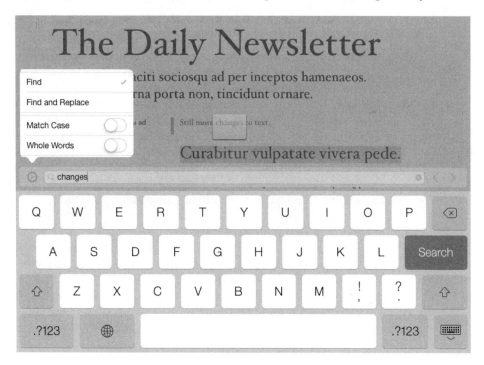

To find and replace text in a document using Pages for iOS:

1. Tap the Tools icon (wrench) in the toolbar and then tap Find.
2. Tap the action menu (gear icon) on the left side of the search window and tap Find & Replace.
3. Type the word, character, or phrase you're looking for in the first field. Pages highlights matches for your search term as you type. Narrow your search results by enabling one or both of the Whole Words and Match Case search tools.
4. Type the replacement text, character, or phrase in the second field. If you leave the second field blank, the text in the first field will be deleted.
5. Use the buttons at the bottom of the Find & Replace window to perform an action on the found text:
   - Replace the selected match by tapping Replace.
   - Replace all matches by tapping-and-holding Replace and then tapping Replace All.
   - Tap the left or right arrow to move to the previous or next match, respectively, without replacing anything.

iCloud

To find text in a document using Pages for iCloud:

1. Click the Tools button in the toolbar and select Show Find & Replace. The Find window will appear at the bottom of the document window.
2. Type the word, character, or phrase you're looking for in the Find field (next to the magnifying glass icon). Pages highlights matches for your search term as you type. Narrow your search results by using the Whole Words (find only the whole words you entered) and/or Match Case (find items that exactly match the capitalization you enter) search tools. To use them, click the action menu (looks like a gear) on the left side of the Find window and click to select one or both options.
3. Click the right or left arrow to see the next or previous match, respectively.

To find and replace text in a document using Pages for iCloud:

1. Click the Tools button in the toolbar and select Show Find & Replace. The Find window will appear at the bottom of the document window.
2. Click the action menu (gear icon) on the left side of the Find window and select Find & Replace from the menu.
3. Type the word, character, or phrase you're looking for in the first field. Pages highlights matches for your search term as you type. Narrow your search results by using one or both of the Whole Words and Match Case search tools.

4. Type the replacement text, character, or phrase in the second field. If you leave the second field blank, the text in the first field will be deleted when you click the Replace button.

5. Use the buttons at the bottom of the Find & Replace window to perform an action on the found text:
   - **Replace**   Replaces the old text with the new.
   - **Arrows**   Click the left or right arrow to move to the previous or next match, respectively, without replacing anything.

Check Your Speling

Dear reader, did you notice the misspelled word in the title of this section? If so, you may not even need this section. However, if you're like me and occasionally overlook a misspelled word, or you type so fast that sometimes one gets by you, continue on to see how to take spelling advice from Pages.

Pages can automatically check for spelling mistakes and correct them, make recommendations for using proper grammar, and even add words to its dictionary. All three versions of Pages allow some degree of spell-checking prowess. High fives all around!

OS X

Pages checks spelling and makes corrections by default in its OS X version. If you misspell a word, Pages will display it with a red-dotted underline. Should you type a misspelled word and Pages picks up on it, it will automatically correct the misspelling and underline it briefly with a blue-dotted line. You can quickly correct a misspelled word manually by CONTROL-clicking (or right-clicking) it and choosing the correct spelling from the pop-up menu.

Click Edit | Spelling & Grammar to see your spell-checking options:

- Show Spelling and Grammar opens the Spelling and Grammar window.
- Check Document Now forces Pages to check spelling.
- Check Spelling While Typing is enabled by default and misspelled words are underlined by a red-dotted line.
- Check Grammar With Spelling causes possible grammatical errors to be underlined with a green-dotted line, and misspelled words are still tagged with the red-dotted underline.

The Spelling and Grammar window offers a few more options than the iOS and iCloud versions can offer:

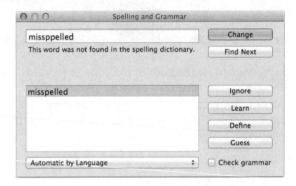

- Misspelled words appear in the top field and possible corrections appear in the lower field. Click the Find Next button to move to the next misspelled word in the document.
- Select a word from the possible corrections and click Change to change to the new word.
- Click Ignore to make Pages look the other way and skip past a word.
- Click the Learn button to add the word to Pages' dictionary.
- Click Define to have Pages look up the meaning of the word in a dictionary.
- Click Guess to ask Pages to offer you some suggestions.
- Check the Check Grammar box to enable this feature.
- Force Pages to automatically correct misspelled words based on a particular language set.

iOS

Spell checking is a pretty simple deal in Pages for iOS:

1. Tap the Tools icon in the toolbar.
2. Tap Settings.
3. Toggle the Check Spelling switch on (green) or off (white). When on, misspelled words will appear with a red-dotted underline.

4. Tap a misspelled word and then tap one of the suggested corrections. If no suggestions are offered, tap the right arrow, tap Replace, and then tap the correct word spelling from the offerings.

iCloud

Checking your spelling is also fairly easy to handle within Pages for iCloud:

1. Turn spell checking on or off by clicking Tools in the toolbar, choosing Settings, and then clicking Check Spelling. Pages is checking spelling when a check mark is next to the option. Misspelled words are tagged with a red-dotted underline.
2. Click a misspelled word and then either:
   - Select the correct spelling from the list.
   - Type the correct spelling.

Utilizing Reference Tools

It may surprise some to learn that Pages doesn't include reference tools, such as a dictionary and thesaurus, of its own, unlike Microsoft's Office suite. However, never fear, for Apple is here!

Apple's computer operating system, OS X, is already locked and loaded with a Dictionary app, which also includes a thesaurus. Dictionary can be found in the Applications folder. Simply type a word into the search field and any references to it are displayed.

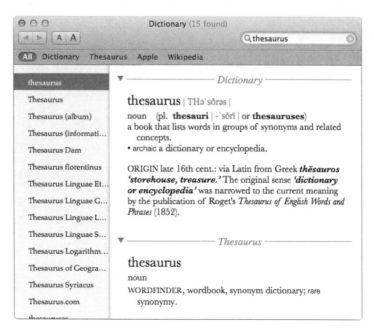

It Turns Out That There Is a Substitute: Using Text Replacement

Have you ever needed to add a character to a document but just couldn't find the darned thing on the keyboard (such as the copyright symbol)? Or is there a particular word that you're just terrible at typing and wish there was a way your computer would automatically insert the word you meant to type all along? The OS X version of Pages (sorry, iOS and iCloud version fans) has a neat feature that allows you to type a string of characters and have Pages substitute something else for them, and this action is called Text Replacement.

To set up and use Text Replacement:

1. Choose Edit | Substitutions | Show Substitutions to open the Substitutions window.
2. Check the box next to Text Replacement, if it's not already checked.
3. Click the Text Preferences button to open the Text tab of the Keyboard preferences (within System Preferences).
4. Click the + button under the Replace list on the left side of the window.
5. Type the string of characters you want to be replaced when they're typed in a document.
6. Press TAB and then type the characters you want to be the substitute for the characters in the Replace list.

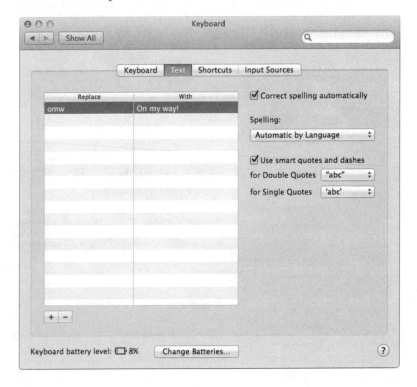

7. Back in the Substitutions window of Pages, click Replace All or Replace In Selection to perform the replacement for text that's already in the document. If Text Replacement is turned on, new text that's entered will automatically be substituted.

Summary

Sadly, it's time to bid adieu to our good friend Pages. This chapter helped you complete documents for your adoring fans to enjoy and fawn over. You are now a certified and bona fide Pages aficionado! (Your certificate's in the mail, but in case it doesn't show up, you could always create one in Pages using your newfound expertise.)

PART III

Creating and Delivering Presentations, the Apple Way

6

Getting to Know Keynote

HOW TO...

- Navigate Keynote's interface
- Set Keynote's preferences
- Create, print, and share presentations
- Choose themes for your presentations
- Master the art of working with presentation slides

Most self-respecting geeks and techno-gurus have seen Steve Jobs deliver one of his famous Macworld Expo keynote addresses, whether in person or through some video medium. Ever wonder how Jobs made such great presentations...and how you could make yours just as great? I thought so, and so did Steve, which is why Apple gives us Keynote, iWork's presentation creation and delivery app.

Sure, Microsoft's PowerPoint has been around for years and, honestly, is a pretty good program, but I'll take Keynote, thank you very much. Keynote, in my humble opinion, offers the kind of elegant simplicity that PowerPoint has been grasping for since the beginning of forever but has failed to obtain simply because it can't shake itself loose from the mayhem that is its legacy and interface. For some reason, perhaps very effective marketing campaigns, many of us have grown to believe that something simple can't be as good as something ridiculously and laughably complex, especially those of us who've labored in the business world for any length of time. "The more bells and whistles (that I'll admittedly never touch, even with your hand) a program has, the better it has to be" has been the business mantra for quite a while now.

Thankfully, since the advent of the iPad and iPhone, that perception has waned a bit. Keynote has been the only usable presentation app on the iPad since its inception in 2010, and iPads are incredibly popular in the business world (thanks in large part to the iPhone), so folks are starting to say "those guys at Apple not only make pretty good phones, but their mobile and computing apps ain't half bad, either."

However, Keynote isn't just gaining in popularity with the business crowd; the more creative among us are also recognizing its capabilities and benefiting from its presentation awesomeness. Again, the simplicity, yet power, of what Keynote offers is exactly what attracts the creative mind.

Please note that when I refer to "simplicity" regarding Keynote (or any of the other iWork apps), I do not mean that it's simplistic or dumbed-down, but quite the opposite. The simplicity I refer to is the ability for Apple to pack so much power into such a tight, easy-to-use, beautifully crafted, and intuitive interface.

Getting Around In Keynote

Enough jibber jabber; let's kick the tires on this Keynote thing! This section shows you the basic layout of Keynote in each of its supported platforms, OS X, iOS, and iCloud, and provides a bit of explanation for much of what you see.

Figure 6-1 shows Keynote from within OS X. Each of the options I point out to you will be covered at some point throughout this book. Also, Chapter 1 has already introduced you to many of the callouts in Figure 6-1.

 The contents of the Format bar will change depending on the element you've selected in the slide. If you select an image, image-formatting options are displayed; if you select text, text-related options show up, and so on.

Figure 6-2 shows the same presentation, only this time it's open in Keynote for iOS.

FIGURE 6-1 A map of Keynote's interface in OS X

Presentations   Slide navigator   Undo   Slide window   Format inspector   Add   Tools   Share   Play   Coaching tips

Add a slide

FIGURE 6-2   The same presentation as shown in Figure 6-1, shown this time in Keynote for iOS

If you've read Chapter 1 already, you're familiar with many of the callouts in Figure 6-2, but there are still a couple I need to familiarize you with. Tapping Presentations in the upper left corner of the screen takes you to the Presentations manager screen, where you can create new presentations or open some you've already created. The Play button in the upper right corner allows you to play your presentation.

iCloud is also home to a version of Keynote, and as you can see in Figure 6-3, I've opened the same presentation in it as well. The presentation looks the same in all three versions, and anytime you make a change in one version, it's instantly reflected in the others (assuming you're saving your presentation to iCloud, that is).

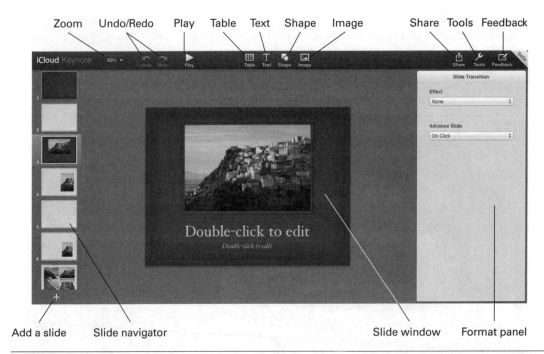

FIGURE 6-3 Presentations look the same in Keynote for iCloud as they do in Keynote for iOS or OS X.

Setting Keynote's Preferences

Keynote includes options, called preferences, that you can set as you like according to the way you work. All three versions of Keynote have preferences, and I'll happily give you a tour of them (it won't take long, promise).

 If the same preference option is available within multiple versions of the app, you'll need to set the option in each version in order for it to be consistent across platforms. Being logged in to iCloud doesn't mean you can set a preference in OS X, for example, and have the same preference changed automatically in iOS.

OS X Preferences

To open the preferences in Keynote for OS X, press ⌘-, (the COMMAND key and comma key simultaneously). You can also click the Keynote menu in the upper left of your screen (to the immediate right of the Apple menu) and select Preferences. There are four tabs within the Preferences window: General, Slideshow, Rulers, and Remotes.

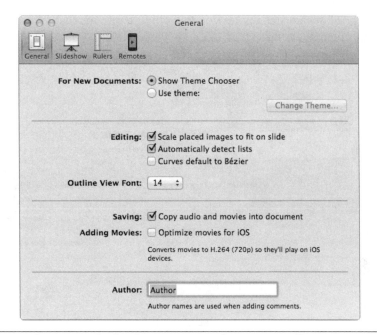

FIGURE 6-4   The General tab of Keynote's Preferences window

Figure 6-4 shows the General tab of Keynote's Preferences window, from which you can make the following adjustments:

- **For New Documents**   Select either Show Theme Chooser or Use Theme as the default action when you begin to create a new presentation. Selecting Show Theme Chooser automatically opens the Theme Chooser, and selecting Use Theme automatically creates a new presentation from a theme you choose by clicking the Change Theme button and selecting it from a location on your Mac.
- **Editing**   This section lets you set default actions for editing a presentation:
  - **Scale placed images to fit on slide**   Speaks for itself, I think.
  - **Automatically detect lists**   Check this box to have Keynote detect when you are typing a list. When a list is detected, Keynote automatically formats it as such.
  - **Curves default to Bézier**   Check this box for Bézier curves to be the default, or leave it unchecked to use smooth curves.
- **Saving**   Check the option Copy Audio And Movies Into Document to do just that, as opposed to linking to them. This ensures the presentation will be playable in its entirety on other computers that might not have the same audio or movie files on them as you have on your Mac.
- **Adding Movies**   Check the Optimize Movies For iOS option when you want to add a movie to your slide and it will be viewed by folks using iOS devices.
- **Author**   Add a name to the available field to use when tracking changes and making comments within a slide.

The Slideshow tab allows you to configure options that are necessary for playback of your presentations.

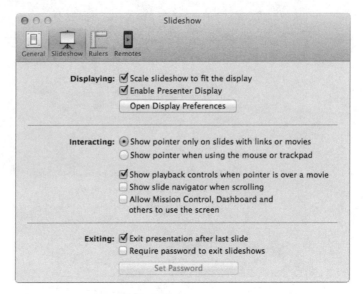

Displaying:

- **Scale slideshow to fit the display**   Does just what it says, gentle reader.
- **Enable Presenter Display**   Check this box to show your presenter notes, slide navigator, and other presenter-related material on your Mac when using an external display to show your presentation. Click the Open Display Preferences button to configure displays in OS X's System Preferences.

Interacting:

- **Show pointer...**   Select one of the two options for allowing the mouse or trackpad pointer to display during your presentation.
- **Show playback controls when pointer is over a movie**   If selected, playback controls (Play, Rewind, etc.) will be visible on the movie within the slide.
- **Show slide navigator when scrolling**   Displays your slide navigator when you scroll on your mouse or trackpad (if it's enabled, of course).
- **Allow Mission Control, Dashboard, and others to use the screen**   Allows Mission Control and other apps to intrude on your presentation; I personally don't care for enabling this option, but you're a grown-up, so by all means do as you please.

Exiting:

- **Exit presentation after last slide**   Select to exit the presentation and return to Keynote once the last slide is presented.
- **Require password to exit slideshows**   This option is a must if you don't want someone to have access to Keynote (not to mention your Mac) should you be letting them view the presentation alone or in a kiosk environment. Security!

The Rulers tab offers options for helping you decide where to place items within your slides.

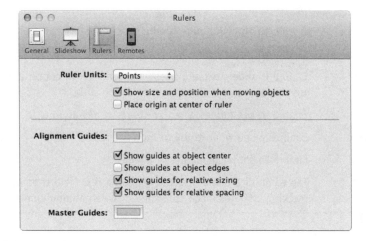

Ruler Units:

- Click the pop-up menu to select a default unit of measurement.
- Check the Show Size And Position When Moving Objects box to see an onscreen prompt that shows you exactly that.
- Check the Place Origin At Center Of The Ruler box to place the ruler's horizontal origin point at the center of the slide.

Alignment Guides:

- Click the button to select a default color for alignment guides.
- Check the respective boxes to enable, or uncheck to disable, the options for showing guides at the center and/or edges of objects in the presentation. These guides make it easier to correctly place an item within the boundaries of the presentation and among other items in it.

Master Guides:

- Click the button to set the default color for master guides.

The Remotes tab in Keynote preferences is used to help set up an iPad or iPhone (that has the iOS version of Keynote installed) to control your presentations remotely. You'll find much more on this subject in Chapter 8.

iOS Settings

The iOS version of Keynote refers to preferences as Settings, but don't be thrown off by that. They still allow you to set app-wide defaults.

TABLE 6-1 Available Options in Settings for iOS Keynote

Option	Description
Check Spelling	Enable to allow Keynote to check your spelling as you type.
Slide Numbers	Enable to display the slide numbers in the lower right corner of the slides.
Center Guides	Enable in order to see guides when one item's center aligns with another item's center, or with the center of the slide.
Edge Guides	Enable to see guides when an item's edges align with another item's edges.
Spacing Guides	Enable to see when three or more items are equally spaced apart on a line.
Comments	Enable to show comments in a slide.
Author Name	Tap to enter a name into the available text field that will be used when tracking changes made to a slide or when adding comments.

Open a presentation, tap the Tools icon (looks like a wrench) in the upper right of the screen, and then tap Settings to access them. The Settings menu, as you can see in Figure 6-5, shows the options defined in Table 6-1. Simply touch the toggle switch to the right of each option to enable it (toggle turns green) or disable it (toggle is white), or tap the option if it has an arrow next to it, indicating it contains suboptions.

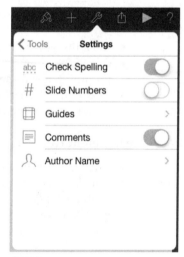

FIGURE 6-5 Preferences are known as Settings in Keynote for iOS.

iCloud Preferences

There are only a half dozen settings (yep, "settings" here too, not "preferences") to cover in Keynote for iCloud, and they can be seen in Figure 6-6. You can access the following settings by opening a presentation and navigating to Tools | Settings from the toolbar:

- **Show/Hide Format Panel** Select to show or hide the format panel on the right side of the screen.
- **Check Spelling** Select to enable or disable automatic spell checking.
- **Center Guides** Select to see guides when one item's center aligns with another item's center, or with the center of the slide.
- **Edge Guides** Select to see guides when an item's edges align with another item's edges.
- **Spacing Guides** Select to see when three or more items are equally spaced apart within a line.
- **Set Password** Select to add a password for the presentation you're currently working in.

FIGURE 6-6   Keynote for iCloud offers several options for setting your defaults.

Working with Presentations

Making new presentations, editing existing ones, punching things up with graphics, and all other manner of creativity are part of working with presentations. You'll find that Keynote will soon be your best buddy when it comes to such tasks.

Creating New Presentations

Creating new presentations seems like the logical place to start when it comes to working with a presentation app, so let's do just that, shall we?

To create a new presentation in Keynote (by format):

- **OS X**   Choose File | New or press ⌘-N to open the Theme Chooser. Select a theme for your new presentation and click Choose in the lower right corner. Note the Standard and Wide buttons at the top of the window, in case you'd like to use a slightly different format.
- **iOS**   From within the Presentations manager (if you're already in a presentation, tap Presentations in the upper left corner), tap the Create Presentation icon to open the Theme Chooser. Tap the theme you want to use and it will open automatically.
- **iCloud**   From within the iCloud Keynote screen, click the Create Presentation icon to open the Theme Chooser. Select the theme you want to use, as illustrated in Figure 6-7, and then click Choose in the upper right corner of the Theme Chooser window to open it.

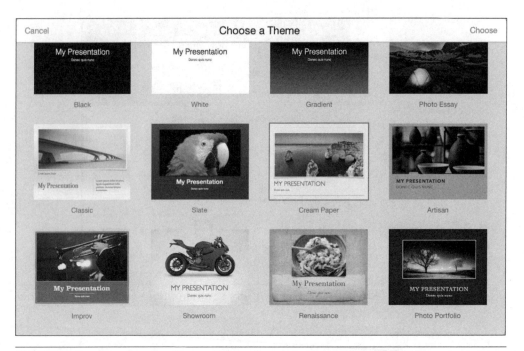

FIGURE 6-7   Opening the Cream Paper theme in Keynote for iCloud

Saving and Renaming Presentations

Since building presentations and not saving them is just silly (yep, I said it), let's see how we go about saving (and renaming) them:

- **OS X**   Press ⌘-s or choose File | Save to save a presentation. If this is the first time saving this presentation, the Save As window will open. Simply give the presentation a title, choose a location in which to keep it, and click the Save button. To rename a presentation, choose File | Rename, type the new name for your presentation (the presentation title in the middle of the window will be highlighted blue), and press RETURN; your presentation is now renamed.

Tip   If you don't see in the pop-up menu the location in which you want to keep the presentation, click the small square containing the downward arrow next to the Save As field to expand the window and see more options.

- **iOS**   Keynote automatically saves your presentations, but it gives them boring names like "Presentation" or "Presentation 2" by default, so you'll be pleased with the ability to easily rename presentations. Open the Presentations manager and tap the name of the presentation you want to rename. Enter the name of your presentation in the field provided in the Rename Presentation screen and tap Done on the screen.

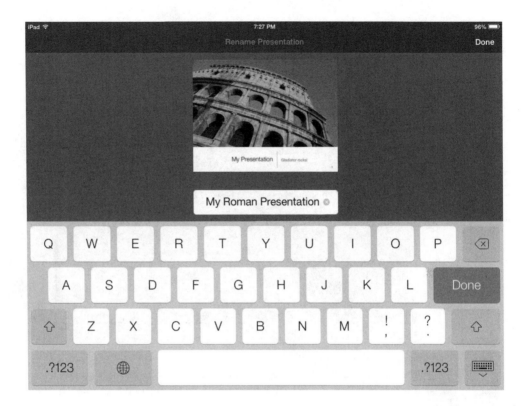

- **iCloud**   Keynote for iCloud automatically saves your presentations, but like iOS you start off with names like "Presentation." Thankfully, it's just as simple to rename the new presentation. Open the Presentations manager, select the name of the presentation you want to rename, enter the new name in the field provided, and press RETURN.

Opening Existing Presentations

Okay, so you've already created some presentations and simply want to know how to go about opening them on the various Keynote platforms—here's how!

OS X

To open presentations that are in iCloud or on your Mac:

1. Press ⌘-O or choose File | Open.
2. Select iCloud or On My Mac in the upper left corner of the window, depending on where the presentation resides.

3. Click once on the presentation you want to open, and then click the Open button in the lower right corner of the window to open it. You can also double-click a presentation within the window to quickly open it.

 Choose File | Open Recent to see a list of presentations that you've recently opened in Keynote. Just click the presentation in the list to open it.

iOS and iCloud

Opening an existing presentation is performed in the same way for both iOS and iCloud versions of Keynote. Just open the Presentations manager and select the presentation you want to open (you'll need to double-click the presentation in iCloud; simply tap it in iOS).

Which View Is for You?

Keynote for OS X (sorry, but not for iOS and iCloud) allows you to view your presentation in four different ways, each of which is useful under certain situations:

- **Navigator view (default)** See all of your slides in the slide navigator on the left side of the window, and the currently selected slide in the slide window. Drag slides up and down the navigator to reorganize them.
- **Slide only view** As its name indicates, this view displays only the currently selected slide in the window, and you cannot navigate to other slides.
- **Light table view** Arranges all the slides as if you had them laid out on a light table, as shown in Figure 6-8. This allows you to quickly view and reorganize the slides by dragging and placing slides into a different order.
- **Outline view** Allows you to work with slide texts within the slide navigator.

FIGURE 6-8 Light table view arranges your slides as if on a light table.

Locking Presentations and Using Passwords

Keynote is quite security-conscious, thank you very much. Who wants other folks messing with their presentations anyway, right? Well, Keynote allows you to use a password to prevent those who don't know it from changing your presentation, and even allows you to lock your presentation to prevent anyone from messing with it at all.

Using Passwords

A password protects your presentation from spies and other dastardly folks, and also from innocents who might accidentally change its contents. Once a password is assigned to a presentation, no one can open it, much less change it, without knowing the password.

 OS X and iOS versions of Keynote offer ways for Keynote to remember a presentation's password so that you don't have to enter it every time you open the presentation. This is not the best idea if you want your presentations to truly be secure.

To assign a password to a presentation:

- **OS X** Choose File | Set Password to open the password dialog. Enter the password in the Password and Verify fields, enter a hint in the Password Hint field if so desired (Apple recommends it, but I don't), and click the Set Password button.

- **iOS**   Open the presentation, tap the Tools icon, and tap Set Password. Enter the password in the Password and Verify fields, enter a hint in the Password Hint field if so desired (Apple recommends it, but again, I can't imagine why), and tap the Go button on the onscreen keyboard. Even if you don't enter a hint, you'll need to tap the Hint field before the blue Go button becomes visible.
- **iCloud**   Open the presentation, select the Tools icon, and then click Set Password. Enter the password in the Password and Verify fields, enter a hint in the Password Hint field if you like (Apple recommends it, but come on... why?), and click the Set Password button.

To open a password-protected presentation, simply type the password when prompted. If you don't know the password, you're up the proverbial creek without the proverbial paddle.

Locking Presentations

Locking a presentation prevents anyone from editing, renaming, moving, or deleting it. You must understand, though, that locking a presentation is an option that's only available within the OS X version of Keynote.

To lock a presentation:

1. Hold the mouse pointer over the title of the presentation (it must be open in Keynote to be locked) until you see a small gray arrow next to it; click the gray arrow.
2. Select the Locked check box to lock the presentation. Click outside the window to return to the presentation. Whenever you try to change an element of the presentation, you will be reminded that it is locked.

 Locking a presentation isn't nearly as secure as protecting it with a password. You can still delete a presentation by ignoring the warnings given you by OS X if you try to do so, and you can easily unlock a presentation by simply unchecking the Locked box in the title bar.

Moving Presentations to and from iCloud

Moving your presentations to iCloud makes them available to yourself and others anywhere you (or they) can connect to the Internet with a computer or iOS device. Moving presentations away from iCloud has the exact opposite effect, so use caution.

To move a presentation from your computer to iCloud, or vice versa:

1. Choose File | Move To.
2. Select a location from the pop-up menu. If you don't see the location you want in the menu, choose Other at the bottom of the menu to browse your hard drive.
3. Click the Move button. Your presentation will be physically moved, not copied, from its old location to the one you specified.

This feature is available only in the OS X version of Keynote.

Sharing Presentations with iCloud

Keynote allows you to share a presentation located in iCloud with anyone by sending them a link to the presentation.

 Make sure you protect your presentation with a password before sharing it (as described earlier in this chapter) if you only want authorized users to make changes to it. If you just send a link to an unprotected presentation, anyone with access to the link can make whatever changes they like. Scary.

When you share a presentation via iCloud, you are actually sending a web link to the presentation's location within iCloud. Anyone with Keynote (either on a Mac, an iOS device, or a Windows PC using iCloud) will be able to click the link and open (and edit) the presentation, and any changes they make will be saved to it, so be careful whom you share it with.

The links can be sent through email, Messages, Twitter, Facebook, or any other method you can think of to get the link to your intended recipient.

OS X

To share a presentation via iCloud from OS X Keynote:

1. Open the presentation you want to share. Protect the presentation with a password, if you haven't already done so!
2. Click the Share button in the toolbar.
3. Select the method you want to use to share the iCloud link to your presentation using the Share Link Via iCloud context menu.

Once the link is sent to the recipient(s), the Share icon in the toolbar is changed from the white box with the upward arrow to a couple of green-colored people, which simply indicates that the presentation is now being shared.

Click the Share button when in shared mode to do the following:

- Change the password for the presentation by using the Change Password button.
- Discontinue sharing of the presentation by clicking the Stop Sharing button.
- Send the link to someone else by clicking the Send Link button and selecting a method from the pop-up menu.

- Hold your mouse pointer over the link until you see a gray button called Copy Link, click the Copy Link button to copy the link to your Mac's clipboard, and then paste the link into any presentation or other sharing mechanism you like.

iOS

To share a presentation via iCloud from iOS:

1. Open the presentation you want to share (and please password-protect it).
2. Tap the Share button in the toolbar.
3. Tap the Share Link Via iCloud option. Decide which method you want to use to share the iCloud link to your presentation. You'll notice that AirDrop is another method of sharing that can be used from an iOS device in order to share the link with other iOS devices.

 AirDrop sharing isn't currently supported for exchanging files from OS X to iOS devices or vice versa. Hopefully, this will change in the near future, but as of this writing it's unsupported.

As in OS X, the Share icon has changed to a couple of green guys, which shows you the presentation is in shared mode. Tap the Share button when in shared mode, and then tap the Share Settings option to do the following:

- Change the password for the presentation by tapping Change Password.
- Discontinue sharing of the presentation by tapping Stop Sharing.
- Send the link to someone else by tapping Send Link and selecting a method from the pop-up menu.
- Tap the link to prompt a dark gray button called Copy, tap the Copy button to copy the link to your device's clipboard, and then paste the link into any presentation or sharing mechanism you like.

iCloud

To share a presentation via iCloud from within Keynote for iCloud:

1. Open the presentation (it's password-protected, right?) you want to share.
2. Click the Share button in the toolbar, and then click the blue Share Presentation button.
3. A window opens that states "This presentation is shared." From within this window, you can perform the following tasks:
    - Change the password for the presentation by using the Change Password button (or add a password by using the Add Password button).
    - Discontinue sharing of the presentation by clicking the Stop Sharing button.
    - Send the link to someone else via iCloud's Mail app by clicking the Email Link button.
    - Click the link once to highlight it, press ⌘-C (Mac) or CONTROL-C (PC) to copy the link to your computer's clipboard, and then paste the link into any presentation or sharing mechanism you like.

To open the "This presentation is shared" window again, click the Share button in the toolbar (the green people are back!), and then click Settings.

Exporting and Importing Presentations

Exporting a presentation from Keynote really has two meanings. One of them is to save the file in a format other than the native one, which is .key. The other meaning of export within Keynote is to transfer files from an iOS device to a computer through iTunes.

Importing presentations is usually as simple as opening them when working in Keynote. Of course, like exporting, importing presentations also has to do with transferring files from iTunes onto your iOS device.

Exporting Files from Keynote

Keynote can export files to multiple formats so they can be viewed and worked with in other apps.

This section of the chapter only deals with exporting files into non-native formats from the OS X and iCloud versions of Keynote; iOS doesn't support this feature.

OS X   To export a presentation using Keynote for OS X:

1. Open the presentation you want to export.
2. Click the File menu and hold your mouse pointer over the Export To menu.
3. Select the format you want to export your file to.
4. When the Export Your Presentation dialog opens, make any selections necessary according to the format you're exporting to, as illustrated in Figure 6-9.
5. Click Next.
6. Choose a location to save your new file, give it a new name if you like, and then click Export.

As indicated in Figure 6-9, file formats supported for export from Keynote for OS X are PDF, PowerPoint, QuickTime, HTML, Images, and Keynote '09.

iCloud   There are two ways to export a presentation using Keynote for iCloud: from within an open presentation and from within the Presentations manager.

To export from within an open presentation:

1. Choose Tools | Download A Copy.
2. Select the format you want to export your file to.
3. Once Keynote finishes formatting the presentation, it will automatically download to your browser's default downloads folder.

FIGURE 6-9   Make selections according to the file format you are exporting to.

To export from within the Presentations manager:

1. Click one time on the presentation you want to export so that it's highlighted.
2. Click the Presentation And Sort Options button (looks like a gear) at the top of the window and select Download Presentation from the menu.
3. Click the format you want to export your file to.
4. Once Keynote finishes formatting the presentation, it will automatically download to your browser's default downloads folder.

 Formats supported by Keynote for iCloud include PDF, PowerPoint, and Keynote.

Importing Files into Keynote

Non-native file formats supported by Keynote include Keynote '09 and PowerPoint. Importing a file into Keynote for OS X is as simple as opening it. To open a presentation file in Keynote for OS X:

1. Press ⌘-o or choose File | Open.
2. Select iCloud or On My Mac in the upper left corner of the window, depending on where the presentation is located.
3. Click once on the presentation you want to open, and then click the Open button in the lower right corner of the window to open it. You can also double-click a presentation within the window to open it.

 You can also simply drag-and-drop a Keynote or PowerPoint presentation onto the Keynote icon in the Dock to open it in Keynote for OS X.

It's also simple to open a presentation file in Keynote for iCloud. The simplest way is to drag-and-drop the file into the Presentations manager (using a supported browser, of course), but you can also upload a file:

1. Click the Settings icon (looks like a gear) and select Upload Presentation.
2. Browse your computer for the file you want to open and click Choose.

To open a presentation file in Keynote for iOS, you must first get the file into the device, and that's where transferring files using iTunes comes into play.

Transferring Files to and from Keynote Through iTunes

iTunes has the ability to transfer files to and from Keynote on iOS devices. This is particularly useful when you don't use, or have access to, iCloud but still need to work on your presentations via a computer.

To transfer files to Keynote for iOS from iTunes:

1. Connect your iOS device to your computer and open iTunes on the computer (not the iOS device).
2. Select your device in iTunes once it appears in the upper right of the window.
3. Select Apps in the toolbar at the top of the window and then scroll to the bottom of the window.
4. Click Keynote in the Apps list under File Sharing.
5. Click the Add button in the lower right and then browse your computer for the file you want to transfer. Once found, select it and then click Add. The file will show up in the Keynote Documents list.

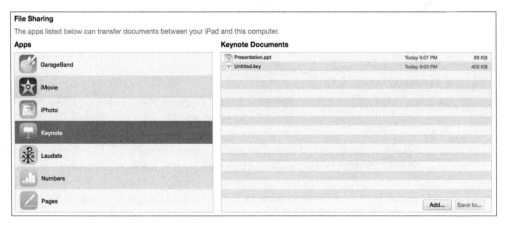

6. Open Keynote on your iOS device.
7. Go to the Presentations manager and click the + in the upper left corner; select Copy From iTunes.

8. When the Copy From iTunes window opens, tap the name of the presentation you want to transfer into Keynote on your iOS device. Once the transfer is complete, the presentation will appear in the Presentations manager, and then can be opened with a simple tap.

To transfer files from Keynote for iOS to iTunes:

1. Connect your iOS device to your computer and open iTunes on the computer (not the iOS device).
2. Select your device in iTunes (it will show up in the upper right of the window) once it appears.
3. Select Apps in the toolbar at the top of the window and then scroll to the bottom of the window.
4. Click Keynote in the Apps list under File Sharing.
5. Open Keynote on your iOS device and do one of the following:
   - If the presentation you want to transfer is not open, tap the Share button in the upper left of the screen (looks like a square containing an upward-pointing arrow) and select Send A Copy from the menu. Tap the presentation you want to transfer to highlight it.
   - If you are working in the presentation you want to transfer, tap the Share button in the upper right of the screen and select Send A Copy from the menu.
6. Tap the iTunes icon to open the Send To iTunes window.
7. Tap the file format you want to use for the presentation. Once the transfer is complete, the presentation will appear in the Keynote Documents list in iTunes. Select the file, click the Save To button in the lower right, select a location in which to save the file on your computer, and click the Save To button.

Printing a Presentation

Printing presentations from Keynote is as simple as from any other app, as you'll soon see.

Printing from OS X

To print presentations from Keynote for OS X, press ⌘-P or choose File | Print to open the Print dialog sheet, and then do the following:

1. Select in the Printer pop-up menu the printer you wish to send the print job to.
2. Make any other changes you deem necessary, such as adjusting the number of copies to print or specifying to print two-sided (if your printer supports such a feature). To see options such as Paper Size, click the Keynote pop-up menu and choose Page Attributes from the options.
3. Click the Print button in the lower right corner to send your job along to the printer.

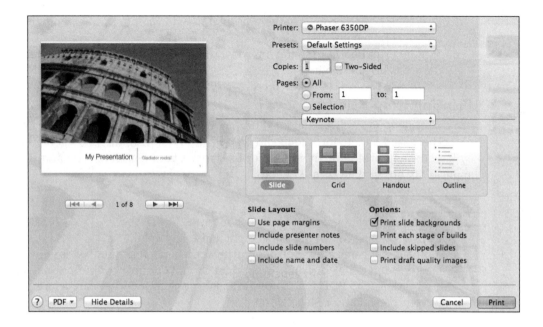

 Tip
If you don't see some of the options you need in the Print dialog sheet, it could be that they are hidden. Click the Show Details button in the lower left of the sheet to see options not available in the standard dialog, including options specific to your printer.

Printing from iOS

Printing from Keynote in iOS is super simple, to be honest (and why on earth would I not be?).

Note
You must have a printer set up to print with your iOS device already. Teaching you how to do this is outside the scope of this book, but you can find more information at http://support.apple.com/kb/HT4356.

To print from Keynote in iOS:

1. Open the presentation you want to print.
2. Tap the Tools icon in the upper right and tap Print in the menu.
3. Select the layout options you want to use and tap Next.
4. Tap Select Printer if the one you need isn't already selected. Browse the list of available printers and tap to select the one you wish to use.

5. Decide how many copies of the presentation you want to print and tap the + or – button correspondingly.

6. Tap the Print button to send your job to the printer. Go to the printer and enjoy the fruits of your labor.

Printing from iCloud

Printing from Keynote for iCloud is different from printing from Keynote for OS X or iOS because Keynote for iCloud can only print PDFs. Also, the PDFs generated by Keynote will print directly from your browser or your computer's default PDF application, not straight from Keynote itself.

To print from iCloud:

1. Open the presentation that you wish to print.
2. Click the Tools icon in the upper right and select Print.
3. Keynote will generate a PDF of your presentation. Once the PDF is generated, click the Open PDF button to open the PDF in your browser or your default PDF application. The PDF generation can take a long time if there are a lot of slides in your presentation, so be warned.

4. Print as you normally would from your browser or PDF app.

Chutes and Ladders: Working with Slides

Get it? "Chutes and ladders"... "Slides"... Sorry, I couldn't resist.

Now that you have the basics of creating, opening, and sharing your slides, it's appropriate to actually learn how to work within the slides themselves, don't you think? Let's get started.

Adding Slides and Slide Numbers

Adding slides to a presentation takes no major feat: simply click or tap the + at the bottom of the slide navigator and select the slide you want from the menu (it works the same in all three versions). Done.

You can quite easily show or hide slide numbers when playing your presentation by doing one of the following:

- To show or hide slide numbers for all the slides in your presentation, select Slide | Show/Hide Slide Numbers On All Slides from the menu.
- To show or hide slide numbers on individual slides, check or uncheck the Slide Number box in the Appearance section of the Format inspector.

Keeping It Together: Reorder and Group Slides

Reordering slides, regardless of which format of Keynote you're using, is a no-brainer. Simply click-and-drag a slide in the slide navigator and drop it where you want.

Grouping slides is quite useful to help keep like slides together; reordering slides is much simpler this way if you have slides that are meant to stick together no matter what else is going on with the rest of them. Grouping is performed the same way in all three versions of Keynote:

1. Drag-and-hold one or more slides to the right under the first slide you want them to be grouped with. Once the dragged files are considered grouped with the first slide, you'll see a line appear to the left of the subordinate slides (a blue arrow shows, too, in iCloud).
2. Simply let go of the mouse or screen to finish grouping the slides. The grouped slides appear indented under the first slide.

To ungroup grouped slides, just select the indented files and drag them to the left until the line (or blue arrow in iCloud) disappears. The slides will no longer be indented, indicating they're not grouped any more.

Editing a Master Slide

Keynote uses master slides in themes to keep the look and feel consistent in presentations. You can edit master slides in Keynote for OS X quite easily, just as you would a normal slide, but when you edit the master, all slides based on it will be modified to reflect the change. For example, if you format the text in a master slide, the same formatting will appear in every slide based on that master.

To edit master slides, just select View | Edit Master Slides, choose the master you want to edit, and edit away.

Skipping Slides

The big day is here: it's time to deliver your presentation to a live audience! All of a sudden, upon opening the presentation, you notice that there are some slides which you'd like to keep in your presentation but not show to this particular audience. What to do? Why, skip the slides, of course. To skip slides:

- In OS X or iCloud, right-click or CONTROL-click the slide(s) you want to skip and select Skip Slide(s) from the menu.
- In iOS, tap the slide or slides you want to hide, tap them again, and tap Skip in the menu.

Summary

All right, you've gotten your feet wet in the deep, clear pool of presentation refreshment known as Keynote. Now it's time to take the plunge: headlong into Chapter 7!

7

Pleasantly Pleasing Presentations

HOW TO...

- Work with objects and media in your presentations
- Format text within your slides
- Use tables to convey information succinctly
- Add charts to spruce up your information

Some presentations require just the bare bones, such as titles and bullet points, to get their points across. However, most folks understand that adding some spice to a presentation, such as cool images and highly stylized text, can get an audience's juices flowing and make otherwise great information phenomenal. This chapter will focus on helping you add said spice to your presentations, making your audience truly sit up and take notice.

Enhancing Slides with Objects and Media

As stated, media such as pictures and video, and objects such as shapes, can really move a presentation from pretty good status to WOW status in just a few clicks of the mouse or taps of the screen. Keynote is cognizant of this fact, and ready and willing to provide the assistance needed to make your presentations pop, or better yet—POP!

Inserting Images

Themes are a great way to start building a presentation, and most come with image placeholders just aching for you to replace them with images of your own.

While Keynote themes make it super simple to place images into slides, you don't have to utilize prebuilt themes every time you create presentations. You're free to start with a blank slide and place images in it wherever you darn well please, thank you very much.

Let's check out how to place and work with images in each version of Keynote.

Adding Images to a Slide

Adding images to slides is a snap with any version of Keynote, with or without a placeholder. Remember, a placeholder is just an idea anyway; a nice page design expert at Apple created the theme and placed its placeholders simply to give you ideas to build your own slide. You're not honor-bound to keep the images in the same places or even at the same sizes as in the original unaltered theme.

OS X There are four simple ways you can get images into your slides when working in Keynote for OS X:

- Drag an image from the Finder into your slide and just drop it in.
- Click the Insert menu and select Choose, browse your Mac for the image you want, and click Insert.
- Click the image button in the lower right corner of an image placeholder (looks like an illustration of a mountain and the sun) and select an image from your iPhoto or Aperture library, as shown in Figure 7-1.
- Click the Media button in the toolbar and choose an image from your iPhoto or Aperture library.

FIGURE 7-1 Click the image button in a placeholder to place an item from your iPhoto or Aperture library.

iOS   Adding images in Keynote for iOS is simple:

1. Tap + in the toolbar and then tap the Media tab, or tap + in an image placeholder (lower right corner).
2. Tap an image to select it; Keynote only shows you images that are stored on your device.

iCloud   Do one of the following to add an image to a slide in Keynote for iCloud:

- Drag an image from the Finder (or your desktop if using a PC) and drop it in the slide.
- Click the Image button in the toolbar, click the Choose Image button, browse your computer for the desired image, and then click Choose.

Masking (Cropping) an Image

When you mask an image, you hide parts of the image you don't want to be seen in your slide, while not changing the actual image. This feat is performed much the same way in all three versions of Keynote:

1. Double-click (or double-tap if in iOS) the image you want to mask to show the masking controls. The default mask is set to the original size of your image.
2. Do one of the following to mask your image:
   - Drag the slider to resize the image.
   - Drag the image itself to reposition it within the mask window.
   - Drag the mask's border to move the mask.
   - Drag the mask's handles to resize it.
3. Click or tap Done when finished masking the image.

Removing Parts of an Image

The Instant Alpha tool in Keynote for OS X or iOS (iCloud doesn't participate in the fun of this feature, I'm afraid) can help hide parts of an image you'd rather not have populate your slide. Instant Alpha doesn't monkey with the original image, so no worries there.

OS X To use Instant Alpha in Keynote for OS X:

1. Click the image to select it.
2. Click the Instant Alpha button in the Image tab of the Format bar.
3. Use the targeting tool (looks like a square containing cross hairs) to find the color you want to remove from the image.
4. Click to begin removing the selected color from your image. Drag to remove more of the color (and those surrounding it). Hold down the OPTION key while dragging and all instances of the color will be removed from the image instantly. You can also hold the SHIFT key while dragging and colors will be added back to your image.
5. Click Done when finished.

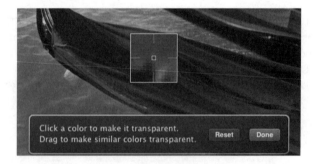

 Zoom into the image for more precise control of color removal.

iOS To use Instant Alpha in Keynote for iOS:

1. Select the image.
2. Tap the Format inspector (paintbrush) icon in the toolbar.
3. Tap Image, and then tap Instant Alpha.
4. Touch-and-drag your finger over the area (or color) in the image that you want to remove. The more you drag, the more of the color, and those surrounding it, is removed.
5. Tap Done when finished.

Adjusting Color Levels in an Image

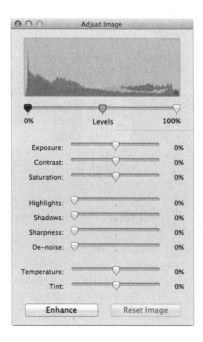

Keynote for OS X affords the ability to adjust color levels in an image, but this feature is sadly missing from the iOS and iCloud versions. To make color adjustments to an image in Keynote for OS X:

1. Select the image.
2. Click the Image tab in the Format bar.
3. Make basic adjustments with the Exposure and/or Saturation sliders, or click Enhance to have Keynote make automatic adjustments to the image.
4. Click the slider button (found between the Enhance and Reset buttons) for more advanced color features. Clicking this button opens the Adjust Image window, which offers up to 12 different options, including the ability to reset the image to its default color settings.

Placing and Adjusting Shapes

Incorporating shapes, such as boxes, circles, and lines, into your slides enhances them more subtly than images, but the effect can be just as powerful. Keynote lets you throw in as many shapes as you like, and offers quite a hefty range to select from. And if that's not enough, you can even draw your own shape if what you're looking for isn't to be found as part of Keynote (OS X only, though).

Adding Shapes to Your Slides

Each flavor of Keynote is adept at adding shapes, so let's take a look at them one at a time.

OS X   To add a shape using Keynote for OS X:

1. Click the Shape button in the toolbar.
2. Select a shape from the pop-up menu by clicking it. Click the gray dots at the bottom of the menu or click the left and right arrows found on either side of the menu to scroll through all the options.
3. Click-and-drag the shape to place it anywhere within your slide.
4. Click-and-drag the handles surrounding the shape to adjust its size.

iOS   To add a shape using Keynote for iOS:

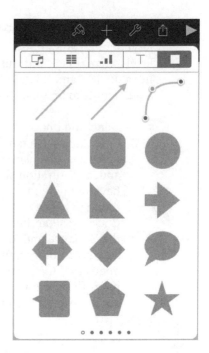

1. Tap the + button in the toolbar.
2. Tap the Shape button (looks like a square). Swipe to the left or right to see more shapes in the menu.
3. Tap a shape to drop it in your slide.
4. Drag the shape to the location you want it to occupy in your slide.
5. Drag the handles to adjust the size of the shape.

iCloud   To add a shape using Keynote for iCloud:

1. Click the Shape button in the toolbar.
2. Click-and-drag the shape to place it into position within the slide.
3. Use the options in the Shape tab of the format panel (right side of the window) to change the color and other attributes of the shape.

Adding Text to Shapes

With Keynote for OS X and iOS (but not iCloud as of this writing), you can add text inside of a shape. This is similar to adding text to a text box, but instead of just a square you can type in whatever shape you choose.

To add text to a shape using Keynote for OS X or iOS:

1. Double-click (OS X) or double-tap (iOS) the shape.
2. Type your text once the cursor appears inside the shape. Should your text not fit the shape, you can simply trim your text, change the font size, or resize the shape by dragging its selection handles.

Editing a Shape's Curves

OS X's version of Keynote allows you to edit the curves of an image using sharp lines or curved lines, enabling you to make some really unique and interesting shapes.

To edit the curves of a shape using Keynote for OS X:

1. Select the shape in your slide.
2. Choose Format | Shapes And Lines from the menu (not the Format button in the toolbar) and select Make Editable from the list.

3. When the handles appear on the edges of your shape, you can drag them to create whatever shape you like. Double-click a handle to change the kind of line it produces:
   - A square handle lets you know the handle creates sharp (straight) lines.
   - A circle handle tells you the handle creates curved lines.
4. Click outside the shape when you're finished editing the curves.

 Hover your mouse over the edges of the shape when editing curves to see hidden handles that you can use to make further changes.

Changing Attributes of Some Shapes

Some shapes (the star, pentagon, arrows, speech balloons, and the rounded-corner square, to be exact) in the OS X and iOS versions of Keynote allow you to make changes to them. You can change the number of points in a star, or you can modify the shape of an arrow; the options available depend on the shape you're using.

To change a shape's attributes:

1. Select the shape.
2. Notice the handles: there's at least one, and possibly more, in particular that stands out due to the fact that it's green.
3. Drag the green handle any which way you can to discover the different ways in which you can toy with the shape. Figure 7-2 shows three arrows that started the same way (the one in the middle is the default shape), but those on the left and right have been altered by dragging the green handle.
4. Click (OS X) or tap (iOS) outside of a shape to stop modifying it.

Drawing Your Own Shapes

The pen is mightier than the sword, or so I've heard (I've yet to see a pen factor heavily in a pirate battle, to be honest). The Pen in Keynote allows you to draw your own shapes, so if you hold that ability to be better than that of defending your boat

FIGURE 7-2   The left and right arrows have been modified from the default shape (in the middle).

against buccaneers, today's your lucky day. Let's see how to wield this powerful weapon (in OS X's version only, I'm afraid):

1. Click the Shape button in the toolbar and select Draw With Pen from the menu.
2. Click the area on the page where you want to begin your drawing. This action creates the first point on the screen, which is a red square.
3. Click another area on the screen to place the second point. This action will draw a straight line between the points. To create a curved line, click the area where the second point goes and begin dragging.
4. To finish creating your shape, click the first point made to close it, or press ESC to leave it open.

 Practice makes perfect when it comes to the Pen tool, which can be a bit tricky at first.

Adding Video and Audio

OS X and iOS versions of Keynote (not iCloud, sorry) allow you to use the coolest media around, video and audio, to make your presentations sing (and with some audio and video files, that could be taken literally)!

OS X

Add audio or video to a slide using Keynote for OS X in one of two ways:

- Drag the audio or video file from the Finder and drop it into the slide wherever it is needed.
- Click the Media button and select a file from either the Music tab or Movies tab.

You can easily adjust playback options by selecting the audio or video in the slide and clicking the Audio tab or Movie tab in the Format bar. Available options include

- **Controls** Forward, Reverse, Play, and Volume are all available.
- **Edit Audio/Movie** Trim the audio or movie to play only the parts you want. If you are using a movie, you will see a Poster Frame option, which allows you to select which frame of the video displays when the video isn't playing.
- **Repeat** Select None to play the file only once, Loop to continuously play the file from beginning to end over and over, or Loop Back And Forth to have the file play forward and then backward over and over again.

If you want your movies to play on an iPad or iPhone you'll need to go into Keynote for OS X's preferences and enable the option to Optimize Movies For iOS. I highly recommend this option; you can never be certain where your audience will want to view their presentation, or what device they'll be using to do so, so it's best to cover all the bases.

iOS

To add a video using Keynote for iOS:

1. Tap the + button in the upper right.
2. Tap the Media button (looks like a musical note).
3. Tap either Camera Roll or My Photo Stream and find the video you want.
4. Tap the video and then tap Use to place it in your slide.

Adjust playback options of audio and video files in Keynote for iOS by doing the following:

1. Tap the audio or video.
2. Tap the format inspector icon (paintbrush) and then tap the Movie tab (regardless of whether it's an audio file or a video file).
3. Choose from the following playback options: None, Loop, or Loop Back And Forth.

Aligning, Moving, Resizing, and Rotating Objects

Keynote is a wiz at helping you quickly and simply position objects in your slides. The position of an object is as key to the flow of information in a slide as is the textual information it contains. Let's see how to move things around in our slides, making them easier to understand and helping to convey information to the audience.

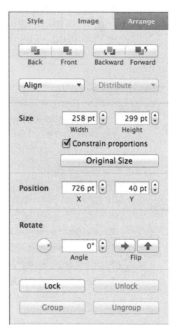

OS X

There are several ways to position objects in Keynote for OS X:

- Position objects based on page coordinates:
    1. Select the object.
    2. Click the Arrange tab in the Format bar.
    3. Enter x and y coordinates in the Position fields. x coordinates are measured from the object's upper left corner to the left edge of the slide, and y coordinates are measured from the object's upper left corner to the top edge of the slide. Coordinates are displayed on screen when you click-and-drag an object within the slide.

- Position objects on a vertical or horizontal axis:
  1. Select the object.
  2. Click the Arrange tab in the Format bar.
  3. Click the Align pop-up menu and choose an option.

- Position objects equally:
  1. Select three or more objects.
  2. Go to the Arrange tab in the Format bar.
  3. Choose an option from the Distribute pop-up menu. The Evenly option places even spacing between all the objects vertically and horizontally. The Horizontally option only spaces them evenly on a horizontal axis, and the Vertically option spaces them evenly on a vertical axis.

- Position objects one or more points at a time:
  1. Select the object.
  2. Press an arrow key once to move one point at a time. Hold down the SHIFT key while pressing the arrow key to move ten points at a time.

iOS

Alignment guides help you see how items line up together visually on a touch screen. There are three types of alignment guides in Keynote for iOS:

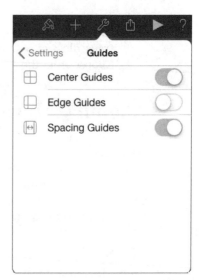

- **Center** Displays when the center of the selected object aligns with the center of another object or the center of the page
- **Edge** Displays when the edges of the selected object align with the edges of another object
- **Spacing** Displays when three or more items are spaced equally apart on a straight line

To turn on alignment guides, tap the Tools icon (looks like a wrench), tap Settings, tap Guides, and finally, toggle the switches next to the guide types you want to enable (green indicates enabled).

Your positioning can be more precise by moving objects one or more points at a time. Touch-and-hold an item with one finger, and then swipe anywhere else on the screen with another finger in the direction you want to move it. You can even move the item several points at a time when swiping with two or more fingers:

- 2 fingers = 10 points
- 3 fingers = 20 points
- 4 fingers = 30 points
- 5 fingers = 40 points

iCloud

As in Keynote for iOS, alignment guides make it so much simpler to position objects in Keynote for iCloud. The same three types of alignment guides populate Keynote in iCloud:

- **Center**   Displays when the center of the selected object aligns with the center of another object or the center of the page
- **Edge**   Displays when the edges of the selected object align with the edges of another object or the edges of the page
- **Spacing**   Displays when three or more items are spaced equally apart on a straight line

Enable alignment guides by clicking Tools in the toolbar, holding your pointer over Settings, and clicking each guide type you want to work with.

You can also position objects based on page coordinates in iCloud:

1. Select the object.
2. Click the Arrange tab in the format panel.
3. Enter x and y coordinates in the Position fields.

Layering and Grouping Objects

Grouping objects allows you to move multiple items together at one time. As a father to four children, I sometimes wish grouping was something available to me as a parent, but I digress.

The task of grouping items in Keynote for OS X and iCloud is similar:

1. Select the items you want to group together:
    - In OS X, hold down the SHIFT key while clicking each item.
    - In iCloud, hold down the ⌘ key (Mac) or CONTROL key (PC) while clicking items.
2. Click the Arrange tab in the Format bar (OS X) or format panel (iCloud).
3. Click the Group button. On the flipside, click the Ungroup button to undo the grouping.

Grouping is performed a little differently in Keynote for iOS:

1. Touch-and-hold the first item.
2. Tap other items while continuing to hold the first.
3. Lift both fingers from the screen.
4. Tap Group in the pop-up menu to group the items (tap Ungroup to undo the grouping).

Group will only be available as an option in step 4 if each of the objects you're selecting is set to stay on the page. To enable this setting, turn off the Move With Text option for each item: tap the object, tap the Format inspector icon (paintbrush), tap the Arrange tab, tap Wrap, and then toggle the Move With Text switch to off.

Animating Objects

If you want to grab the attention of an audience and hold it for a bit, nothing does the trick quite like animating an object. Keynote isn't going to turn your objects into the next Bugs Bunny or anything like that, but it will get them moving (how it moves them depends on the type of object they are). It looks like Keynote for iCloud is left out of this party, though, so we'll concentrate on OS X and iOS.

Using Build Effects

The effect used when animating an object is called a build effect, and (as mentioned) the available effects depend on the object being animated. There are three types of builds:

- **Build in**   Moving an item onto a slide
- **Build out**   Moving an item off of a slide
- **Action build (OS X only)**   Moving an item around a slide

Build Effects in OS X   To move an object on and off a slide in OS X:

1. Select the object you want to animate.
2. Click the Animate inspector button (right side of the toolbar, near Format), and do one of the following:
   - **Build in**   Click the Build In tab, click the Add An Effect button, and select an effect from the list. A really great feature is the Preview option offered to the right of each effect. Before you choose an effect, simply click Preview to see how the effect will work with your object.
   - **Build out**   Click the Build Out tab, click the Add An Effect button, and select an effect from the list. Preview is also available for these options. Woo-hoo!
3. Once you choose an effect, use its controls to decide how the effect interacts with the object it's attached to.

To move an object within a slide in OS X:

1. Select the object you want to animate.
2. Click the Animate inspector button and then click the Action tab.
3. Click the Add an Effect button and choose an effect from the list. Remember to use the Preview option to get a quick peek at how the effect works with the object you selected.
4. Once you choose an effect, use its controls to adjust the animation.

 You can add more than one action build to an object, which helps create some unique animations. For example, you could add a Jiggle and a Bounce to a star. Click the Add Action button to add multiple action builds to an item, and even change the order of an action by selecting a number from the Order pop-up menu.

What happens if you want to change the order in which effects are displayed? Easy as pie:

1. Select the slide containing the animations you want to reorder.
2. Click the Animate inspector button and then click the Build Order button at the bottom.
3. Perform the following actions on the builds listed:
   • Click-and-drag them into the order you like.
   • Select one to change its controls.
   • Click the Preview button to see how the new order affects your slide.
4. Close the Build Order window by clicking the red circle in its upper left corner.

Build Effects in iOS

To move an object on and off a slide in iOS:

1. Start by either:
   - Tapping the object, and then tapping Animate in the menu.
   - Tapping the Tools icon in the toolbar, tapping Transitions And Builds, and then tapping the object.
2. When the two blue + buttons appear, tap either the one for build in or the one for build out, depending on what animation you want to invoke.
3. In the menu that appears, find the effect you want to use (you may need to scroll to see all the options) and tap it. Tap Play in the upper right of the menu to see a preview of the effect on the selected object.

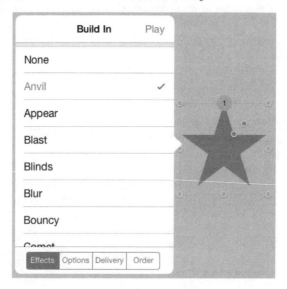

4. In the same menu, tap the Options tab and/or the Delivery tab at the bottom to view and change controls for the effect. You can also tap the Order tab to change the order in which effects in the selected slide are displayed.
5. When finished, tap Done in the upper right corner of the blue bar.

Building Items One Element at a Time

Still another way to animate objects is to build them on the screen one element at time. For example, if you have a table in your slide, you can choose to show one row at a time, or if you have a pie chart, you can show one "slice" of it at a time, until the entire table or chart is built.

To build one element at a time in OS X:

1. Select a text block, a table, or a chart that has an animation.
2. Open the Animate inspector and select the Build In tab.
3. Click the Delivery menu and select from the available options. The options will vary depending on the type of item selected in step 1.

To build one element at a time in iOS:

1. Select a text block, a table, or a chart, and then tap Animate in the menu.
2. Tap Build In or Build Out.
3. Tap the effect you want to use in the menu.
4. Tap the Delivery tab at the bottom of the menu and select one of the options. The options will vary depending on the type of item selected in step 1.

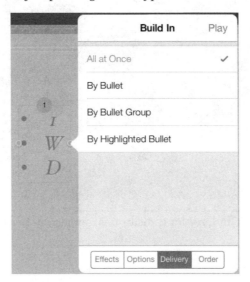

Taking Advantage of Neat Slide Transitions

A transition is the effect that occurs when moving from one slide to another during a presentation. Transitions can be as simple as a fade in or as cool as rippling pools of water (try the Droplets effect for this one, which you can see in Figure 7-3). Transitions are simple but very effective means of giving a presentation that special POP that makes it stand out to the audience, even after it's over.

Basic Transitions

All three versions of Keynote can apply transitions, but the options available vary.
To apply transitions in Keynote for OS X and iCloud:

1. Select the slide you want to begin with. The transition is placed between this slide and the next one in the slide navigator.
2. Add a transition:
   - In iCloud:
     a. Select a transition effect from the Slide Transition pane on the right side of the window, using the Effect pop-up menu. You may need to scroll to see all the effects.
     b. Use the controls in the Slide Transition pane to modify how the transition effect works.

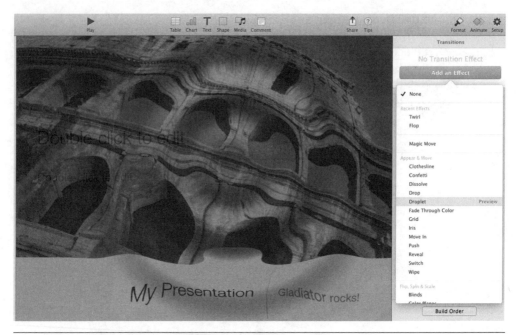

FIGURE 7-3 The Droplet transition is a neat way to dissolve from one slide to the next.

- In OS X:
  a. Click the Animate inspector in the toolbar.
  b. Click the Add An Effect button and select one from the list (you may need to scroll to see them all).
  c. Use the controls in the Transitions pane of the Format bar.

 Slides that contain a transition appear in the slide navigator with a blue triangle in their lower right corner.

To apply transitions in Keynote for iOS:

1. Select the slide you want to add the transition to (the effect occurs when switching between this slide and the next one in the slide navigator).
2. Select a transition in one of two ways:
   - Tap the slide again, tap Transition in the menu, and tap a transition in the list (swipe up or down to see more).
   - Tap the Tools icon, tap Transitions And Builds, tap None next to the selected slide, and tap a transition in the list.

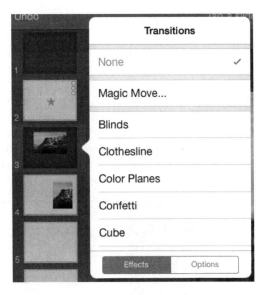

3. Tap the Options tab at the bottom of the Transitions window to modify how the transition effect works in your presentation.
4. Continue to add transitions to other slides if you like, and tap Done in the upper right corner of the screen when you're finished.

Magic Move Transitions

There's yet one more kind of transition, and it's one that apparently Gandalf invented, based on its name: the Magic Move transition. The Magic Move transition (I feel like I should be wearing a pointed hat and carrying a wooden staff every time I type it) is one in which it appears that some common elements among your slides are moving from one place to the next with each transition. And it's also a transition that's not available in iCloud.

The way to make a Magic Move transition is to create a new slide and add elements to it, then duplicate the slide and rearrange or resize the common elements. Elements that remain on the slide but have been moved will move during the transition. Elements in slide 1 that are not in slide 2 are simply faded out during the transition, and those that were not in slide 1 but are in slide 2 fade in.

Here's how you go about making a Magic Move transition in OS X:

1. Create a slide and add elements you need.
2. Duplicate the slide by pressing ⌘-D.
3. Make any changes necessary to the duplicate slide.
4. Click the first slide (from step 1).
5. Click the Animate inspector to see the Transitions pane, click the blue Add An Effect button, and then select Magic Move.
6. Utilize the controls in the Transitions pane to help modify how the transition will affect your presentation.

Here's how to make a Magic Move transition in iOS:

1. Select the slide (tap it in the slide navigator) you want to begin the transition with, tap it a second time to open the menu, and then tap Transition.
2. Tap Magic Move in the Transitions pane.
3. In the Duplicate Slide window, tap Yes if you haven't duplicated the slide yet, or tap No if you already have duplicated it.
4. Go to the duplicate slide and make any changes or rearrangements necessary.
5. Tap the first slide, and then tap Magic Move to open the Transitions pane again.
6. Tap the Options tab at the bottom of the pane and use the controls to adjust how the transition affects your presentation.

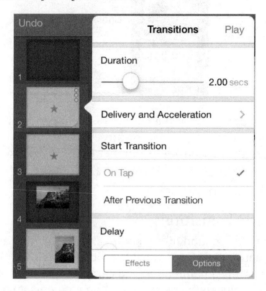

7. Tap Done in the upper right corner of the screen when you've completed the transition creation.

Hitting the Links: Linking Objects

Often in a presentation, the presenter will include links to things like websites, email addresses, other slides in the presentation, or just about anything else they want. Keynote for OS X and iOS makes it simple to add links to objects, but iCloud doesn't perform that task (at least not as of this writing).

To add a link to an object in OS X:

1. CONTROL-click or right-click the object (text, images, what have you) and select Add Link from the list.
2. Select the type of link you want to provide using the Link To pop-up menu.
3. Make any settings necessary based on the type of link provided.
4. Click outside the link to get back to your slide.

To add a link to an object in iOS:

1. Tap the Tools icon in the toolbar.
2. Tap the Presentation Tools option, and then tap Interactive Links.
3. Tap the object you want to attach the link to and then select the type of link you're providing from the tabs at the bottom of the Link window (Slide, Webpage, or Mail).
4. Enter the information needed for the link you're providing.
5. Tap outside the Link window, and then tap Done in the upper right corner of the screen when finished.

Work That Text!

Slides and text go together like peanut butter and chocolate. It's too bad that some folks tend to use way too much of either, instead of striking just the right balance. Who wants to eat a peanut butter cup that's 95 percent peanut butter? Well, actually, it might be quite good, but you get my point, right? Moving on.

Text in a presentation can be a real boon or a real bust. I'm not referring to just the amount of text either; let's face it, some of us just aren't cut out to be writers (that's why I'll reiterate my love for my McGraw-Hill editors right here in this very section). Let's discover how to add text to our presentations in Keynote before I say something else that will get me into trouble.

Adding Text to Slides

Adding text to a slide isn't exactly rocket science, but I'm more than happy to show you how so that you can avoid some of the missteps I've made along the way. As you've already discovered, in the act of creating a new presentation or adding a new slide, you'll see text boxes that are already formatted and ready for you to fill full of information. Simply click or tap a text box and go to town with your keyboard. They all say "double-click to edit" or "double-tap to edit" anyway, so even I figured this thing out rather quickly.

Of course, you may want to add your own text box to the slide, which is perfectly legal in most countries (or perhaps all... I'm not certain). Anyway, here's how to go about that in each version of Keynote.

OS X

To create a text box in OS X:

1. Click the Text button in the toolbar; its icon looks like a T.
2. Choose which type of text box you'd like to add to the slide, and simply drag-and-drop it from the Text window into your slide, or just click it and it will appear in the middle of the slide window.
3. If you want to move the text box, simply click-and-hold the text and drag the box to where you'd like it to be.

iOS

To create a text box in iOS:

1. Tap the + in the toolbar.
2. Tap the Text tab in the window; it looks like a T.
3. Choose which type of text box you'd like to add to the slide, and then tap it to add it to the slide.

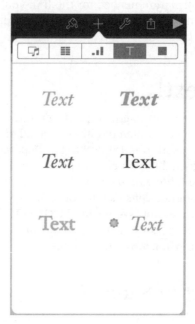

4. If you want to move the text box, tap-and-hold the text and drag the box to its new home.

iCloud

To create a text box in iCloud:

1. Click the Text button in the toolbar; its icon looks like a T. The text box instantly appears in the slide.
2. Format the text box using the Shape, Text, and Arrange tabs in the format panel on the right side of the window.
3. If you want to move the text box, simply click-and-hold the text and drag the box to where you'd like it to be.

Formatting a Slide's Text

All three versions of Keynote offer you some measure of control over the formatting of your text. Formatting your text properly is the best way to look way smarter than you actually are (at least it's worked for me sometimes).

OS X

Just like in Pages, the Format bar is the place to go to format your slide's text in Keynote for OS X. The text options show up on the right side of the slide window whenever you select text in the slide, assuming you have the Format inspector selected in the toolbar.

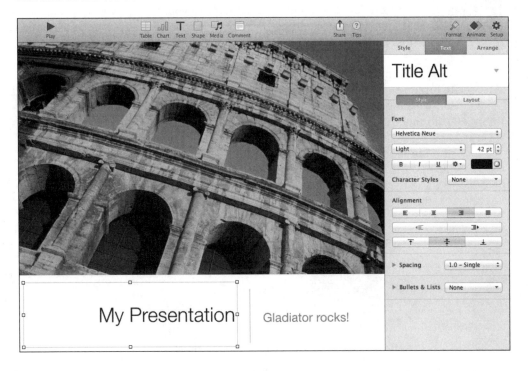

The Style tab in the Format bar allows you to make formatting selections for the text box itself. You can add and adjust elements such as borders, fills, shadows, and more.

To choose a font for your slide, click the Font pop-up menu in the Text tab (click the Style button if it's not already selected) of the Format bar and select one from the list. This list is WYSIWYG, so you'll be able to easily see what's what. Adjust the appearance of the font by changing its typeface, size, color, and so forth from within the Text tab. There's plenty of other options in the Layout section of the Text tab, too, which you can use to set up indents, tabs, columns, and the like.

Tip   Click the gear icon in the Style section of the Text tab to access advanced options such as baseline, ligatures, strikethrough, and the like.

The Arrange tab of the Format bar allows you to align the text to the left side, center, or right side of your slide, as well as justify the text (which aligns it to both the left and right margins).

iOS

Keynote is just as adept at working with text in iOS as it is in its desktop forms, but things do work a tad differently.

You may not have available in Keynote for iOS all the fonts you have available in Keynote for OS X if you've added fonts to your Mac, so you may want to keep that in mind when choosing them for your slides if they are to be used and edited across platforms.

You can make adjustments to text formatting in a couple of different ways: you can either make wholesale changes to the entire text box or manually change the text itself working within the text box.

To make changes to the entire text box at once:

1. Tap the text box to select it.
2. Tap the Format inspector icon in the toolbar (looks like a paintbrush).
3. Use the options at your disposal under the Style, Text, and Arrange tabs to format the text of your entire box.

To make manual changes to text while working within a text box:

1. Tap the text inside the box to select it.
2. Tap the Format inspector icon in the toolbar (looks like a paintbrush).

3. Use the options at your disposal under the Style, List, and Layout tabs to format the text.

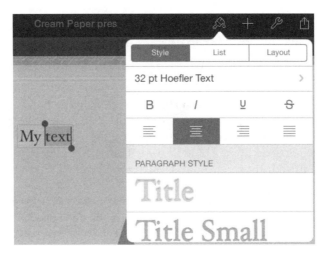

iCloud

Changing the appearance of text in Keynote for iCloud is super similar to doing so in Keynote for OS X. Select text in the slide to open the format panel, which offers the same functionality as the Format bar in Keynote for OS X, even though you may not have as many fonts to choose from.

 To make changes to the entire text box at once, just select the box and not the text within it.

Using and Formatting Lists

Perhaps in no other type of application are lists used more than within presentation apps, such as Keynote. Since lists are used to quickly show the main points of the presenter, Apple has made sure Keynote is a pro when it comes to working with them. Keynote can do much of the list formatting all on its own by default, but, of course, you have full reign to turn off automatic lists (see "Setting Keynote's Preferences" in Chapter 6) and make adjustments to them manually.

Lists in OS X

To create a list in Keynote for OS X:

1. Click the Text option in the toolbar (looks like a T) and click the bullet option from the list (has a bullet point in front of the word "Text"). Alternatively, you can drag-and-drop the bullet option from the list into the desired location in your slide.

2. Type the first item in your list.
3. Press RETURN, and Keynote automatically launches into list mode.
4. Continue to add items to your list by typing them out and pressing RETURN after each one.
5. To quit generating the list, press RETURN twice or press the DELETE key.

Once your list is typed, you can easily change the hierarchy of a list by clicking-and-dragging items in the list left or right, or change the order by clicking-and-dragging an item up or down the list. When you start to click-and-drag an item, a blue arrow will appear and help you navigate to where it should go in your list.

 Tip Further customize your lists by using the Bullets & Lists section in the Text tab of the Format bar (click the Style button if you don't see it). Select an item in your list and click the arrow next to Bullets & Lists to see available formatting options.

Lists in iOS

To create a list in Keynote for iOS:

1. Tap + in the toolbar and then tap the Text tab (looks like a T).
2. Tap a text style that begins with a bullet point.
3. Double-tap the newly placed text box and begin typing your first item in the list.
4. When finished, tap Return, and Keynote automatically goes into list mode.
5. Continue to add items to your list by typing them out and tapping Return after each one.
6. To quit generating the list, tap Return twice or tap outside the text box.

Changing the hierarchy of a list is done by touching-and-dragging items in the list left or right, or you can change their order by touching-and-dragging an item up or down the list. When you start to click-and-drag an item, a blue arrow appears, along with blue alignment guides, to help with item placement.

Lists in iCloud

To create a list in Keynote for iCloud:

1. Type the first item in your list and press RETURN (Mac) or ENTER (PC). Repeat this step until all of your items are listed.
2. Select the text you want to include in your list.

3. Scroll near the bottom of the Text format pane to see the Bullets & Lists menu. Click the menu and select one of its styling options for your list.
4. You may continue to add items to your list by typing them out and pressing RETURN (or ENTER) after each one. You can change the hierarchy of an item in the list by using the indent buttons at the bottom of the Text format pane.
5. To quit generating the list, choose None from the Bullets & List menu in the Text format pane.

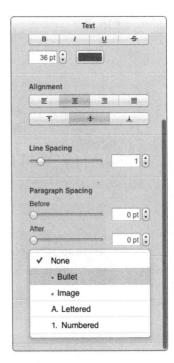

Creating Paragraph Styles

Paragraph styles are simply text that has been preformatted, and there are several to select from within Keynote, all three versions of it. However, what if you want to create a unique paragraph style for your presentations? Well, that's not a problem at all, at least not for the OS X version of Keynote. iOS and iCloud will have to take a back seat during this section of the chapter.

To create a new paragraph style in Keynote for OS X:

1. Create the paragraph you want to base the new style on and select it.
2. In the Text tab of the Format inspector, click the name of the paragraph style currently in use to open the Paragraph Styles menu.
3. Click the + at the top of the menu.
4. Enter a name for the new paragraph style, and then click outside the menu to close it.

Use your new style at any time by selecting the paragraph you want to apply it to, and then choosing its name from the Paragraph Styles menu.

Turning the Tables

Tables can be a key element of slides, so Apple made Keynote a table-wielding machine, capable of throwing tables into any old slide you want it to, regardless of which platform you're using.

Adding a Table

Adding a table is quite a simple task in Keynote. Let's see how to do so in all three of its incarnations.

OS X

To add a table to a slide in Keynote for OS X:

1. Place the cursor where you'd like the table to appear in the slide.
2. Click the Table icon in the toolbar.
3. Click to choose a table from the options, or drag one from the menu and drop it into the slide. Click the left and right arrows in the menu to see different types of tables.

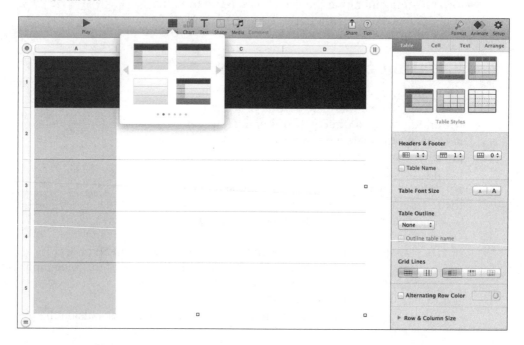

4. Click a cell and begin typing to add content to it.
5. To move a table, click it to activate it, then click-and-drag the circle in its upper left corner.
6. Delete a table by clicking the circle in its upper left corner, and then press the DELETE key.

iOS

To add a table to a slide in Keynote for iOS:

1. Tap + in the toolbar and then tap the Table icon to see a menu of different tables.
2. Tap to select a table from the options, or drag one from the menu and drop it into the slide. Swipe to the left or right to see different types of table styles.
3. Tap a cell and begin typing to add content to it.
4. To move a table, tap it to activate it, then tap-and-drag the circle in its upper left corner.
5. Delete a table by tapping it and then tapping Delete in the menu.

iCloud

To add a table to a slide in Keynote for iCloud:

1. Click the Table icon in the toolbar.
2. Click to choose a table from the options.
3. Click a cell and begin typing to add content to it.
4. To move a table, click it to activate it, then click-and-drag the square in its upper left corner.
5. To delete a table, click its upper left corner to select it, and then press the DELETE key.

Adding or Removing Rows and Columns

Typically, the default number of rows and columns in Keynote's tables doesn't fill the bill for your needs (of course, it's not really meant to, but that's neither here nor there). Thankfully, it's silly-simple to add or remove both as needed.

Working with Rows and Columns in OS X

To add or remove the rows and columns of a table in Keynote for OS X:

1. Click to select the table.
2. Do one of the following to add or remove rows or columns:
   - To add a column to the right side of the table or to add a row to the bottom of it, click the circle containing the two parallel lines and use the arrow to increase the number of columns or rows. Simply decrease the number to remove the rightmost column or bottommost row.
   - Move the pointer over the column or row bar (lettered or numbered, respectively) of the column or row to which you want to make an addition. When you see a small gray arrow appear, click it to see a pop-up menu. Select to add a column before or after the one you're working with, or add a row above or below the one you're working with. To remove the column or row you're working with, simply select Delete Column or Delete Row.

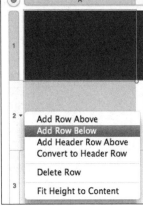

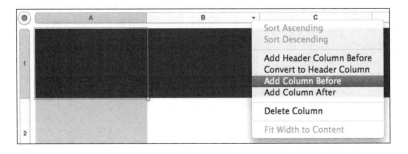

Working with Rows and Columns in iOS

To add or remove the rows and columns of a table in Keynote for iOS:

1. Tap to select the table.
2. To add a column to the right side of the table or to add a row to the bottom of it, tap the circle containing the two parallel lines and use the arrow to increase the number of columns or rows. Simply decrease the number to remove the rightmost column or bottommost row.

Working with Rows and Columns in iCloud

To add or remove the rows and columns of a table in Keynote for iCloud:

1. Click to select the table.
2. Do one of the following to add or remove columns and rows:
   - To add a column to the right of the table or to add a row to the bottom of it, click the handle to the right of the columns and/or the handle at the bottom of the rows. Use the resulting arrows to increase or decrease the number of columns and rows.
   - Move the pointer over the column or row bar (lettered or numbered, respectively) of the column or row to which you want to make an addition. When you see a small black arrow, click it to see a pop-up menu. Select to add a column before or after the one you're working with, or add a row above or below the one you're working with. To remove the column or row you're working with, simply select Delete Column or Delete Row.

Formatting Cells

Customizing a table or cell means dictating how data looks and operates within it. You can customize an entire table at once or one cell at a time, depending on your needs, of course.

There are tons of options available for customization; I suggest tinkering with them all to see how you can use them in your slides. The set of options available in each version of Keynote varies widely, just so you know.

OS X

To customize a table in Keynote for OS X:

1. Select which part of the table you want to customize:
   - For the entire table, click the circle in the upper left corner of it.
   - For a single cell, click within that cell.
   - For multiple cells, click-and-drag to select the cells, or hold the ⌘ key while clicking the individual cells.

2. To make table-wide customizations, click the Table tab in the Format inspector. Options available in the Table tab include
   - **Table Styles**   Change the entire look of a table using the predefined styles.
   - **Headers & Footer**   Increase or decrease the number of headers and footers, and enable the table's name (appears at the top of the table).
   - **Table Font Size**   Set the default font size for the table.
   - **Table Outline**   Determine whether to apply an outline to the table's outer boundaries, and what that outline should look like.
   - **Grid Lines**   Apply boundary lines to the interior grids of your table.
   - **Alternating Row Color**   Alternate the color of the rows for easier viewing.
   - **Row & Column Size**   Set the default height of rows and width of columns.
   - **Resize rows to fit cell contents**   Does just what it says.
3. To make changes to single cells or groups of cells, click the Cell tab in the Format inspector. Cell tab options are as follows:
   - **Data Format**   Determine how data in a cell appears and is used throughout the slide based on what type of data it is. You can allow Keynote to automatically format the data according to the type of data entered, or you can select the type of data a cell is to use. Data types are Number, Currency, Percentage, Fraction, Numeral System, Scientific, Text, Date & Time, and Duration.
   - **Fill**   Adjust the color fill of the cell(s).
   - **Border**   Adjust the color of the cell borders.
   - **Conditional Highlighting**   Automatically highlight cells when they match the criteria you set for them.

4. To make changes to the text of a cell or table, click the Text tab in the Format inspector.
5. To make changes to the arrangement of the table or selected cells within the rest of the slide, use the options in the Arrange tab.

iOS

To customize a table in Keynote for iOS:

1. Select which part of the table you want to customize:
   - For the entire table, tap the circle in its upper left corner.
   - For a single cell, tap within that cell.
   - For multiple cells, tap the first cell to see the blue outline showing the selected cell, including the blue dots in the upper left and lower right of it. Tap-and-drag the blue dots to select the desired cells.
2. To make table-wide customizations:
   a. Select the table as described in step 1.
   b. Tap the format inspector icon in the toolbar.
   c. Tap the Table, Headers, or Arrange tab in the Format bar and make the desired changes.

Items available in the Table tab include
- **Table Styles** Change the entire look of a table using the predefined styles.
- **Table Options** Enable or disable the Table Name, Table Outline, and Alternating Rows, as well as Grid Options such as Horizontal or Vertical Lines, Header Column Lines, and Header Row Lines. You can also make table-wide font settings from here.

Items in the Headers tab allow you to increase or decrease the number of Header Rows, Header Columns, and Footer Rows.

Items available in the Arrange tab include
- **Move to Back/Front** Allow you to position the table within the layers of the slide.
- **Lock/Unlock** Prevent or allow the table to be edited and/or moved.

3. To make changes to a single cell or a group of cells:
   a. Select the cell(s) as described in step 1.
   b. Tap the format inspector icon in the toolbar.
   c. Tap the Table, Headers, Cell, or Format tab in the Format bar and make desired changes:
      - Items available in the Table and Headers tabs are the same as for table-wide changes, as described in step 2.
      - Items in the Cell tab allow you to adjust the look of the text within the cell, as well as its fills and borders.

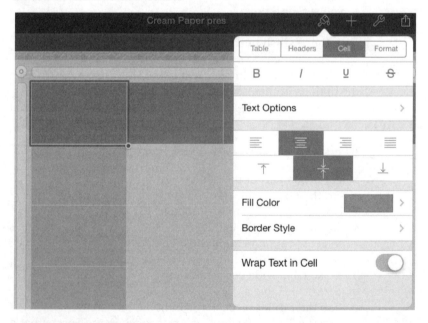

   - Items available in the Format tab lets you determine how Keynote formats the data in a cell (or cells) according to the type of data entered, or you can select the type of data a cell is to use. Data types are Number, Currency, Percentage, Text, Date & Time, and Duration.

iCloud

To customize a table in Keynote for iCloud:

1. Select the table and then select the part of it you want to customize. When you move your pointer over a table, the cursor changes to look like a white cross. Click once on a cell to select it, or click-and-drag over multiple cells to select them.
2. To make table-wide customizations:
   a. Select the entire table as discussed in step 1.
   b. Click the Table tab in the format panel. Options available in the Table tab include
      • **Table Styles**   Change the entire look of a table using the predefined styles.
      • **Headers & Footer**   Increase or decrease the number of headers and footers.
      • **Table Font Size**   Change the default font size for the entire table.
      • **Table Options**   Enable the table's name (appears at the top of the table).
3. To make customizations to a cell or cells:
   a. Select an individual cell or a group of cells as discussed in step 1.
   b. Click the Cell tab in the format panel. Options available in the Cell tab include Font, Alignment, and Fill, all of which you're already familiar with. You will also see Merge Cells if you have selected more than one cell, but we'll discuss this in the upcoming section.
   c. Click the Data tab to select what type of data the cell(s) are formatted to handle. The options are Automatic, Number, Currency, Percentage, Date & Time, Fraction, Scientific, and Text.

Merging and Unmerging Cells

Merging cells allows you to combine the content of two or more cells, and unmerging them has the opposite effect.

Merging cells will cause the following to occur:

• Should only one of the selected cells contain content before the merger, the merged cell will keep the content and formatting of that cell.
• Should more than one of the cells have content, all of the content is kept, however it is all converted to text.
• If the top left cell (of those selected) contains a fill color, the merged cell keeps that color.

When you unmerge cells, the formatting of the previously merged cell is kept throughout the unmerged cells.

To merge cells:

1. Select the cells to be merged.
2. Follow the specific procedure for the Pages version you're working in:
   • **OS X**   Choose Format | Table | Merge Cells (using the Format menu, not the Format button in the toolbar).

- **iOS**   Tap Merge in the pop-up menu.
- **iCloud**   Click the Cell tab in the format panel and click the Merge button at the bottom.

To unmerge cells:

1. Select the cells to be unmerged.
2. Follow the specific procedure for the Pages version you're working in:
   - **OS X**   Choose Format | Table | Unmerge Cells (using the Format menu, not the Format button in the toolbar).
   - **iOS**   Tap Unmerge in the pop-up menu.
   - **iCloud**   Click the Cell tab in the format panel and click the Unmerge button at the bottom.

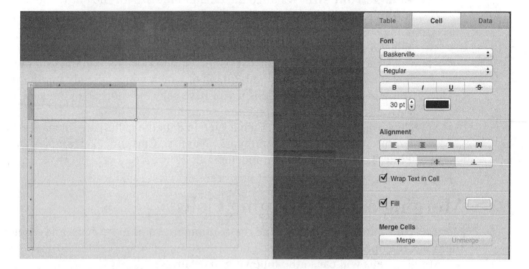

The Basics of Formulas

Often, a person who uses tables will want to combine numbers from a column to get a total (for example, if a presenter wanted to show the total number of children in a school by class grades). Keynote for OS X and iCloud (not iOS, sorry) are loaded with 250 predefined mathematical functions, which makes it simple for you to find the function you need to complete a formula for the cells in a table.

Tip   We'll cover the basics of using formulas and functions in this section of the chapter, but you'll definitely want to go to Apple's online resource for the topic to dig in deep. You can access the Formulas and Functions Help page at http://help.apple.com/functions/mac/4.0/.

To enter your own mathematical formula into a cell:

1. Select the cell in which you want the result of the formula to display.
2. Press the = key on the keyboard to open the formula editor.
3. Create your formula:
   a. Select the first cell that you want to use for the first value in the formula (when you click it, the combined name of the column and the row appears, such as A2, B4, etc.), or manually enter a value.
   b. Enter the mathematical operator you need for your formula, such as + (add), - (subtract), * (multiply), or / (divide).
   c. Select the next cell that you want to use for the next value in the formula, or manually enter a value.
   d. Continue the process above until all the cells you need for your total are included in the formula.
4. Press the RETURN key or click the green check mark in the formula editor to complete the formula creation. Clicking the red × will cause you to lose the changes you've made.

You can also use the predefined functions that come with Keynote instantly when you select a cell and press the = key on your keyboard. This action opens the Functions panel in both the OS X and iCloud versions of Keynote, shown in Figure 7-4. Here's how to use the Functions panel:

1. Search for functions by entering their names in the search field, denoted by the magnifying glass, or...
   Select a type of function from the left side of the functions list, and then select a function from within that type to see its description (and several examples of how it is used in a formula) at the bottom of the panel.
2. Click the Insert Function button to place the function in your formula.

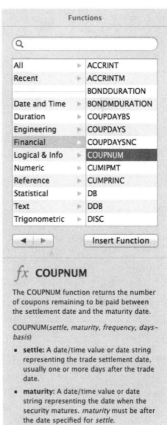

FIGURE 7-4 The Functions panel offers 250 functions for you to plug into your formulas.

Pop Charts

Charts are great ways to convey information both beautifully and informatively. They especially suit the format of a presentation, when the info has to come fast and furious, as well as put on a pretty face. Charts are easily implemented and manipulated within Keynote for OS X and iOS, but they are not yet available in Keynote for iCloud.

To add a chart to slides in the OS X version of Keynote:

1. Click the Charts button in the toolbar.
2. Click either the 2D, 3D, or Interactive tab to select a chart type.

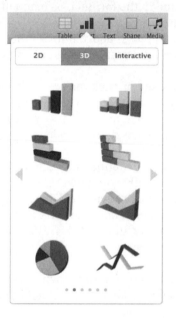

3. Choose a chart by clicking it in the pop-up menu or by dragging-and-dropping it into the slide. Click the right and left arrows to peruse the chart variations. If you select a 3D chart, you can click-and-drag the rotation controls in its center to rotate it to the angle you want to use.
4. Click the Edit Chart Data button to change the headings and data within the chart, and then begin entering your own information. Click the red dot in the upper left corner to close the editor.
5. Drag the chart anywhere you like to place it in the slide.

Delete a chart by selecting it and pressing your keyboard's DELETE key.
To add a chart to slides in the iOS version of Keynote:

1. Tap + in the toolbar and then tap the Charts tab (looks like three bars, progressing from smaller to larger) in the menu.
2. Select either the 2D, 3D, or Interactive tab to choose a chart type.

3. Choose a chart by tapping it in the pop-up menu or by dragging-and-dropping it into the slide. Swipe to the right or left to browse the chart versions. If you select a 3D chart, you can tap-and-drag the rotation controls in its center to rotate it to the angle you want to use.

4. Tap the chart and then tap Edit Data in the menu to change the headings and data within the chart, and then enter your own data in the Editor Chart Data window. Should you want to change which data, rows or columns, is plotted as your data series, tap the gear icon in the upper left of the toolbar and tap the option you want to use. Regain the use of a full keyboard by toggling the switch next to the option for it. Tap Done in the upper right corner to close the editor.

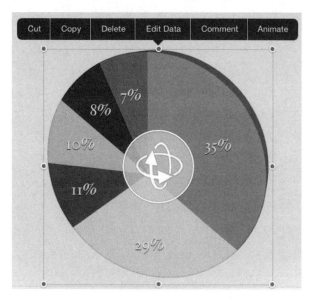

5. Drag the chart anywhere you like to place it in the slide.

Delete a chart by tapping it and then tapping Delete in the menu.

Summary

Text and tables and charts, oh my! Shapes and images and animations, my goodness! You've learned how to really make a presentation take off in this chapter. We'll wrap up some of the finer details of presentation creation in Chapter 8, so let's mosey on over.

8

Getting Your Presentation to the Masses

HOW TO...

- Find and replace text, and check its spelling
- Use reference tools
- Make comments and highlights in text
- Play your presentations

You've written a presentation so compelling that it could persuade a mouse to visit a hungry cats' convention—unarmed, no less. The next step is making sure that you've edited it (even though the chances of mistakes are almost nil, right?) and that you can actually deliver your presentation to the mouses—I mean, masses! Sorry.

In this chapter, I'll show you how to edit the (very few) mistakes you and/or your collaborative team have made, as well as how to play your presentation, both manually and automatically.

Squaring the Whole Thing: Editing Presentations

Even the best writers in the world need editors, and you'll find none better than those at McGraw-Hill (yes, I'm surfing for brownie points, okay?). But even with the great editors at McGraw-Hill, I still need help double-checking my own spelling and the like. Keynote makes it super easy to do the necessary editing tasks, so let's get started.

Chop, chop! That presentation of yours won't edit itself (but I think Apple's working on that for Keynote's next version...)!

Finding and Replacing Text

Keynote is a wiz at finding text in your presentation. Using Find and Replace, you can even replace that text as you find it, should the notion strike.

OS X

To find text in a presentation using Keynote for OS X:

1. Click the View button in the toolbar and select Show Find & Replace.
2. Type the word, character, or phrase you're looking for in the search field (denoted by the magnifying glass and the word Find). Keynote highlights matches as you type. Narrow your search results by using the Whole Words (find only the whole words you entered) and/or Match Case (find items that exactly match the capitalization you enter) search tools. Click the action menu (looks like a gear) on the left side of the Find & Replace window and click to select one or both options.

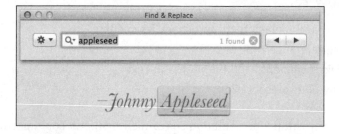

3. Click the right or left arrow to see the next or previous match, respectively.

To find and replace text in a presentation using Keynote for OS X:

1. Click the View button in the toolbar and select Show Find & Replace.
2. Click the action menu on the left side of the Find & Replace window and select Find & Replace.
3. Type the word, character, or phrase you're searching for in the first field. Keynote highlights matches as you type. Narrow your results by using one or both of the Whole Words and Match Case search tools.
4. Type the replacement text, character, or phrase in the second field. If you leave the second field blank, the text in the first field will be deleted during this process.

5. Use the buttons at the bottom of the Find & Replace window to perform an action on the found text:
   - **Replace All**   Replaces every match at once.
   - **Replace & Find**   Replaces the first match and moves on to the next.
   - **Replace**   Replaces the first match and does not move to the next.
   - **Arrows**   Click the left or right arrow to move to the previous or next match, respectively, without replacing anything.

iOS

To find text in a presentation using Keynote for iOS:

1. Tap Tools (the wrench icon) in the toolbar and then tap Find.
2. Type the word, character, or phrase you want to find in the search field, which appears right above the keyboard. Keynote highlights matches as you type. Narrow your results by using the Whole Words (find only the whole words you entered) and/or Match Case (find items that exactly match the capitalization you enter) search tools. To use them, tap the action menu (looks like a gear) on the left side of the search window and toggle the switches to enable one or both of them.

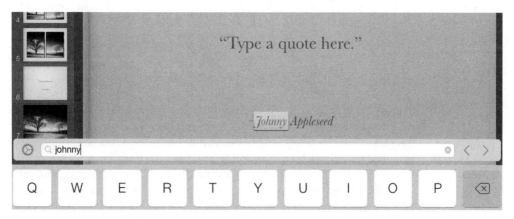

3. Tap the right or left arrow to see the next or previous match, respectively.

To find and replace text in a presentation using Keynote for iOS:

1. Tap Tools (the wrench icon again) in the toolbar and then tap Find.
2. Tap the action menu (gear icon) on the left side of the search window and tap Find & Replace.
3. Type the word, character, or phrase you're wanting to replace in the first field. Keynote highlights matches as you type. Narrow the search results by enabling one or both of the Whole Words and Match Case search tools.
4. Type the replacement text, character, or phrase in the second field. If you leave the second field blank, the text in the first field will be deleted.

5. Use the buttons at the bottom of the Find & Replace window to perform an action on the found text:
   - Replace the selected match by tapping Replace.
   - Replace all matches by tapping-and-holding Replace, and then tapping Replace All.
   - Tap the left or right arrow to move to the previous or next match, respectively, without replacing anything.

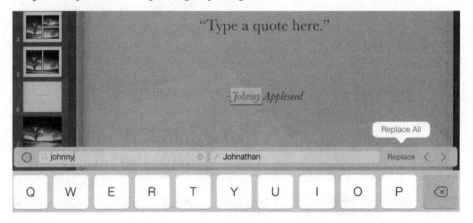

iCloud

To find text in a presentation using Keynote for iCloud:

1. Click the Tools button in the toolbar and select Show Find & Replace. The Find window opens at the bottom of the presentation window.
2. Type the word, character, or phrase you need in the Find field. Keynote highlights matches for your search terms as you type. Narrow the results by using the Whole Words (find only the whole words you entered) and/or Match Case (find items that exactly match the capitalization you enter) search tools. To use them, click the action menu (looks like a gear) on the left side of the Find window and click to select one or both options.
3. Click the right or left arrow to see the next or previous match, respectively.

To find and replace text in a presentation using Keynote for iCloud:

1. Click the Tools button in the toolbar and select Show Find & Replace. The Find window opens at the bottom of the presentation window.
2. Click the action menu (gear icon) on the left side of the Find window and select Find & Replace from the menu.
3. Type the word, character, or phrase you need to replace in the first field. Keynote highlights matches for your terms as you type. Narrow the results by using one or both of the Whole Words and Match Case search tools.
4. Type the replacement text, character, or phrase in the second field. If you leave the second field blank, the text in the first field will be deleted when you click the Replace button.

5. Use the buttons at the bottom of the Find & Replace window to perform an action on the found text:
   - **Replace**   Replaces the old text with the new.
   - **Arrows**   Click the left or right arrow to move to the previous or next match, respectively, without replacing anything.

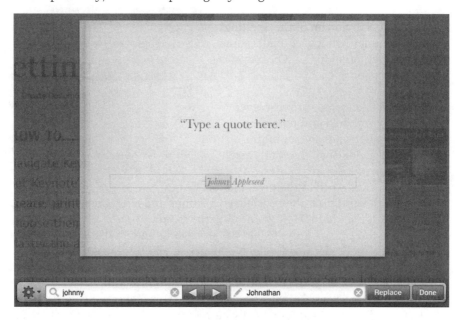

Chek Your Spelling

Let's not pretend: we all misspell words. Yes, I'm talking to you, friend. We both do it, so let's just be transparent with one another.

Luckily for us all, Keynote can automatically check for spelling mistakes and replace them. It can also help us with our grammar! No worries, though, all you copy editors out there; no software can replace a human—yet.

OS X

Keynote checks spelling and makes corrections by default in its OS X incarnation. If you misspell a word, Keynote displays it with a red-dotted underline. If you happen to type a misspelled word and Keynote catches it, it automatically corrects the misspelling and temporarily underlines it with a blue-dotted line. You can also correct a misspelled word yourself by CONTROL-clicking (or right-clicking) it and choosing the correct spelling from the pop-up menu.

Click Edit | Spelling & Grammar in the menu to view spell-checking options:

- Show Spelling and Grammar opens the Spelling and Grammar window.
- Check Document Now forces Keynote to check spelling immediately, which is great for you impatient folks (he typed, looking in the mirror).

- Check Spelling While Typing is enabled by default and misspelled words are underlined by the aforementioned red-dotted line.
- Check Grammar With Spelling causes possible grammatical errors to be underlined with a green-dotted line, and misspelled words are still displayed with ye olde red-dotted underline.

The OS X version of the Spelling and Grammar window contains some options not found in the iOS and iCloud versions:

- Misspelled words are displayed in the top field and possible corrections are shown in the lower field. Click the Find Next button to move to the next misspelled word in the presentation.
- Click a word from the possible corrections and click Change to use it.
- Click Ignore to make Keynote skip the word.
- Click the Learn button to add the word to Keynote's dictionary (if Keynote doesn't have a particular word in its dictionary, it will think it's misspelled).
- Click Define to have Keynote look up the meaning of the word in a dictionary.
- Click Guess to have Keynote make suggestions to you.
- Check the Check Grammar box to enable this feature.
- Force Keynote to automatically correct misspelled words based on a particular language set.

iOS

Spell checking is simple in Keynote for iOS:

1. Tap the Tools icon (wrench) in the toolbar.
2. Tap Settings.
3. Toggle the Check Spelling switch on (green) or off (white). Misspelled words are displayed with a red-dotted underline when this feature is enabled.
4. Tap a misspelled word and then tap one of the suggested corrections. If no suggestions are offered, tap the right arrow, tap Replace, and then tap the correct word spelling from the offerings.

iCloud

Keynote for iCloud makes checking your spelling a breeze, too:

1. Turn spell checking on or off by clicking Tools in the toolbar, choosing Settings, and then clicking Check Spelling. Keynote is checking spelling when a check mark is next to the option. Misspelled words are displayed with a red-dotted underline.

2. Click a misspelled word and then either:
   - Select the correct spelling from the list.
   - Type the correct spelling.

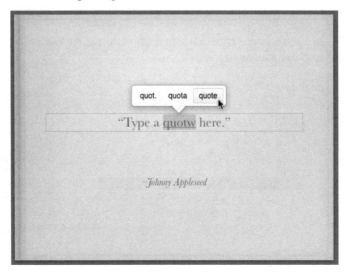

Playing It Smart with Reference Tools

Like Pages, Keynote in OS X uses the Dictionary app that's already built into OS X not only to define words, but also to find words of similar meaning via the Dictionary app's thesaurus. You can quickly look up a word by selecting it, right-clicking (or CONTROL-clicking) it, and then selecting Look Up *selected word*.

Similarly, Keynote for iOS allows you to define a word on-the-fly, but there is no thesaurus available (there may be a good thesaurus app available for download in the App Store, but it won't be interactive with Keynote, I'm afraid). Tap a selected word and tap Define from the menu to see a thorough definition of the word.

Keynote for iCloud doesn't include access to a dictionary or thesaurus on its own, but the operating system you're accessing it from may (we already know OS X does, of course).

Substituting Text On-the-Fly

The OS X and iOS versions of Keynote (sorry iCloud version fans) have a neat feature called Text Replacement that lets you type a string of characters and have Keynote substitute something else for them. For example, you can type "supcal" (minus the quotes) and have Keynote replace it with supercalifragilisticexpialidocious (assuming you've set it up to do so, of course).

To set up and use Text Replacement in OS X:

1. Choose Edit | Substitutions | Show Substitutions to open the Substitutions window.
2. Check the box next to Text Replacement (it may already be checked).

3. Click the Text Preferences button to open System Preferences to the Text tab of the Keyboard preferences window.
4. Click the + button under the Replace list on the left side.
5. Type the string of characters you want to be replaced when they're typed in a presentation.
6. Press TAB and type the characters you want to be the substitute for the characters in the Replace list.

7. Back in the Substitutions window of Keynote, click Replace All or Replace In Selection to perform the replacement for text that's already in the presentation. If Text Replacement is turned on, new text that's entered will automatically be substituted.

iOS offers the same feature, but it's referred to as keyboard shortcuts (not to be confused with keyboard shortcuts in OS X). These shortcuts do the exact same thing as the Text Replacement option in Keynote for OS X, allowing you to type a few key letters that cause an entire word to appear. To add shortcuts to iOS:

1. Starting from your iOS device's home screen, open Settings.
2. Tap General and then tap Keyboard (you'll have to scroll down the screen, most likely).
3. Scroll to the bottom of the Keyboard window and find the Shortcuts section.

4. Tap the Add New Shortcut... option.
5. In the Phrase field, enter the text you want to appear when the shortcut is typed.
6. In the Shortcut field, enter the string of characters you want to translate into the text in the Phrase field.
7. Tap Save in the upper right corner of the window, just underneath the battery life indicator.

Tip   If you're using the same iCloud account on your Mac and iOS devices, these shortcuts will synchronize.

Making Comments and Highlighting Text

To place comments or highlights in a presentation while working in Keynote for OS X:

1. Click in the presentation anywhere that you want to add your comment, or select the text you want to highlight.
2. Click Comment in the toolbar to open a comment window. To highlight selected text, choose Insert | Highlight.
3. Enter comments, if you are indeed commenting and not simply highlighting.

4. Click outside the comment window to make it disappear. The comment is still in the presentation, but it's now hidden until someone clicks the small yellow box to open it.

To work with a comment or highlight in a presentation in Keynote for OS X:

- Hover your mouse pointer over the commented or highlighted item to see its contents.
- Click the commented/highlighted text or item to open the comment and leave it open (click outside of it to make it disappear again).
- Discard the comment or highlight by opening it and then clicking Delete in the lower left of the comment window.

To place comments or highlights in a presentation while working in Keynote for iOS:

1. Tap your presentation in the location or on the item that you want to add your comment to, or select the text you want to highlight.
2. Tap Comment or Highlight in the pop-up menu to open a comment window.
3. Enter your comments if working with a comment window.
4. Tap outside the comment window to make it disappear.

To work with a comment or highlight in a presentation in Keynote for iOS:

- Tap the commented object to open its comment.
- Discard a comment from the presentation by tapping the comment and then tapping Delete in the lower left of the comment window. Discard a highlight by tapping it and then tapping Remove Highlight in the pop-up menu.

Presenting Your Presentations

You've spent three weeks of blood, sweat, tears, and espressos on this presentation. All T's are crossed, I's are dotted (except the capitals, of course), and it's time to deliver your creation to a breathless audience. You walk into the conference room, pop open your MacBook Pro, launch Keynote, and then...

And then...?

Well, if you're not sure what happens after "and then," you're about to find out. You'd better hurry up and read this section of the chapter; your boss appears to be getting antsy.

Playing a Presentation

Here's the answer to "and then": play that presentation, my friend! "How?" I'm glad you asked. Let's see how to do so, using your trusty Mac, faithful iPad, or dependable iCloud.

OS X

To play your presentation using Keynote for OS X:

1. Click the slide you want to begin the presentation with and then click the Play button in the toolbar.

2. To move through your presentation:
   - Press the RIGHT ARROW key to move to the next slide.
   - Press the LEFT ARROW key to move to the previous slide.
   - To move to a different slide, type a number on the keyboard to open the slide navigator. Type the number of the slide you want to jump to and press RETURN (or click the Go button in the upper left of the screen).
3. Press the ESC key at any time to quit playing the presentation.

 You can also move to the next slide by pressing the SPACEBAR or clicking the left mouse button.

iOS

To play your presentation using Keynote for iOS:

1. Tap the slide you want to begin the presentation with and then tap the Play button in the right side of the toolbar.
2. To move through your presentation:
   - Tap the currently viewed slide to move to the next slide.
   - Swipe to the right to move to the previous slide. If you go too far to the left of the screen when swiping, you might accidentally open the slide navigator. This won't cause a major disruption, but might throw your timing off a bit.
   - To move to a different slide, tap the left side of the screen to open the slide navigator, and then simply tap the slide you want to jump to, as shown in Figure 8-1.
3. Pinch anywhere on the iPad's screen to quit playing the presentation.

iCloud

To play your presentation using Keynote for iCloud:

1. Click the slide you want to begin the presentation with and then click Play in the toolbar. Your screen goes into full screen mode during the presentation.
2. To move through your presentation:
   - Press the RIGHT ARROW key or the SPACEBAR to move to the next slide.
   - Press the LEFT ARROW key to move to the previous slide.
   - To move to a different slide, type a number on the keyboard and press RETURN or ENTER to jump to it. You may also move your pointer all the way to the left side of the screen to open the slide navigator and click a slide to jump to it.
3. Press the ESC key at any time to quit playing the presentation.

 Make sure you're using a supported browser for best results during presentation playback. We can't have some rogue browser or a beta version of a supported browser mucking up our presentation, now can we? That's a big huge NO, in case you're wondering.

FIGURE 8-1 Open the slide navigator and simply tap a slide to jump to it during your presentation.

 Press the ? key to show onscreen keyboard shortcuts you can use to navigate your presentation.

Utilizing Links-Only or Self-Playing Presentations

Sometimes it's nice to have your presentation play back automatically, either upon launch or by someone clicking or tapping a link. You can easily set your presentations to exhibit this independent behavior on both the OS X and iOS versions of Keynote, but not iCloud (as of this writing, at least).

To set a presentation to play its slide automatically:

1. Open the Setup inspector in Keynote for OS X by clicking its icon on the right side of the toolbar, and then click the Presentation tab. In iOS, tap the Tools icon and then tap Presentation Tools.
2. Set up the presentation based on platform:
   - **For OS X** Click the Presentation Type menu and select one of the following options:
     - **Normal** Move through slides manually with the press of a key.
     - **Links Only** Moves through or to slides when a link is clicked.

- **Self-Playing**   Moves through slides automatically, based on settings made for Transition Delay and Build Delay (in the Setup inspector).
- **For iOS**   Tap the Presentation Type option and select one of the following options:
  - **Normal**   Move through slides manually with the tap of the screen.
  - **Links Only**   Moves through or to slides when a link is tapped.
  - **Self-Playing**   Moves through slides automatically, based on settings made for Transition Delay and Build Delay (in the Tools | Presentation Tools | Presentation Type menu, shown in Figure 8-2).

FIGURE 8-2   Adjusting a self-playing presentation's settings in Keynote for iOS.

Setting Presentation Playback Options

There are a few other options that help you set a presentation for customized playback. You can make these settings in the following places depending on platform:

- **OS X**   Open the Setup inspector in Keynote for OS X by clicking its icon on the right side of the toolbar, and then click the Presentation tab.
- **iOS**   Tap the Tools icon and then tap Presentation Tools.

You can set a presentation to continue playing on a loop by checking the Loop Slideshow check box in OS X or by toggling the Loop Presentation switch in iOS.

If you'd like your presentation to play automatically after sitting idle for a predetermined amount of time:

- **OS X**   Check the Restart Show If Idle For check box and then adjust the amount of idle time (in minutes) using the up or down arrows (you can also manually enter a time).
- **iOS**   Toggle the switch for Restart Show If Idle to on and then drag the slider for the desired amount of idle time.

Using Your Presenter Notes

Even the best of actors needs a cue for a forgotten line, so it only stands to reason that even the best presenters could use a cue, as well. Instead of another actor or a director giving you a cue, though, you'll rely on good ole Keynote for that helping hand, by using presenter notes. Presenter notes, which aren't visible to the audience, allow you to give yourself cues to what you want to speak about. Presenter notes will work when playing your presentation using the OS X or iOS version of Keynote, but poor iCloud is left out of the fun.

Presenter notes are only available in your presentation if you have a display connected to your Mac or iOS device.

Adding and Editing Presenter Notes

To add or edit presenter notes in a slide using Keynote for OS X:

1. Open the slide you want to add the notes to.
2. Click View (in the toolbar, not the menu) and select Show Presenter Notes.
3. Enter your notes into the white space that appears under the slide.

To add or edit presenter notes in a slide using Keynote for iOS:

1. Open the slide you want to add the notes to.
2. Tap the Tools icon and then tap Presenter Notes.
3. Enter your notes into the supplied space. Notice that slides containing presenter notes are displayed with a gray box in the corner of their thumbnail images in the slide navigator. This gray box only appears when in Presenter Notes mode.

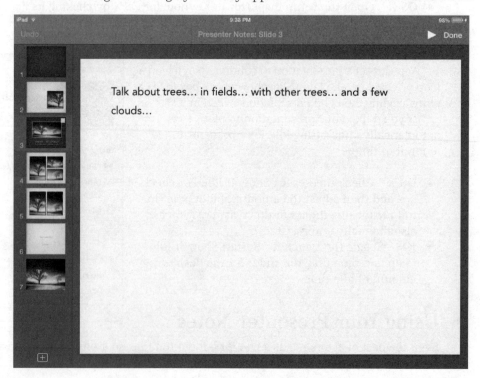

4. Tap the next slide you want to add notes to and then do so, and continue this process until you're done adding notes.
5. Tap Done in the upper right of the blue toolbar when finished.

Viewing Presenter Notes

To view your notes during a presentation using Keynote for OS X:

1. Click the Play button to begin your presentation.
2. Click the Layout button, which looks like two gray squares on top of a single gray rectangle, and select Presenter Notes.
3. Move through your presentation as normal.

To view your notes during a presentation using Keynote for iOS:

1. Tap the Play button in the toolbar.
2. Tap Layout and then tap Notes.
3. Move through your presentation as normal.

Driving with Keynote Remote

One very cool feature of Keynote is the ability to use an iPad, iPhone, or iPod touch to remotely control a presentation being played from a Mac or another iOS device.

 You must have Keynote installed on all devices, and each device must be connected to the same Wi-Fi network.

Setting Up an iOS Device to Work with Another iOS Device

To set up an iOS device to work as a remote for another iOS device:

1. Open Keynote on the iOS device to be used as the remote.
2. Tap the Remote button (looks like an iOS device with a small Play button at the bottom) in the upper left corner of the presentation manager, and then tap Continue to open the Set Up Remote screen.
3. Open the presentation you want to show on the iOS device that is hosting the presentation.
4. Tap the Tools icon and then tap Presentation Tools. Tap Allow Remote Control and then toggle the switch to Enable Remotes.
5. Tap Link next to the device you want to use as the remote. You can also come back here later and tap Unlink to unlink a device.
6. A four-digit code appears on both devices: verify they match and tap Confirm. The devices are now linked, and you can remotely control one from the other.

Setting Up an iOS Device to Work with a Mac

To set up an iOS device to work as a remote for a Mac:

1. Open Keynote on the iOS device to be used as the remote.
2. Tap the Remote button (looks like an iOS device with a small Play button at the bottom) in the upper left corner of the presentation manager, and then tap Continue to open the Set Up Remote screen.
3. Open Keynote on your Mac. Select Keynote | Preferences.
4. Select Remotes in the Preferences window, and then check the Enable box.
5. Clink the Link button next to the device you want to use as the remote. You can also come back here later and tap Unlink to unlink a device.

6. A four-digit code appears on both the Mac and the iOS device: verify they match, click Confirm, and then close the Preferences window. The devices are now linked, and you can remotely control the Mac from the iOS device.

Remotely Controlling a Presentation

To remotely control a presentation using an iOS device:

1. Open the presentation on the Mac or iOS device that is hosting it.
2. Open Keynote on the iOS device being used as the remote.
3. Tap the Remote button (looks like an iOS device with a small Play button at the bottom) in the upper left corner of the presentation manager, and then tap Play.

4. Control playback using the following options:
   - To move to the next or previous slide, swipe to the left or right.
   - To jump to a specific slide, open the slide navigator by tapping the slide number in the upper left corner. Tap the slide you want to show from within the navigator.
5. To stop the presentation, tap the × button in the upper right corner.

Narrating a Self-Playing Recording

Let's throw in one more really cool trick before we end our little trip through Keynote Land. Be warned that this little trick is only available in Keynote for OS X, though.

The little trick I speak of is the ability to narrate your presentation using a microphone and your Mac. You can use either the Mac's built-in microphone or another one that you've attached to one of its handy-dandy ports.

To record a narration for your presentation:

1. Open the presentation to the slide that you want to begin the narration in.
2. Open the Setup inspector and click the Audio tab.
3. Click the Record button to enter recording mode, shown in Figure 8-3.
4. Click the recording button (the one with the red dot) at the bottom of the screen to begin recording your audio. When you first click the recording button, Keynote gives you an onscreen three-second countdown so you'll know when to begin your narration. Thanks, Keynote!

FIGURE 8-3   The recording mode screen lets you record narrations for your slides.

5. Speak into your microphone and record your audio. Press the RIGHT ARROW key to move through your slides when you're ready. You can also pause recording by clicking the Pause button; continue recording with another click of the recording button.
6. Click the recording button again to stop recording.
7. Click the × button in the upper right to save your recording and exit the recording mode screen.

 Click the Layout button in the upper right corner of the recording mode screen to change how you view slides in recording mode.

Summary

Gently close this book (until you're ready to move on to the section on Numbers), set it aside, breathe in and out slowly ten times, and then scream like a banshee! Why? Because Keynote is now your presentation playground, having discovered the bells and whistles that'll make you and your presentations stand out above the crowd. Booyah.

PART IV

Working with Spreadsheets, the Apple Way

9

Juggling Numbers

HOW TO...

- Get around in the land of Numbers
- Adjust preferences to your liking
- Create, save, and share spreadsheets
- Secure spreadsheets from prying eyes
- Export and import spreadsheets
- Print spreadsheets

Numbers is Apple's answer to Microsoft's Excel spreadsheet application, and it is a loud and unmistakably confident answer, at that. Numbers is able to do what Excel hasn't up to now: make working with spreadsheets almost a *fun* thing to do. That's right: working with spreadsheets doesn't *have* to be a slavishly boring and menial task, I don't care what accountants may tell you.

Like its word processing and spreadsheet making iWork cousins, Numbers is available for OS X, iOS, and iCloud, so, as has been the case in previous chapters of this book, we'll look at how to perform tasks on all three versions (if applicable).

Getting Around in Numbers

Let's get things started by exploring how to get around in the world of Numbers. Numbers isn't your dad's spreadsheet application, so if that's what you're used to, you may be in for a surprise. Of course, for consistency's and sanity's sake, the Numbers interface is as close to those in Pages and Keynote as possible, so it won't be all that foreign to you if you've already worked with those two apps.

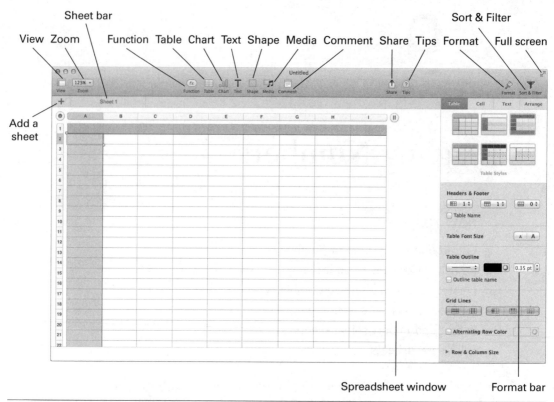

Sheet bar

Sort & Filter

View Zoom   Function Table Chart Text Shape Media Comment Share Tips Format   Full screen

Add a
sheet

Spreadsheet window   Format bar

FIGURE 9-1 The lay of the land in Numbers-ville, OS X-style

Figure 9-1 shows the top-down view of Numbers from within OS X, and it acts as a guide to Numbers-ville. You were given a brief explanation of many of these callouts in Chapter 1.

The contents of the Format bar will change depending on the element you've selected in the spreadsheet. For example, if you select a cell, cell formatting options appear, and if you select text, text-related options show up.

Figure 9-2 shows what the same spreadsheet looks like when opened in Numbers for iOS.

If you've read Chapter 1, you have a general knowledge of each of the callouts in Figure 9-2 except Spreadsheets and Sheet bar, which are specific to Numbers. If you

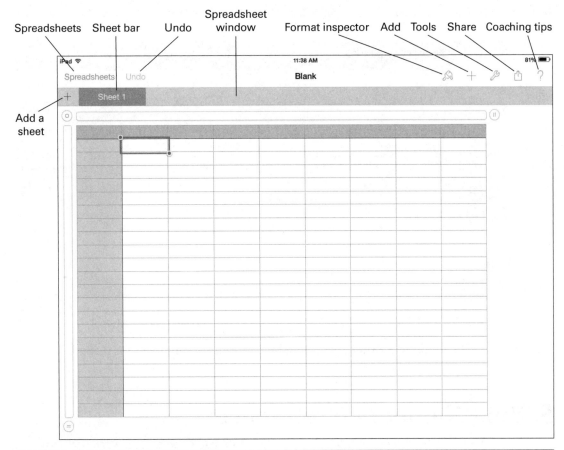

FIGURE 9-2   The same spreadsheet as in Figure 9-1, but now in Numbers for iOS

tap Spreadsheets in the upper left corner, you'll be taken to the Spreadsheets manager screen, where you can create new spreadsheets, open spreadsheets you've previously worked with, and more. Numbers allows you to have multiple sheets within a single spreadsheet, sort of like having multiple chapters in a book. You can access these sheets via the Sheet bar, and you can add new sheets by clicking the Add A Sheet button (looks like a + in the upper left corner of the screen, not to be confused with the Add button in the upper right of the screen).

Figure 9-3 shows the same spreadsheet, but this time in Numbers for iCloud.

Add a sheet Zoom Undo/Redo   Table Text Shape Image Format panel Share Tools Feedback

Sheet tab

Spreadsheet window

FIGURE 9-3 The same spreadsheet yet again, but this time in Numbers for iCloud

Setting Numbers' Preferences

Numbers is a friendly spreadsheet app, so it wants you to be able to work within it in the ways that suit you best. To this end, Numbers offers you preferences that allow you to make some settings work just the way you want them to.

Note If the same preference option is available within multiple versions of the app, you'll need to set the option in each version of the app in order for it to be consistent across platforms. The different versions of apps don't synchronize their settings, even if you're logged in to iCloud.

OS X Preferences

To open the preferences in Numbers for OS X, press ⌘-, (that's the COMMAND key and comma key simultaneously). You can also click the Numbers menu in the upper left of your screen and select Preferences.

The General tab of Numbers' Preferences window is shown in Figure 9-4. Several options are available for your customization:

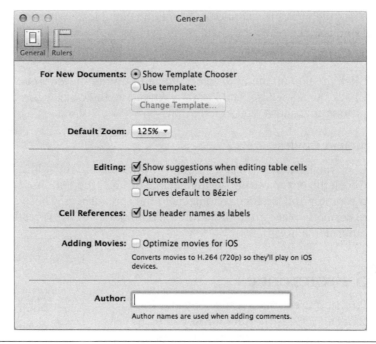

FIGURE 9-4   The General tab of Numbers' Preferences window

- **For New Documents**   Select either Show Template Chooser or Use Template as the default action when you begin to create a new spreadsheet. Selecting Show Template Chooser does just what it says, and selecting Use Template will automatically create a new spreadsheet from a template you choose by clicking the Change Template button and selecting it from a location on your Mac.
- **Default Zoom**   Choose what the default zoom setting will be for new spreadsheets.
- **Editing**   This section lets you set default actions for editing a spreadsheet:
  - **Show suggestions when editing table cells**   Check this box to have Numbers offer advice to you based on information in other cells of the same column.
  - **Automatically detect lists**   Check this box to have Numbers detect when you are typing a list. When a list is detected, Numbers automatically formats it as such.
  - **Curves default to Bézier**   Check this box for curves to be Bézier curves by default, or leave it unchecked to use smooth curves.
- **Cell References**   Check the Use Header Names As Labels box to allow Numbers to label items in charts and formulas with the names of column and row headers (A4, B3, etc.).
- **Adding Movies**   Check the Optimize Movies For iOS box when you want to add a movie to your spreadsheet and it will be viewed by folks using iOS devices.
- **Author**   Add a name to the available field to use when tracking changes and making comments within a spreadsheet.

The Rulers tab offers options for helping you decide where to place items within your spreadsheet:

Ruler Units:

- Click the pop-up menu to select a default unit of measurement.
- Check the Show Size And Position When Moving Objects box to see an onscreen prompt that shows you exactly that.

Alignment Guides:

- Click the button to select a default color for alignment guides.
- Check the box to enable, or uncheck to disable, the options for showing guides at the center and/or edges of objects in the spreadsheet. These guides make it easier to correctly place an item within the boundaries of the spreadsheet and among other items in it.

iOS Preferences

"Preferences" are actually called Settings in Numbers for iOS (as they are for Keynote and Pages in iOS), but they perform the same function of creating app-wide defaults.

Access Settings by opening a spreadsheet, tapping the Tools icon (looks like a wrench) in the upper right of the screen, and then tapping Settings. The Settings menu, shown in Figure 9-5, offers us several items, which are described briefly in Table 9-1. Touch the toggle switch to the right of each option to enable it (green) or disable it (white).

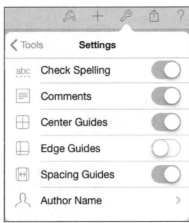

FIGURE 9-5 Preferences are known as Settings in Numbers for iOS.

TABLE 9-1 Available Options in Settings for iOS Numbers

Option	Description
Check Spelling	Enable to allow Numbers to check your spelling as you type.
Comments	Enable to show comments in a spreadsheet.
Center Guides	Enable in order to see guides when one item's center aligns with another item's center, or with the center of the page.
Edge Guides	Enable to see guides when an item's edges align with another item's edges.
Spacing Guides	Enable to see when three or more items are equally spaced apart on a line.
Author Name	Tap to enter a name into the available text field that will be used when tracking changes made to a spreadsheet or when adding comments.

iCloud Preferences

iCloud's version of Numbers also refers to its preferences as Settings (as does the iOS version), which must make OS X's version of Numbers feel like it's missing something. I think the relationship will survive their differences, though.

Click the Tools button in the toolbar and hold your pointer over Settings to see the options shown in Figure 9-6:

- **Show/Hide Format Panel**   Select to show or hide the format panel on the right side of the screen.
- **Check Spelling**   Select to enable or disable automatic spell checking.
- **Center Guides**   Select to see guides when one item's center aligns with another item's center, or with the center of the page.
- **Edge Guides**   Select to see guides when an item's edges align with another item's edges.
- **Spacing Guides**   Select to see when three or more items are equally spaced apart within a line.
- **Set Password**   Select to add a password for the spreadsheet you're currently working in.

Changes made to Settings in Numbers for iCloud only hold while the spreadsheet is open, with the important exception of Set Password.

FIGURE 9-6   Numbers for iCloud offers a handful of options for setting your defaults.

Working with Spreadsheets

Despite all the neat stuff Numbers can do, its raison d'être is to be the best darned spreadsheet app out there. That's right, Excel; the gauntlet has been thrown down!

Since spreadsheets are the number one reason Numbers exists on this planet, let's get down to business and discover how to utilize them.

Creating New Spreadsheets

To create a new spreadsheet in Numbers:

- **OS X** Choose File | New or press ⌘-N to open the Template Chooser. Click a template for your new spreadsheet and then click Choose in the lower right corner.
- **iOS** From within the Spreadsheets manager (if you're in a spreadsheet already, just tap Spreadsheets in the upper left corner to get to this screen), tap the Create Spreadsheet icon (can't miss that big + in the middle of it) to open the Template Chooser. Tap the template you want to use and it will open up for you.
- **iCloud** From within the iCloud Numbers screen, click the Create Spreadsheet icon to open the Template Chooser. Select the template you want to use, as I'm doing in Figure 9-7, and then click Choose in the upper right corner of the Template Chooser window to open it.

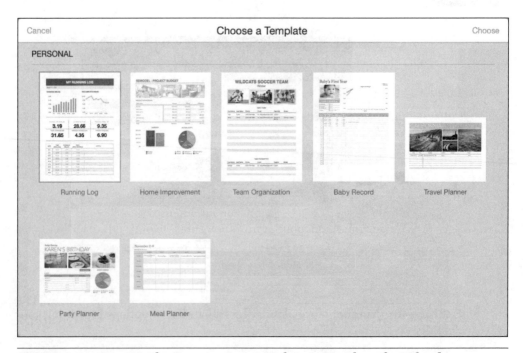

FIGURE 9-7 Opening the Running Log template in Numbers for iCloud

Saving and Renaming Spreadsheets

Why would someone create a spreadsheet, go to all the trouble of formatting it and filling it out, and then fail to save it? To avoid falling into the category of one so foolish, follow these simple instructions to save and rename your precious information before disaster strikes:

- **OS X**   Press ⌘-s or choose File | Save to save a spreadsheet. If this is the first time saving this spreadsheet, the Save As window opens. Give the spreadsheet a fancy title (or not so fancy, whichever), choose a location in which to keep it, and then click Save. If you want to rename a spreadsheet, choose File | Rename, enter the new name for your spreadsheet (the spreadsheet title in the top middle of the window will be highlighted blue, and that's where you'll be typing), and press RETURN; your spreadsheet is now renamed.

 If the location you want to keep the spreadsheet in isn't in the pop-up menu, click the small square containing the downward arrow next to the Save As field to expand the window and see more options.

- **iOS**   Numbers automatically saves your spreadsheets, but by default it saves them with their original name (unless there are multiples of the same name, in which case a 2, 3, or other appropriate number is tacked on to the name's end). Open the Spreadsheets manager and tap the name of the spreadsheet you want to rename. Enter the name of your spreadsheet in the field provided in the Rename Spreadsheet screen and tap Done on the keyboard.

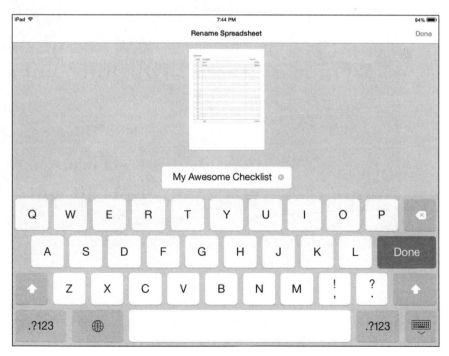

- **iCloud** Numbers for iCloud automatically saves your spreadsheets, but like iOS you start off with generic names. To rename a spreadsheet, open the Spreadsheets manager, select the name of the spreadsheet you want to rename, enter the new name in the field provided, and press RETURN.

Opening Existing Spreadsheets

In order to open existing spreadsheets (from your computer or via iCloud), you'll need a can of WD-40, an antique bottle-opener, and a leather chamois (no ShamWows, please).

Okay, maybe not. It's actually so simple as to be almost silly. I just felt you might need a little perking up at this point in the chapter.

OS X

To open spreadsheets that exist within iCloud or on your Mac:

1. Press ⌘-o or choose File | Open.
2. Select iCloud or On My Mac in the upper left corner of the window, depending on where the spreadsheet is located.
3. Click one time on the spreadsheet you want to open, and then click the Open button in the lower right corner of the window to open it. You can also double-click a spreadsheet within the window to immediately open it.

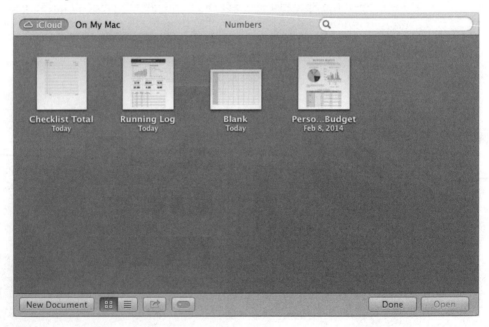

 Choose File | Open Recent to see a list of spreadsheets that you've recently opened in Numbers. Just click the spreadsheet in the list to open it. (You can also click Clear Menu to wipe it clean.)

iOS and iCloud

Opening an existing spreadsheet is performed in the same way for both iOS and iCloud versions of Numbers. Simply open the Spreadsheets manager and select the spreadsheet you want to open (double-click the spreadsheet in iCloud).

Adding and Organizing Sheets

A spreadsheet can contain many multiple sheets within it, which is useful for keeping similar information together. You can use multiple sheets for as many reasons as you can think of, from keeping accounting information for every department in your organization to tracking your children's grades throughout the school years.

Adding a sheet to a spreadsheet is shamefully simple: just click the + in the Add a sheet bar (OS X and iOS) or tab (iCloud), which is found near the upper left of the spreadsheet window (see Figures 9-1, 9-2, and 9-3).

Here are a few things you can do with your sheets within the Sheet bar:

- Click-and-drag a sheet's tab left or right to change its order in the Sheet bar.
- Double-click the name of a sheet to rename it.
- Hold your pointer over the right side of a tab and click the arrow that appears. From it, you can perform several tasks, some of which are germane to every tab, and others that are unique to specific tabs (depending on the type of information it contains).

What to do if you have more sheet tabs than will fit in the Sheet bar?

- If you're in OS X, you'll see two arrows on the right side of the bar. Click the right or left arrow to navigate through the sheet tabs.
- If you're in iOS, you unfortunately don't get much of a heads-up that you have multiple sheet tabs. You can swipe left or right in the Sheet bar to see if there are more tabs, though.
- If you're in iCloud, you'll notice a scroll bar underneath the tabs; simply scroll from left to right to see your tabs.

Locking Spreadsheets and Using Passwords

Security is (or should be) a big deal to all of us, but it can be a particularly big deal when it comes to spreadsheets, as they often contain sensitive information, such as financial data. Numbers utilizes passwords and/or a locking system to keep your info secure to only those who need to know it.

Using Passwords

A password is the first line of defense when it comes to protecting your spreadsheet from prying eyes and from others who might accidentally change its contents (hi, kids!). Once a password is assigned to a spreadsheet, no one can even open it (and certainly can't change it) without knowing the password.

Both the OS X and iOS versions offer you a way to have Numbers remember a spreadsheet's password so that you don't have to enter it every time you open the spreadsheet. DO NOT use this option if you want your spreadsheets to truly be secure; it just doesn't make any sense, in my opinion.

To assign a password to a spreadsheet:

- **OS X**   Choose File | Set Password to open the password dialog, shown in Figure 9-8. Enter the password in the Password and Verify fields, enter a hint in the Password Hint field if so desired (why, Apple, why?), and click the Set Password button.
- **iOS**   Open the spreadsheet, tap the Tools icon, and then tap Set Password. Enter the password in the Password and Verify fields, enter a hint in the Password Hint field if you want (Apple recommends it, but I don't), and tap the Go button on the onscreen keyboard (or Done in the upper right corner of the window).
- **iCloud**   Open the spreadsheet, select the Tools icon, and then click Set Password. Enter the password in the Password and Verify fields, enter a hint in the Password Hint field if you like (or follow my advice and don't), and click Set Password.

To open a password-protected spreadsheet, type the password when prompted. Folks who don't know the password will be in a bit of a pickle, to say the least.

Locking Spreadsheets

Locking prevents anyone from editing, renaming, moving, or deleting a spreadsheet. It's also an option only available within the OS X version of Numbers.

To lock a spreadsheet:

1. Hold the mouse pointer over the title of the spreadsheet until you see a small gray arrow next to it, and then click the arrow.
2. Select the Locked checkbox to lock the spreadsheet, and then click outside the window to return to the spreadsheet.

Require a password to open this spreadsheet:

Password: •••••

Verify: •••••

Password Hint: (Recommended) DON'T USE THIS OPTION, FOR GOODNESS SAKE! (or the one below this, either, for that matter)

☐ Remember this password in my keychain

Cancel   Set Password

FIGURE 9-8   Please notice my not-so-subtle warnings in this figure!

Locking a spreadsheet does not prevent it from being deleted, or from being as unlocked as easily as it was locked. A password is still the recommended way to go when it comes to securing spreadsheets.

Moving Spreadsheets to and from iCloud

Moving spreadsheets to iCloud makes them available anywhere you (or others you share them with) can connect to the Internet with a computer (Mac or PC) or iOS device. Of course, moving a spreadsheet from iCloud will eliminate online access.

To move a spreadsheet from your computer to iCloud, or vice versa (this can only be accomplished from the OS X version of Numbers):

1. Choose File | Move To.
2. Select a location from the pop-up menu. If you don't see the location you want in the menu, choose Other at the bottom of the menu to browse your computer for it.
3. Click the Move button and your spreadsheet will be physically moved (not copied) from its previous location to the one you specified.

Sharing Spreadsheets with iCloud

Numbers allows you to share a spreadsheet with other folks by sending them a link to the spreadsheet, which is physically stored in iCloud. When you share a spreadsheet from iCloud, you are basically sending a web link to the spreadsheet's location within iCloud. Anyone with Numbers (any version, any platform) will be able to click the link and open the spreadsheet, as well as make changes to it.

 It's a fine idea to password-protect your spreadsheet before sharing it if you only want authorized users to view and edit it.

OS X

To share a spreadsheet via iCloud from Numbers in OS X:

1. Open the spreadsheet you want to share.
2. Click the Share button in the toolbar.
3. Decide which method you want to use to share the iCloud link to your spreadsheet, and then choose it from the Share Link Via iCloud context menu.

Once the link is sent to the recipient, check out the Share icon in the toolbar. The white box with the upward arrow that once represented the button has now changed to a couple of green people, indicating the spreadsheet is currently being shared.

Click the Share button when in shared mode and select View Shared Settings to do the following:

- Use the Change Password button to change the password for the spreadsheet.
- Quit sharing your spreadsheet by clicking the Stop Sharing button.
- Send the link to someone else by clicking the Send Link button and choosing a sharing method from the pop-up menu.

- Hold your mouse pointer over the link until you see a gray button called Copy Link, click the Copy Link button to copy the link to your Mac's clipboard, and then paste the link into any spreadsheet or sharing mechanism you feel is appropriate.

iOS

To share a spreadsheet via iCloud from iOS:

1. Open the spreadsheet that's itching to be shared.
2. Tap the Share button in the toolbar.
3. Tap the Share Link Via iCloud option and choose which method you want to use to share the iCloud link. AirDrop is available as another method of sharing between iOS devices.

 As of this writing, AirDrop sharing isn't currently supported for exchanging files from OS X to iOS devices or vice versa. Hopefully, this will change in future incarnations of OS X and iOS.

The Share icon has now morphed into two green folks, as it does in the OS X version of Numbers. Tap the Share button when in shared mode to do the following:

- Tap Change Password to change the password for the spreadsheet.
- Discontinue sharing of the spreadsheet by tapping Stop Sharing.
- Send the link to someone else by tapping Send Link and selecting a method from the pop-up menu.

- Tap the link to see a dark gray button called Copy, tap the Copy button to copy the link to your device's clipboard, and then paste the link into any spreadsheet or sharing mechanism you like.

iCloud

To share a spreadsheet from within Numbers for iCloud:

1. Open the spreadsheet you want to share.
2. Click the Share button in the toolbar, and then click the blue Share Spreadsheet button.
3. A window called "This spreadsheet is shared" opens. You can perform the following tasks from it:
   - Change the password for the spreadsheet by using the Change Password button.
   - Discontinue sharing of the spreadsheet by clicking the Stop Sharing button.
   - Send the link to someone else via iCloud's Mail app by clicking the Email Link button.
   - Click the link once to highlight it, press ⌘-c (Mac) or CONTROL-C (PC) to copy the link to your computer's clipboard, and then paste the link into any spreadsheet or sharing mechanism you like.

To access the "This spreadsheet is shared" window again, click the Share button in the toolbar and then click Settings.

Exporting and Importing Spreadsheets

As with Pages and Keynote, when we speak of "exporting" a spreadsheet from Numbers, it can have a couple of different meanings:

- To save the file in a format other than the native one, which is .numbers
- Transferring files from an iOS device to a computer through iTunes

Importing spreadsheets is as simple as opening them in Numbers (any method will do), as long as its file format is supported by Numbers, of course. Importing spreadsheets does have a second meaning too (like exporting), which means to transfer files from iTunes onto your iOS device.

Exporting Files from Numbers

Numbers is blessed with the ability to export files to multiple formats so they can be viewed and worked with in other apps. By the way, this is only supported in OS X and iCloud versions; iOS is left in the cold this time, sorry.

To export a spreadsheet using Numbers for OS X:

1. Open the spreadsheet you wish to export.
2. Click the File menu, hold your mouse pointer over the Export To menu, and then select the format you want to export your file to.

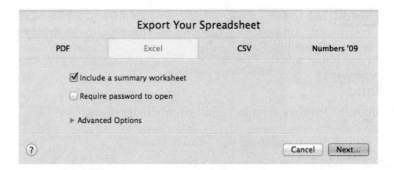

FIGURE 9-9 Options vary depending on the file format you're exporting to.

3. When the Export Your Spreadsheet window opens, make any selections you need according to the format you're exporting to, as shown in Figure 9-9.
4. Click Next.
5. Choose a location to save your new file, give it a new name (otherwise, all manner of confusion could abound), and then click Export to complete the process.

 File formats supported for export from Numbers for OS X are PDF, Excel, CSV, Numbers '09, and ZIP. Formats supported by Numbers for iCloud include PDF, Excel, and Numbers.

There are two ways to export a spreadsheet using Numbers for iCloud: from within an open spreadsheet and from within the Spreadsheets manager.

To export from within an open spreadsheet:

1. Choose Tools | Download A Copy.
2. Select the format you want to export your file to.
3. Once Numbers finishes formatting the spreadsheet, it automatically downloads to your browser's default downloads folder.

To export from within the Spreadsheets manager:

1. Click one time on the spreadsheet you want to export so that it's highlighted.
2. Click the Document And Sort Options button (looks like a gear) at the top of the window and select Download Spreadsheet from the menu.
3. Click the format you want to export your file to.
4. When Numbers finishes formatting the spreadsheet, it automatically downloads to your browser's default downloads folder.

Importing Files into Numbers

Non-native file formats supported by Numbers include Numbers '09, Excel, CSV (Comma Separated Values), and tab-delimited text files. As noted earlier, importing a file into Numbers for OS X is as simple as opening it. You must get a file into Numbers for iOS and Numbers for iCloud before they can even make the attempt to open it, though, which brings us to our discussion of transferring files to and fro using iTunes.

Transferring Files to and from Numbers with iTunes

Anyone with an iOS device, regardless of what kind of computer they use to synchronize it, is familiar with iTunes. While adept at syncing devices and downloading and playing music, videos, or whatnot, iTunes can also transfer files to and from Numbers on the previously mentioned iOS devices.

To transfer files to Numbers for iOS from iTunes:

1. Connect your iOS device to your computer and open iTunes on your computer.
2. Select your device in iTunes once it appears (it should show up in the upper right of the window).
3. Select Apps in the toolbar at the top of the window and scroll to the bottom of the window.
4. Click Numbers in the Apps list under File Sharing.
5. Click the Add button in the lower right and browse your computer for the file you need to transfer. When you find the file, select it and then click Add. The file now shows up in the Numbers Spreadsheets list.
6. Open Numbers on your iOS device.
7. Go to the Spreadsheets manager and tap + in the upper left corner, and then tap Copy From iTunes.
8. When the Copy From iTunes window opens, tap the name of the appropriate spreadsheet to transfer it into Numbers on your iOS device. The Copy From iTunes window will indicate the file is importing, and once finished, the file appears in the Spreadsheets manager.

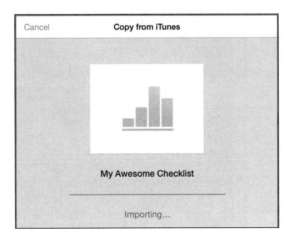

To transfer files from Numbers for iOS to iTunes:

1. Connect your iOS device to your computer and open iTunes on the computer (not the iOS device).
2. Select your device in iTunes (it will show up in the upper right of the window) once it appears.
3. Select Apps in the toolbar at the top of the window and then scroll to the bottom of the window.
4. Click Numbers in the Apps list under File Sharing.
5. Open Numbers on your iOS device and do one of the following:
   - If the spreadsheet you want to transfer is not open, tap the Share button in the upper left of the screen (looks like a square containing an upward-pointing arrow) and select Send A Copy from the menu. Tap the spreadsheet you want to transfer to highlight it.
   - If you are working in the spreadsheet you want to transfer, tap the Share button in the upper right of the screen, and then select Send A Copy from the menu.
6. Tap the iTunes icon to open the Send To iTunes window.
7. Tap the file format you want to use for the spreadsheet: Numbers, PDF, Excel, or CSV. When the transfer (really, it's a copy, but we'll stick with Apple's terminology) is finished, the spreadsheet will appear in the Numbers Spreadsheets list in iTunes. Select the file, click the Save To button in the lower right, choose a location in which to save the file on your computer, and click the Save To button.

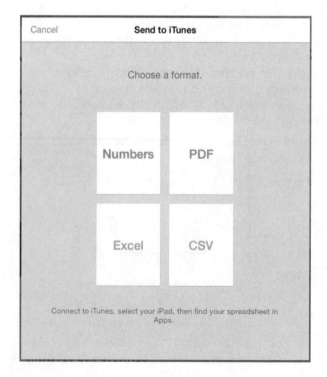

Printing a Spreadsheet

Some bosses still prefer to have a printed spreadsheet in their hands (go figure), and printed spreadsheets can be downright handy (literally) in a meeting, so let's see how to get a hard copy from our beloved versions of Numbers.

Printing from OS X

To print spreadsheets from Numbers for OS X:

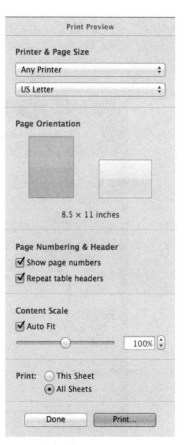

1. Press ⌘-P or choose File | Print to open the Print Preview pane on the right side of the window, and also show a preview of the sheets to be printed. From here, you can do the following:
   a. Choose a printer and page size.
   b. Select the desired page orientation. The preview window will instantly show you what will happen with your spreadsheets when printed.
   c. Make selections in the Page Numbering & Header and the Content Scale sections.
   d. Determine whether to print just the selected sheet or all the sheets.
   e. Click Print when you're ready to go to the OS X Print dialog sheet.
2. From the OS X Print dialog sheet, you can do the following:
   a. Select the printer you wish to send the print job to in the Printer pop-up menu. You actually should have done this already in step 1a, but you can always change your mind, I guess.
   b. Make any other selections you need using the available options. If you don't see some of the options you need in the Print dialog sheet, they could be hidden. Click the Show Details button in the lower left of the sheet to see the hidden (advanced) options not available in the standard dialog.
   c. Click the Print button in the lower right corner to print the job.

Printing from iOS

Printing from Numbers in iOS is as basic as printing gets. You tell it to print and it does. Done.

Okay, fine, you talked me into getting a little more detailed.

You must already have a printer set up to print with your iOS device. Find more information for doing so at http://support.apple.com/kb/HT4356.

To print from Numbers in iOS:

1. Open the spreadsheet you want to print.
2. Tap the Tools icon in the upper right and tap Print in the menu. Numbers opens to a print preview screen, denoted by the blue background.
3. Set options at the bottom of the preview screen, such as Portrait or Landscape, as well as the size of the spreadsheet on the page.
4. Tap the Options icon (looks like a gear) in the upper right to open the Options window, which allows you to choose to print page numbers, repeat table headers on each page, and select a paper size for the job.

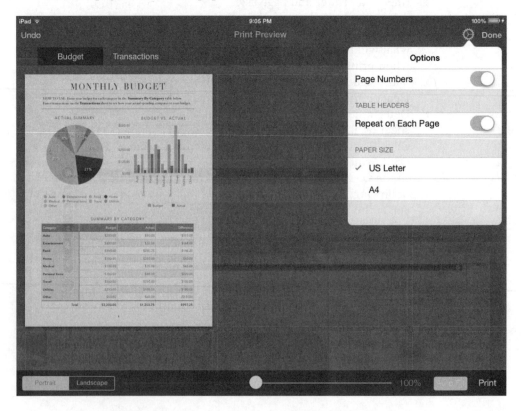

5. Tap Print in the lower right corner of the screen, and then tap Printer to select a printer to send the print job to.
6. Decide how many copies of the spreadsheet you want to print and tap the + or − buttons accordingly.
7. Tap the Print button to send your job along to the printer.

Printing from iCloud

Numbers for iCloud doesn't print your spreadsheet from its native file format, but rather, it creates a PDF and prints it. Actually, these PDFs print directly from your browser or your computer's default PDF application, not from Numbers itself.

To print from iCloud:

1. Open the spreadsheet that you need to print.
2. Click the Tools icon in the upper right and select Print.
3. Numbers generates a PDF of your spreadsheet. When the PDF generation is complete, click the Open PDF button to open the PDF in your browser or your default PDF application.
4. Print as you normally would from your browser or PDF app.

Summary

All right! We've covered the "beginner's basics" of Numbers, such as learning the lay of the land, importing and exporting spreadsheets, sharing your information, and more, but now it's time to get your nails dirty. Chapters 10 and 11 will continue our quest for better spreadsheets, so head on over when you're ready.

10

Filling in All Those Cells

HOW TO...

- Work with tables and cells
- Use formulas within your spreadsheets
- Display information using charts

Okay, it's time to get our hands dirty with the real business of Numbers: getting data into cells, rows, and columns, and clearly representing that data with charts and graphs. Up to now, you've learned the basics of getting around in Numbers, but now we'll actually get some work done.

A Seat at the Table

Anyone who's ever touched a spreadsheet app knows darned good and well that tables are the quintessential part of a spreadsheet. Heck, a spreadsheet *is* a table, for all intents and purposes. Since tables are so integral to Numbers, it stands to reason that adding and working with them is just as easy as Apple could possibly make it. Let's get busy "setting the table" in all three versions of Numbers, shall we?

Adding a Table

Well, here's the deal: when you create a new spreadsheet in Numbers, you're automatically going to have a table in it. Whether you choose a preformatted template in the Template Chooser or create a blank spreadsheet, a table will be present in the sheet.

Having said that, you can add as many tables to a sheet as you like, so adding a table is an essential element of working in Numbers. All three versions allow you to easily add tables.

OS X

To add a table to a spreadsheet in Numbers for OS X:

1. Click the Table icon in the toolbar.
2. Choose a table from the options, or drag one from the menu and drop it into the spreadsheet, as I've done in Figure 10-1 (note that the coordinates appear when placing the table). Click the left or right arrows in the menu to see different styles of tables.
3. To move a table, click it to make it active, then click-and-drag the circle in its upper left corner to its new position.
4. Delete a table by clicking the circle in its upper left corner and then pressing the DELETE key.

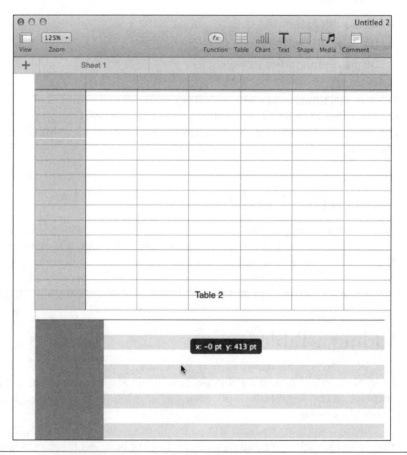

FIGURE 10-1 I've just dragged a table from the Table icon in the toolbar and placed it under the original table in the spreadsheet.

iOS

To add a table to a spreadsheet in Numbers for iOS:

1. Tap + in the toolbar and then tap the Table icon to see a menu of different table styles. Swipe left or right to see more styles.
2. Tap to select a table from the options, or drag one from the menu and remove your finger from the screen to drop it into the spreadsheet.
3. To move a table, tap it to make it active, then tap-and-drag the circle in its upper left corner to its new location in the spreadsheet.
4. To delete a table, tap it, and then tap Delete in the menu.

iCloud

To add a table to a spreadsheet in Numbers for iCloud:

1. Click the Table icon in the toolbar.
2. Choose a table style from the options and click it.
3. To move a table, click it to make it active, then click-and-drag the square in its upper left corner to its new home in your spreadsheet.
4. Delete a table by clicking its upper left corner to activate it and then pressing the DELETE key.

Adding Rows and Columns

Tables are like egos: they can vary greatly in size. Numbers is quite skilled at easily helping you to maximize or minimize the numbers of rows and columns in your tables, regardless of the version you decide to utilize.

Working with Rows and Columns in OS X

To add or remove table rows and columns in Numbers for OS X:

1. Select the table.
2. Do one of the following to add or remove rows or columns:
   - To add a column to the right side of the table or to add a row to the bottom of it, click the circle containing the two parallel lines. You can also click-and-drag the circle to add or remove columns and/or rows.
   - Move the pointer over the column or row bar (lettered or numbered, respectively) of the column or row to which you want to make an addition.

When you see a small gray arrow appear, click it to see a pop-up menu. Choose to add a column before or after the one you're working with, or add a row above or below the one you're working with. To remove the column or row you're working with, simply select Delete Column or Delete Row.

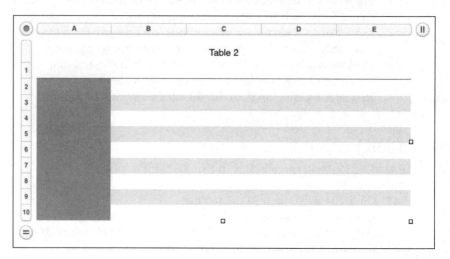

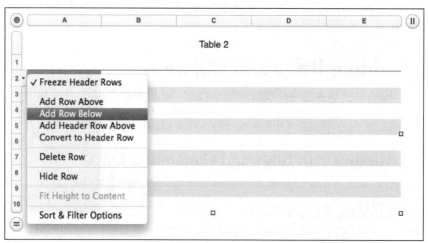

Working with Rows and Columns in iOS

To add or remove table rows and columns in Numbers for iOS:

1. Select the table.
2. To add a column to the right side of the table or to add a row to the bottom of it, tap the corresponding circle containing the two parallel lines once for every column or row you want to add. You can also tap-and-drag the circles to add or remove columns and/or rows.

Working with Rows and Columns in iCloud

To add or remove table rows and columns in Numbers for iCloud:

1. Select the table.
2. Do one of the following to add or remove columns and rows:
   - To add a column to the right side of the table or to add a row to the bottom of it, click the handle to the right of the columns and/or the handle at the bottom of the rows.
   - Move the pointer over the column or row bar (lettered or numbered, respectively) of the column or row to which you want to make an addition. When you see a small black arrow, click it to open a pop-up menu. Choose to add a column before or after the one you're working with, or add a row above or below the one you're working with. To remove the column or row you're working with, select Delete Column or Delete Row.

Working with Cell Contents

Columns and rows are fun (aren't they?), but the real action in a table is the content of its cells. Cells are denoted by their column and row delineations; for example, cell A5 is at the intersection of column A and row 5 in your table.

Numbers helps you quickly determine the name of the cell you've selected: the column and row headers are highlighted, as shown in Figure 10-2.

Placing content into a cell is no brain-buster: click a cell and start typing. Bada-bing, bada-boom. However, that's not all there is when it comes to working with the contents of cells (otherwise, this would be a ridiculously short section).

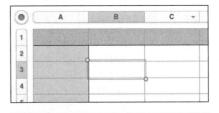

FIGURE 10-2   Numbers highlights the column and row headers of selected cells, helping you quickly distinguish which cell you're working in.

Selecting Cells

Sometimes you need to make changes to or work with more than one cell at once, and Numbers makes it simple to select more than one cell.

To select cells in OS X:

- Click a single cell to select it.
- Select multiple contiguous cells by clicking-and-dragging the selection handles (small white dots) on a selected cell.
- Select multiple noncontiguous cells by clicking the first cell you want and then holding down the COMMAND key (⌘) while clicking the additional cells (shown in Figure 10-3). Release the ⌘ key when finished making selections.

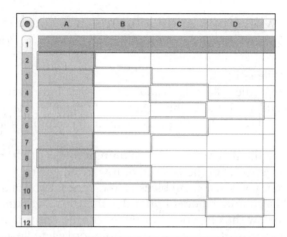

FIGURE 10-3 Multiple noncontiguous cells have been selected here.

To select cells in iOS:

- Tap a cell to select it; double-tap to edit it.
- Select multiple contiguous cells by dragging the selection handles (small blue dots, in this case) on a selected cell.

To select cells in iCloud:

- Click a single cell to select it.
- Select multiple contiguous cells by clicking-and-dragging the selection handles (back to small white dots, as in OS X) on a selected cell.

Copying and Pasting Cells

Copying and pasting cells is a task some of us will find ourselves frequently using, especially if we're working with others in building a spreadsheet and data is being added on-the-fly. All three versions are adept at cutting and pasting from cells in Numbers, but OS X affords many more options than its counterparts.

Some basic things to know when copying and pasting cells:

- When you copy or move a cell, all of its properties are copied, too. This includes all its data, formatting, fill, and so forth.
- If the cells you're copying contain hidden data, said hidden data is also copied, and will subsequently be pasted as well.

OS X   There are quite a number of cool things you can do when it comes to copying and pasting cells in Numbers for OS X. First, select the cells you want to copy (or move), and then do one of the following:

- **Move the information**   Click-and-hold the selected cells until they detach from the table (as illustrated in Figure 10-4), then drag the cells to their new location. If you drop the selected cells onto cells that already contain information, the new will overwrite the old.
- **Make a new table**   Click-and-drag the selected cells somewhere outside of the table that currently houses them. When you drop them, a new table is instantly created for them.
- **Paste and overwrite existing data**   Choose Edit | Copy or press ⌘-c. Click the top left cell where you want to paste the copied information, then choose Edit | Paste (or press ⌘-v). If the cells you selected contain formulas, choose Edit | Paste Formula Results to retain them.
- **Paste without overwriting existing data**   Choose Edit | Copy (or press ⌘-c), select the cells you're pasting to, and then choose Insert | Copied Rows or Insert | Copied Columns. New rows or columns will be added for the copied cells.
- **Paste a cell style**   Choose Format | Copy Style, select the cells that you want to copy the style to, and then choose Format | Paste Style.
- **Paste cell contents but not the style**   Choose Edit | Copy (or press ⌘-c), select the cells where you want to paste the copied data, and choose Edit | Paste And Match Style. The data you paste will conform to the style already used in the cell.

	A	B	C	D	E
1	DATE	TIME (MINUTES)	DISTANCE (MILES)	PACE (MINUTES/MILE)	NOTES
2					
3		4/1	20.00	2.00	10.00
4		4/3	25.30	2.25	11.24
5		4/10	30.00	2.50	12.00
6		4/12	30.20	3.25	9.29
7	4/16	4/14 30.70	30.00 3.25	3.00 9.45	10.00
8	4/18	30.00	3.00	10.00	
9	4/21	30.40	4.00	7.60	
10	4/23	30.00	4.35	6.90	
11	4/25	30.00	4.25	7.06	

FIGURE 10-4   Clicking-and-dragging selected cells to a new location in my spreadsheet

iOS

Copying and pasting is not as robust in Numbers for iOS as it is in Numbers for OS X, but it can still get the job done. Select the cells you want to copy (or move), and then do one of the following:

- **Move the information** Tap-and-hold the selected cells until they detach from the table, then drag them to their new location in the table. If you drop the selected cells onto cells that already contain information, the new will overwrite the old, just as it does in OS X.
- **Make a new table** Tap-and-drag the selected cells somewhere outside of their current table. Remove your finger from the screen, and a new table is created for them.
- **Paste and overwrite existing data** Tap Copy (in the pop-up menu that opens when you select the cells), tap the top left cell where you want to paste the copied data, then tap Paste in the pop-up menu. If the cells you selected contain formulas, tap Paste Formulas or Paste Values to retain one or the other (shown in Figure 10-5).

iCloud Copy and paste is pretty cut and dried when it comes to Numbers for iCloud:

1. Select the cell(s) you want to copy, and then press ⌘-c for Mac or CONTROL-C for PC.
2. Select the cell(s) you want to paste the copied cells to, and then press ⌘-v for Mac or CONTROL-V for PC.

Ah, sweet simplicity...

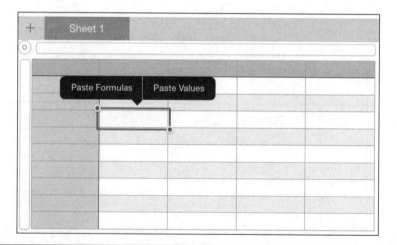

FIGURE 10-5 Determine whether to paste the formulas or just the values when copying and pasting cells containing formulas in Numbers for iOS.

Formatting Tables and Cells

Formatting, or customizing, a table or cell is the act of determining how information looks and works within it. You can format an entire table at once or one cell at a time, whatever the situation calls for. All three versions of Numbers allow you to format cells to some extent, with OS X offering the most options, iOS offering quite a few options, and iCloud offering just a few simple options. The only way to master any of these options and discover how you can most effectively use them in your spreadsheets is to play, play, play with them. Go ahead: your boss won't mind this kind of playtime when she sees the kind of spreadsheets you can generate from good old Numbers.

OS X

To format a table and its cells in Numbers for OS X:

1. Select which part of the table you want to format:
   - For the entire table, click the circle in the upper left corner of it.
   - For a single cell, click within that cell.
   - For multiple cells, click-and-drag to select the cells, or hold the ⌘ key while clicking the individual cells.
2. To make table-wide changes, click the Table tab in the Format bar. Options available include:
   - **Table Styles**   Change the entire look of a table by selecting one of the predefined styles.
   - **Headers & Footer**   Increase or decrease the number of headers and footers, and enable the table's name (appears at the top of the table).
   - **Table Font Size**   Set the default font size for the table.
   - **Table Outline**   Determine whether to apply an outline to the table's outer boundaries, and what that outline should look like.
   - **Grid Lines**   Apply boundary lines to the interior grids of your table.
   - **Alternating Row Color**   Alternate the color of the rows for easier viewing.
   - **Row & Column Size**   Set the default height of rows and width of columns.
   - **Fit buttons for rows and columns**   Click to resize rows and columns to fit cell contents.

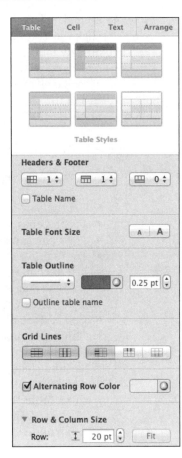

3. To make changes to single cells or groups of cells, click the Cell tab in the Format bar to see the following options:

- **Data Format** Determine how data in a cell appears and is used throughout the spreadsheet based on what type of data it is. You can allow Numbers to automatically format the data according to the type of data entered, or you can select the type of data a cell is to use. Data types are Number, Currency, Percentage, Fraction, Numeral System, Scientific, Text, Date & Time, and Duration.
- **Fill** Adjust the color fill of the cell(s).
- **Border** Adjust the color of the cell borders.
- **Conditional Highlighting** Automatically highlight cells when they match the criteria you set for them.

4. To make changes to the text of a cell or table, click the Text tab in the format bar (you're already familiar with the options offered here since you've seen them in Chapters 3 and 7).

5. To make changes to the arrangement of the table or selected cells within the rest of the spreadsheet, use the options in the Arrange tab (which you're already familiar with).

iOS

To format a table and its cells in Numbers for iOS:

1. Select the part of the table you want to format:
   - For the entire table, tap the circle in its upper left corner.
   - For a single cell, tap within that cell.
   - For multiple cells, tap the first cell to see the blue outline showing the selected cell, including the blue dots in the upper left and lower right of it. Tap-and-drag the blue dots to select the desired cells.

2. To make table-wide changes:
   a. Select the table as described in step 1.
   b. Tap the Format inspector icon (paintbrush) in the toolbar.
   c. Tap the Table, Headers, or Arrange tab in the Format bar and make the desired changes.
      - Items available in the Table tab include
        - **Table Styles** Change the entire look of a table by selecting one of the predefined styles.
        - **Table Options** Enable or disable the Table Name, Table Outline, and Alternating Rows, as well as Grid Options such as Horizontal or Vertical Lines, Header Column Lines, and Header Row Lines. You can also make table-wide font settings from this section.

- Items in the Headers tab allow you to increase or decrease the number of Header Rows, Header Columns, and Footer Rows. Toggle the Freeze Rows and Freeze Columns switches to prevent addition or removal of rows and columns from a table.
- Items available in the Arrange tab include
  - **Move to Back/Front**   Allow you to position the table within the layers of the spreadsheet.
  - **Lock/Unlock**   Prevent or allow the table to be edited and/or moved.

3. To make changes to a cell or group of cells:
   a. Select the cell(s) as described in step 1.
   b. Tap the format inspector icon (paintbrush) in the toolbar.
   c. Tap the Table, Headers, Cell, or Format tab in the Format bar and make desired changes:
      - Items available in the Table and Header tabs are the same as for table-wide changes, as described in step 2.
      - Items in the Cell tab allow you to adjust the look of the text within the cell, as well as its fills and borders.
      - Items available in the Format tab let you determine how Numbers formats the data in a cell (or cells) according to the type of data entered, or you can select the type of data a cell is to use. Data types are Number, Currency, Percentage, Text, Date & Time, Duration, Slider, Stepper, Pop-Up Menu, Checkbox, and Star Rating.

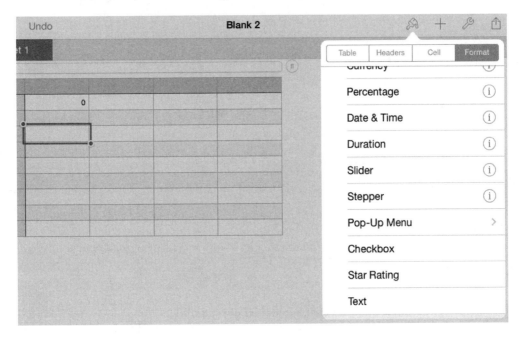

iCloud

To format a table and its cells in Numbers for iCloud:

1. Select the table and then select the part of it you want to format. When you move your pointer over a table, the cursor changes to look like a white cross. Click once on a cell to select it, or click-and-drag over multiple cells to select them.
2. To make table-wide changes:
   a. Select the entire table as discussed in step 1.
   b. Click the Table tab in the format panel. Options available in the Table tab include
      - **Table Styles**   Change the entire look of a table using the predefined styles.
      - **Headers & Footer**   Increase or decrease the number of headers and footers.
      - **Table Font Size**   Set the default font size for the table.
      - **Table Options**   Enable the table's name (appears at the top of the table)
3. To make changes to a cell or cells:
   a. Select an individual cell or a group of cells as discussed in step 1.
   b. Click the Cell tab in the format panel. Options available in the Cell tab include Font, Alignment, and Fill, all of which you're already familiar with. Checking the Wrap Text In Cell checkbox causes the text in a cell to appear on multiple lines within it, if necessary. You will also see Merge Cells if you've selected more than one cell, and we'll discuss that option a bit later in this chapter.

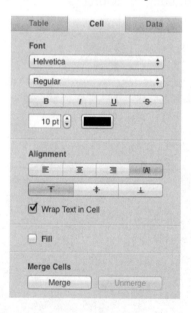

   c. Click the Data tab to select what type of data the cell(s) are formatted to use. The options are Automatic, Number, Currency, Percentage, Date & Time, Fraction, Scientific, Text, Checkbox, Star Rating, Slider, and Stepper.

Adding Controls to Cells

Numbers allows you to add controls to cells; these controls act to constrain the values in a table's cells to your specifications. For example, if you want only monetary values to appear in a cell. you'll want to restrict the number of characters that can be displayed and whether some of those numbers are rounded up or down.

 Numbers for OS X and iOS offer the same types of controls, while iCloud doesn't allow the addition of pop-up menus.

OS X

There are several different kinds of controls that you can utilize in your spreadsheet via Numbers for OS X, so let's take them one at a time.

Checkboxes and Star Ratings   Checkboxes force a cell to keep its values to binary 1 (true) or binary 0 (false), or selected and unselected, respectfully. Simply clicking within a cell with a checkbox control will either cause the cell to display a check mark (the first click) or not (the second click).
Star ratings allow you to rate items from best (5) to worst (0); a cell with this control applied to it can only be populated by stars. Click the dots that appear in the cell to make your rating.

To apply a checkbox or star rating control to a cell in OS X:

1. Select the cell or cells.
2. Click the Cell tab of the Format inspector and select either Checkbox or Star Rating using the Data Format pop-up menu.

Sliders and Steppers   Sliders and steppers are just two different ways of allowing someone to enter data into a cell without using the keyboard. Sliders use a slider menu, in which you slide a control up and down the bar to increase or decrease the amount in the cell. Steppers allow you to click either the up or down arrow to increase or decrease the amount in the cell.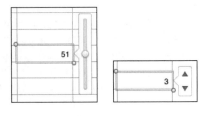
You can make modifications to the settings for both by clicking the Cell pane in the Format inspector. To add a slider or stepper to a cell:

1. Select the cell or cells.
2. Click the Cell tab of the Format inspector and select either Slider or Stepper using the Data Format pop-up menu.

Pop-up Menus Pop-up menus give a reader a list of items they can choose from to populate a cell, and they're simple to set up:

1. Select a cell or cells.
2. Click the Cell tab of the Format inspector and choose Pop-up Menu in the Data Format pop-up menu (coincidence?).
3. Edit the list of options from within the Cell pane. If the cells you selected in step 1 contain data, that data will populate the list, but you can change them if you need to. Double-click an item in the list to edit it.
4. You can add (up to 250) or remove items from the list by clicking the + or – button, respectively.
5. Use the pop-up menu under the list to specify the default state of a pop-up menu cell (Start With First Item or Start With Blank).

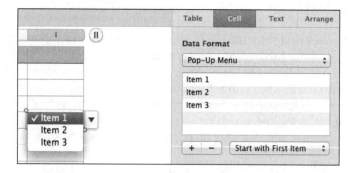

iOS

Numbers for iOS allows you to apply the same kind of controls to cells as does Numbers for OS X, but the steps differ enough that it warrants a separate section (in my humble opinion).

Checkboxes and Star Ratings Checkboxes force a cell to keep its values to binary 1 (true) or binary 0 (false), or selected and unselected, respectfully. Tapping within a cell with a checkbox control applied to it will either cause the cell to display a check mark (the first tap) or not (the second tap).

Star ratings allow you to rate items from best (5) to worst (0); stars can only populate a cell with this control applied to it. Tap the dots that appear in the cell to make your rating.

To apply a checkbox or star rating control to a cell in iOS:

1. Select the cell or cells.
2. Tap the Format inspector icon (paintbrush) and then tap Format.
3. Tap Checkbox or Star Rating (you may have to swipe up or down to see them in the list).

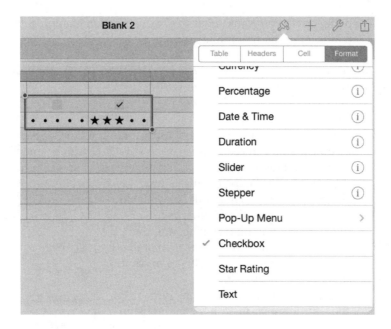

Sliders and Steppers   Sliders and steppers allow two different ways for someone to enter data into a cell. Sliders use a slider menu, in which you slide a control up and down the bar to increase or decrease the amount in the cell. Steppers allow you to tap either the up or down arrow to increase or decrease the amount in the cell.

To add a slider or stepper to a cell:

1. Select the cell or cells.
2. Tap the Format inspector in the toolbar and then tap Format.
3. Tap the Information icon (looks like an "i" within a circle) to the right of either the Slider or Stepper option (whichever one you want to use for the selected cell(s), of course).
4. In the Slider/Stepper Options window (shown in Figure 10-6), do the following:
   a. Make adjustments to the Minimum Value, Maximum Value, and/or Increment options, if needed.
   b. Tap the Information icon next to the format you want to use (under the Format section of the window) and make any settings adjustments necessary. Tap Back in the upper left of the Options window when finished.

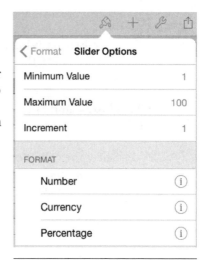

FIGURE 10-6   Adjust settings for Sliders or Steppers using the Options window.

5. Tap the format you want under the Format section to apply it to the selected cell(s).
6. Tap outside of the menu to dismiss it.

Pop-up Menus   Pop-up menus give a reader a list of items they can choose from to populate a cell, and they're simple to set up:

1. Select a cell or cells.
2. Tap the Format inspector in the toolbar and then tap Format.
3. Tap Pop-Up Menu in the list to see the Pop-Up Options window, and then do one or more of the following:

   - Tap an item in the list to edit its text; these are the items that will be available to someone using the spreadsheet.
   - Tap-and-drag the rearrange icon to the right of an item (looks like three parallel lines stacked on one another) to move it up or down in the list.
   - Tap the + button to add a new item or tap the – button next to an item in the list to delete it.
   - Determine the default state of a pop-up menu cell by selecting First Item or Blank in the Initial Value section.

4. Tap Format in the upper left of the Pop-Up Options window and then tap outside the window to dismiss it.

iCloud

While Numbers for iCloud doesn't get to take part in the fun of applying pop-up menus to cells, it does have the pleasure of applying the other controls that are available in the OS X and iOS versions.

Checkboxes and Star Ratings   To apply a checkbox or star rating control to a cell in OS X:

1. Select the cell or cells.
2. Click the Data tab of the format panel on the right side of the window and select either Checkbox or Star Rating using the Data Format pop-up menu.

Sliders and Steppers   To add a slider or stepper to a cell:

1. Select the cell or cells.
2. Click the Data tab of the format panel and select either Slider or Stepper using the Data Format pop-up menu.

3. Use the options in the Data tab to make adjustments to the slider or stepper as needed.

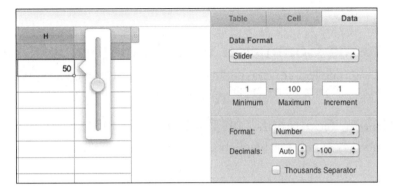

Merging and Unmerging Cells

Merging cells allows you to combine the content of two or more cells, and unmerging them has the opposite effect.

Merging cells will cause the following to occur:

- Should only one of the selected cells contain content before the merger, the merged cell will keep the content and formatting of that cell.
- Should more than one of the cells have content, all of the content is kept, however it is all converted to text.
- If the top left cell (of those selected) contains a fill color, the merged cell keeps that color.

When you unmerge cells, the formatting of the previously merged cell is kept throughout the unmerged cells.

To merge cells:

1. Select the cells to be merged.
2. Follow the procedure for the version of Numbers you're using:
   - **OS X** Choose Format | Table | Merge Cells (using the Format menu, not the Format button in the toolbar).
   - **iOS** Tap Merge in the pop-up menu.
   - **iCloud** Click the Cell tab in the format panel and click the Merge button at the bottom.

To unmerge cells:

1. Select the cells to be unmerged.
2. Follow the specific procedure for the Numbers version you're working in:
   - **OS X** Choose Format | Table | Unmerge Cells (using the Format menu, not the Format button in the toolbar).

- **iOS** Tap Unmerge in the pop-up menu.
- **iCloud** Click the Cell tab in the format panel and click the Unmerge button at the bottom.

Placing Comments and Highlighting in Cells

Commenting text and making highlights to text in Numbers are tasks that can easily be accomplished using the OS X and iOS varieties, but not iCloud, I'm afraid.

Making Comments and Highlights in OS X

To place comments or highlights in a spreadsheet while working in Numbers for OS X:

1. Click in the spreadsheet anywhere that you want to add your comment, or select the text you want to highlight.
2. Click Comment in the toolbar to open a comment window. Highlight selected items by choosing Insert | Highlight from the menu.
3. Enter your comments as desired (which is not necessary if you're simply highlighting an item).

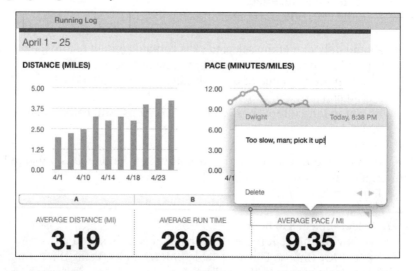

4. Click outside the comment window to make it disappear. The comment is still in the spreadsheet (denoted by a small yellow triangle in the upper right of the cell), but it's out of sight until someone wants to view or edit it.

To work with a comment or highlight in a spreadsheet in Numbers for OS X:

- Hover your mouse pointer over the comment or highlight to see it.
- Click the commented/highlighted text or item to open the comment and leave it open (until you click outside of it to make it disappear again).
- Dismiss the comment or highlight altogether by opening it and then clicking Delete in the lower left of the comment window.

Making Comments and Highlights in iOS

To place comments or highlights in a spreadsheet while working in Numbers for iOS:

1. Tap the spreadsheet in the location or on the item that you want to add your comment to, or select the text you want to highlight.
2. Tap Comment in the pop-up menu to open a comment window, or tap Highlight to do so.
3. Enter your comments if working with a comment window.

4. Tap outside the comment window to make it disappear.

   To work with a comment or highlight in a spreadsheet in Numbers for iOS:

- Tap the commented text or item to open the comment (you can tell if an item has a comment by the yellow flag or box attached to it).
- Remove a comment from the spreadsheet by tapping it and then tapping Delete in the lower left of the comment window. Remove a highlight by tapping it and then tapping Remove Highlight in the pop-up menu.

Sorting and Filtering Data in Columns

Sorting and filtering data in your spreadsheets is a great way to organize information. Sorting helps you arrange data alphabetically or numerically, while filtering lets you see only data that meets your specifications. Sorting can be done in all three versions of Numbers, but filtering can only be achieved through the power of OS X's version.

Sorting Data

Sorting can be done in each of the versions of Numbers, but it's handled a bit differently in each. Let's "sort" it all out, shall we? (I couldn't pass that one up, folks.)

 When you sort data in columns, the rows are reorganized, as you might already suspect.

Sorting in OS X   Numbers in OS X uses sorting rules to apply sorting to columns. Here's how:

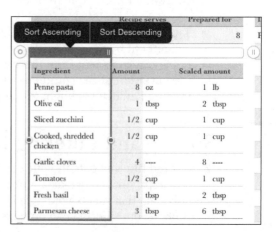

1. Decide what to sort:
   - To sort the entire table, click the table, click the Sort pane in the Sort & Filter inspector, and then click Sort Entire Table in the pop-up menu.
   - To sort only rows you select, select the rows (you already know how, right?), click the Sort pane in the Sort & Filter inspector, and then click Sort Selected Rows in the pop-up menu.
2. Click the Add A Column button in the Sort pane of the Sort & Filter inspector, and then select a column to sort by from the list.
3. Choose Ascending or Descending from the pop-up menu in the Sort By section of the Sort pane.
4. Click the Sort Now button to apply the new rule.
5. Add more rules, if needed, by performing steps 2 through 4 again; continue until you've finished adding rules. You can reorder the rules by moving your pointer over a rule and then dragging the handle (looks like three parallel lines stacked on one another) up or down the list. Delete rules by clicking the trashcan icon.

 Rows containing merged cells cannot be sorted.

Sorting in iOS   Sorting is a shade simpler in iOS, but you also don't have as much control as in OS X. Regardless, here's how we do it:

1. Tap the table.
2. Tap the bar above the column you want to sort.
3. Tap Sort in the menu.
4. Tap Sort Ascending or Sort Descending to sort the column.

Sorting in iCloud   Sorting columns in iCloud is even easier to do than in iOS, but again, you still don't have the level of control that you do with OS X:

1. Click the column you want to sort.
2. Click the black arrow next to the header name.
3. Select Sort Ascending or Sort Descending from the menu.

Filtering Data

Filtering data in a table is a great way to remove all the clutter when you simply want to see only the information you specify. For example, if you're looking at a table that lists your bills for the month, you could apply a filter that only shows you bills that are due this particular week.

 None of the data is removed from your table, so don't have a conniption when some of it disappears when you apply a filter rule. The data is simply hidden until either you modify the rule specifications or delete the filter altogether.

To create a filtering rule (remember, this applies to OS X only):

1. Select the table and then click the Sort & Filter icon in the toolbar.
2. Click the Filter tab and then click the Add A Filter button. Select a column from the list to apply the filter to.
3. Select a rule from the Choose A Filtering Rule menu. Scroll up or down to see the full list, or click the various topics to see different kinds of rules.

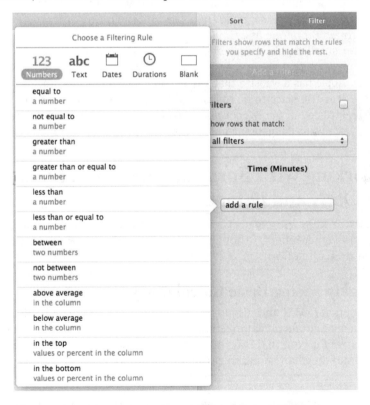

4. You can add more filtering rules by clicking the "or" button under the first rule (and subsequent ones after that).
5. Turn filtering on or off for the table by selecting or unselecting the Filters box on the Filter tab.

You can't create or edit filters in Numbers for iOS, but you can turn filters on or off in spreadsheets you're viewing that contain them (this is a no go in iCloud, though). Tap the table, tap the circle in the upper left corner of it, and then tap Turn Filters On/Off.

Formulas (and Functions) for Success

Formulas and functions are applied to some cells to make them automatically perform calculations based on criteria you specify, and then display the results. They're downright crucial to the creation and usability of some spreadsheets, to say the least. Numbers has you covered when it comes to adding and editing these rascals (all three versions of Numbers are quite skilled at handling them, thank you very much).

Numbers for OS X and iCloud are quite similar in how they work with formulas and functions, but working with them in iOS is a different ballgame.

There are lots of ways to work with formulas and functions in Numbers. Some are crazy-simple to use, and others can simply drive you crazy if you let them. Let's go through them one at a time and I suspect you'll come out of this section of the chapter smelling like a rose by the time we're done.

Apple has a website that I refer to as the Formulas and Functions Bible because it is THE place to go to learn all there is to know about every formula and function included in the iWork suite of apps. Please pay a visit to the following address to see what I'm gabbing about: http://help.apple.com/functions/mac/4.0/.

Working with Formulas and Functions in OS X and iCloud

Since working with formulas and functions is so similar in the OS X and iCloud versions of Numbers, I thought I'd just lump them both together to save us all a little time and effort.

Quickly Seeing Basic Calculations

Numbers for OS X and iCloud allow you to select a range of cells and instantly see basic calculations for them. Simply select some cells, and the values are immediately displayed for you. In OS X, the values are shown at the bottom of the window, while in iCloud they can be found at the top (just underneath the sheet tabs).

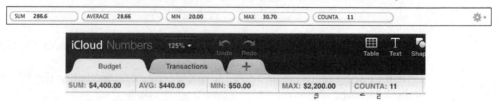

The values that you can view in iCloud are fixed to Sum, Average, Minimum, Maximum, and Count. However, the values you can view in OS X can be changed. Click the gear icon to the right of the values at the bottom of the window and you can select the values you want to display.

Quickly Adding Functions to Cells in OS X (not iCloud)

You can add to a cell a function that will display a value based on cells you select within your spreadsheet. To do so:

1. Select the cell that you want to display the result (called the results cell).
2. Click the Function button in the toolbar and select a function from the pop-up menu.
3. Double-click the results cell; the function editor appears, as does a blue box that encapsulates the selected cells that are used to calculate the value in the results cell. From here, you can
   - Drag the handles on the blue box to resize the selection of cells.
   - Move the selection to new cells (the size of the selection won't change, so no worries there).
4. Click the green check mark to save changes to the cell, or click the red × to remove the changes from the cell.

Performing Basic Arithmetic Functions (Add, Subtract, Multiply, Divide)

You can easily insert simple formulas based on the most basicy-basic (yes, I just coined a new phrase) of arithmetic functions: good ol' addition, subtraction, multiplication, and division. By the way, all four of them are available in both OS X and iCloud. Bonus!
   To add these arithmetic standbys to your spreadsheet:

1. Select the cell where you want the result to display (again, this is the results cell).
2. Type the equal sign (=) to open the formula editor.
3. In iCloud only, enter a left parenthesis, (,to begin your formula.
4. Click a cell to use as your first argument in the formula, or you can enter a value.
5. Enter a basic arithmetic operator (+ , – , *, or /).
6. Click the cell you want to use as the next argument in the formula, or enter a value.
7. Keep adding operators and arguments until you've finished building your formula, as I've done in Figure 10-7.
8. In iCloud only, enter a right parenthesis,), to end the formula.
9. Press RETURN (or ENTER on a PC) or click the green check mark to save the formula to the results cell; clicking the red × will cancel the whole gig.

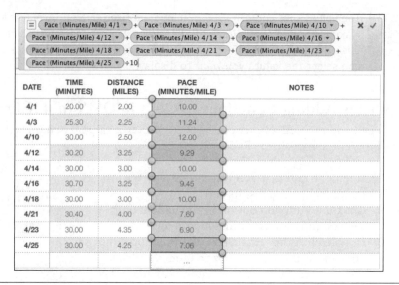

FIGURE 10-7 Creating a formula using the selected cells in the table

Comparing Values in Cells

Numbers in OS X and iCloud can compare the values in cells that you select and enter the result of the comparison in another cell (quick: what's that cell called?).

1. Select the cell that you want to be the results cell.
2. Type the equal sign (=) to open the formula editor.
3. Click the first cell you're using in the comparison, or manually enter a value.
4. Type a comparison operator (>, > =, =, < >, <, or < =).
5. Click the next cell being used in the comparison, or enter a value manually.
6. Press RETURN (or ENTER on a PC) or click the green check mark to save the formula to the results cell; click the red × to cancel the comparison.

The results cell will display TRUE or FALSE, depending on whether the comparison meets the criteria in the formula.

Using Numbers' Predefined Functions

The good folks at Apple have loaded Numbers with 250 functions that they've already defined for you, so you don't have to do all that dirty work yourself (okay readers, drop your books and run around your home, office, library, or wherever you are, waving your arms and shouting "Long live Apple!"). The Function Browser is the tool in Numbers that will help you find the function you're needing for a particular instance.

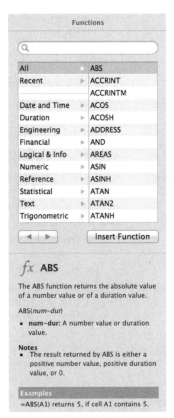

1. Select the cell that you want to be the results cell.
2. Type the equal sign (=) to open the formula editor and the Function Browser (which is displayed on the right side of the window).
3. Type a function name (if you know what you're looking for) in the search field at the top of the Function Browser, or simply browse the list of functions.
4. Double-click the name of the function you want to use, and it will appear in the formula editor.
5. Click an argument within the function.
6. Decide which cells you want to use in your calculation in one of these ways:
   • Click each cell you want to use.
   • Drag across the range of cells you want to use.
   • Select just a single row or column.
7. The cell references are displayed within the formula in the formula editor.
8. Press RETURN (or ENTER if using a PC) or click the green check mark in the formula editor when finished. Click the red × to cancel the entire operation.

Changing Arguments Within Functions

Uh oh! You've built a function but suddenly realize you used the wrong arguments within it! Oh, well...looks like your spreadsheet is hosed and you'll have to start all over, sorry.

Not!

Fixing this is a breeze:

1. Double-click the results cell containing the formula you want to change, and the formula editor opens.
2. Do any of the following:
   • Add more cell references by clicking in the argument area of the function and clicking the cells you want to add.
   • Change a cell reference by clicking the cell reference you need to change and selecting the cell you want to replace it with.

- Remove cell references altogether by clicking in the argument area of the function, clicking the references you want to get rid of, and pressing the DELETE key.

3. Press RETURN (or ENTER if on a PC) or click the green check mark in the formula editor when finished making changes. Simply click the red × if you want to toss your changes to the wind.

Preventing Row and Column References from Changing in Formulas

If you don't want the row and column references in your formulas to be monkeyed with, it's a good idea to lock them down. This is a good way for you to use a formula in other parts of your spreadsheet without having to go into the formula to edit the cell references.

To perform this fantastic feat:

1. Double-click the results cell containing the formula you want to change; the formula editor opens.
2. Click the triangle in the cell range you want to lock down.
3. Click the Preserve Row box and/or the Preserve Column box.

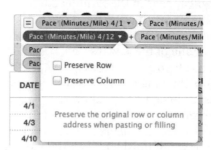

4. Press RETURN (or ENTER on a PC) or click the green check mark in the formula editor to save your changes, or click the red × to cancel the changes.

Working with Formulas and Functions in iOS

I'll bet you were thinking I'd forgotten all about one of our trio of Numbers buddies. No worries; it's time to tackle formulas and functions with Numbers for iOS!

Summing the Values of Selected Cells

You can quickly add the values of cells you select within your spreadsheet:

1. Double-tap the cell that you want to be the results cell (where the results of your formula's calculations appear).

2. Tap the keyboard button (looks like a black circle containing two parallel white lines) to open the functions keyboard.
3. Tap the Sum button.
4. Tap-and-drag the selection handles in the spreadsheet to modify the range of cells used in the calculation. You can also select cells that are discontiguous by tapping one cell and then tapping a discontiguous one.
5. Tap the green check mark in the input bar to accept the changes, or click the red × to cancel them.

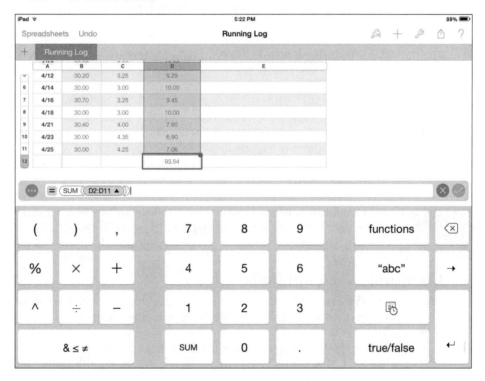

Using Simple Arithmetic Functions to Create Formulas

You can use plain old addition, subtraction, multiplication, and division to build some pretty extensive or fairly simple formulas with Numbers for iOS.

To add these arithmetic basics to your spreadsheet in iOS:

1. Double-tap the cell that you want to be the results cell.
2. Tap the keyboard button (looks like a black circle containing two parallel white lines) to open the functions keyboard.
3. Tap a cell to use as your first argument in the formula, or you can enter a value.
4. Tap a basic arithmetic operator (+, –, *, or /).

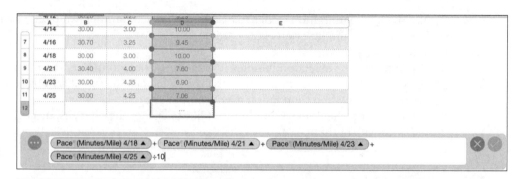

FIGURE 10-8 Creating a formula in Numbers for iOS using the selected cells in the table

5. Tap the cell you want to use as the next argument in the formula, or enter a value.
6. Continue adding operators and arguments until you've finished building your formula, as I've done in Figure 10-8.
7. Tap the green check mark in the input bar to accept the changes, or click the red × to cancel them.

If the cell references in the input bar are too many to fit within its viewing area, simply swipe up or down in the viewing area to see all of them.

Comparing Values in Cells

Numbers in iOS can compare the values in cells that you select and enter the result of the comparison in another of the spreadsheet's cells (the results cell). Here's the skinny:

1. Double-tap the cell that you want to be the results cell.
2. Tap the keyboard button (looks like a black circle containing two parallel white lines) to open the functions keyboard.
3. Tap the first cell you're using in the comparison, or manually enter a value.
4. Tap the button underneath the operators (in the very lower left corner of the screen) to open the keyboard containing the comparison operators.
5. Tap a comparison operator (>, > =, =, < >, <, or < =) to use it in the calculation.
6. Tap the next cell being used in the comparison, or enter a value manually.
7. Tap the green check mark in the input bar to accept the changes, or click the red × to cancel them.

The results cell will display TRUE or FALSE, depending on whether the comparison meets the criteria in the formula.

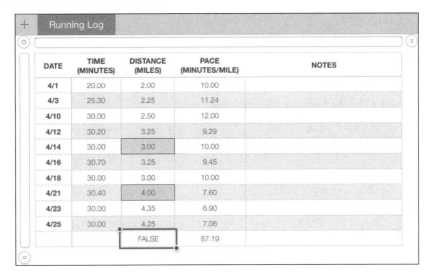

DATE	TIME (MINUTES)	DISTANCE (MILES)	PACE (MINUTES/MILE)	NOTES
4/1	20.00	2.00	10.00	
4/3	25.30	2.25	11.24	
4/10	30.00	2.50	12.00	
4/12	30.20	3.25	9.29	
4/14	30.00	3.00	10.00	
4/16	30.70	3.25	9.45	
4/18	30.00	3.00	10.00	
4/21	30.40	4.00	7.60	
4/23	30.00	4.35	6.90	
4/25	30.00	4.25	7.06	
		FALSE	87.19	

Using Numbers for iOS's Predefined Functions

Just like its desktop cousins, Numbers for iOS has 250 functions built right in that are already defined for you. The Function Browser is the tool in Numbers for iOS that you will use to find the functions you need.

1. Double-tap the cell that you want to be the results cell.
2. Tap the keyboard button (looks like a black circle containing two parallel white lines) to open the functions keyboard.
3. Tap functions in the keyboard, and then tap Categories.
4. Tap a category, and then tap a function to place it in your formula; you'll see it in the input bar. Swipe up and down to see the full list of functions, if needed. You can tap the Information icon (looks like a circle containing an "i") next to a function to learn more about it.
5. Tap the green check mark in the input bar to accept the changes, or click the red × to cancel them.

Changing Arguments Within Functions

Changing an argument within a function you've already created is simple:

1. Double-tap the results cell containing the formula you want to change, and the formula editor and keyboard open.
2. Do any of the following:
   - Add more cell references by tapping in the argument area of the function and tapping the cells you want to add.
   - Change a cell reference by tapping the cell reference you need to change and tapping the cell you want to replace it with.

- Remove cell references altogether by tapping in the argument area of the function, tapping the references you want to get rid of, and tapping the Delete key on the keyboard.

3. Tap the green check mark in the input bar to accept the changes, or click the red × to cancel them.

Preventing Row and Column References from Changing in Formulas

If you want to use a formula in other parts of your spreadsheet without having to go into the formula to edit the cell references, Numbers for iOS allows you to freeze them:

1. Double-tap the results cell containing the formula you want to change; the formula editor opens.
2. Tap the triangle on the token for the cell range you want to freeze.
3. Toggle the Preserve Row switch and/or the Preserve Column switch for the beginning and ending references.

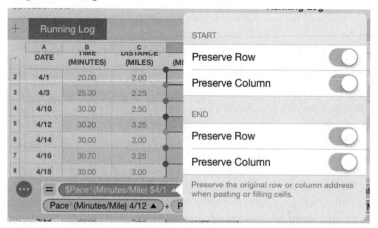

4. Tap the green check mark in the input bar to accept the changes, or click the red × to cancel them.

Using String Operators, Wildcards, Arguments, and Values

Way back in Chapter 1, I mentioned where you go to get help for each of the apps in the iWork suite. Well, here's where you'll put that knowledge to the test.

Numbers' help system, in all three versions, is top notch, and it's where you'll want to go to find out the definitions and descriptions of the types of arguments and values you can use within formulas and functions. You'll also be able to find out how string operators and wildcards can be used to build conditions within said formulas and functions. Discussing these items here would require a forest of trees to print the tomes, and your home or office would need a small warehouse to contain those tomes, so we'll have to leave these to the digital realm.

Charting the Course

Charts hold a special place in the world of spreadsheet apps because they can help someone get an almost instant understanding of the data that populates a spreadsheet. I love the fact that charts are affected by the raw data only; if the data changes, the chart changes—just that simple. There's no need to manually change every bit of data in the chart or manually adjust the graphic representations within the chart. Numbers handles it all on-the-fly. As a matter of fact, you can't change data directly within a chart in Numbers; data in your tables controls that.

Creating charts is limited to the OS X and iOS versions of Numbers. Sorry, iCloud fans.

Understanding Chart Types

Numbers is chock-full of all kinds of chart types, and each one is better at displaying different types of information than another may be. There's a chart to help represent your information in stages, to make broad comparisons, to show how pairs of values work together...you name it, there's a chart for it. You can gain a great understanding of every kind of chart available in Numbers from within Numbers itself. The Template Chooser in all three versions of Numbers contains a template called Charting Basics; this is the manual for knowing what charts you have at your disposal and what kinds of data they're best suited to display. Open the template and click the sheets to discover Numbers' charts.

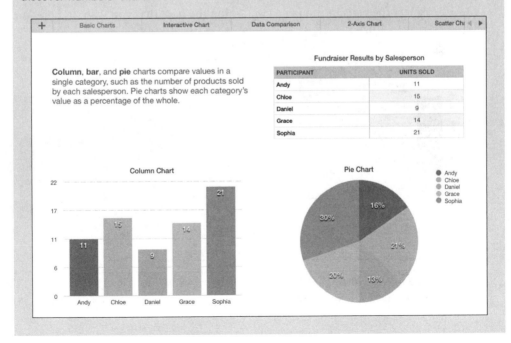

Adding and Placing Charts

You can add charts to spreadsheets in Numbers for OS X and iOS in two ways:

- Create a new chart and add data afterward.
- Create a new chart by using data that already exists.

OS X

To create a chart and add data after:

1. Click the Charts button in the toolbar.
2. Click either the 2D, 3D, or Interactive tab to select a chart type. Choose a chart by clicking it in the pop-up menu or by dragging-and-dropping it into the spreadsheet. Click the right and left arrows to peruse the chart variations. If you select a 3D chart, you can click-and-drag the rotation controls in its center to rotate it to the angle you want to use (pretty cool, huh?).
3. Click the Add Chart Data button.
4. Select the cells within the table that contain the data you want to populate your chart with, as shown in Figure 10-9. Use the pop-up menu in the very lower left of the window to change whether rows or columns are plotted as data series.
5. Click Done at the bottom of the window when you're finished.

Delete a chart by selecting it and pressing your keyboard's DELETE key.
To create a chart using existing data:

1. Select the cells in the table containing the data that you want to populate your chart with.

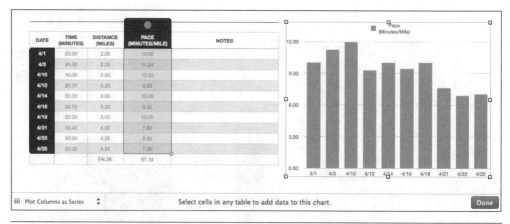

FIGURE 10-9 Notice that the chart on the right is populated with the data I've selected in the table on the left.

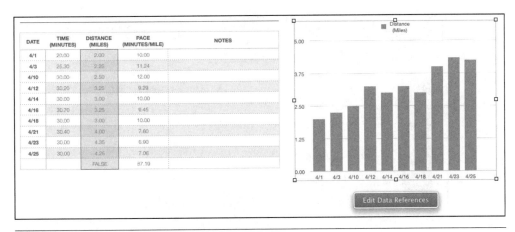

FIGURE 10-10   Click Edit Data References to change the data used in the chart.

2. Click the Charts button in the toolbar. Click either the 2D, 3D, or Interactive tab to select a chart type. Choose a chart by clicking it in the pop-up menu or by dragging-and-dropping it into the spreadsheet. Click the right and left arrows to peruse the chart variations. If you select a 3D chart, you can click-and-drag the rotation controls in its center to rotate it to the angle you want to use.

3. Click the Edit Data References button to change the data used to populate your chart (illustrated in Figure 10-10).

4. Use the pop-up menu in the very lower left of the window to change whether rows or columns are plotted as data series.

5. Click Done at the bottom of the window when you're finished.

iOS

To create a chart and add data after:

1. Tap + in toolbar and then tap the Chart tab.

2. Tap 2D, 3D, or Interactive, and then tap a chart to add it to your spreadsheet. Swipe left or right to see more chart styles.

3. Drag the chart to the location you want it to occupy in the spreadsheet.

4. Tap the chart, and then tap the cells in the table that contain the data you want to populate your chart with, as shown in Figure 10-11.

5. Tap the gear icon in the toolbar to change whether rows or columns are plotted as data series.

6. Tap Done in the toolbar when finished.

Delete a chart by selecting it and tapping Delete in the menu.

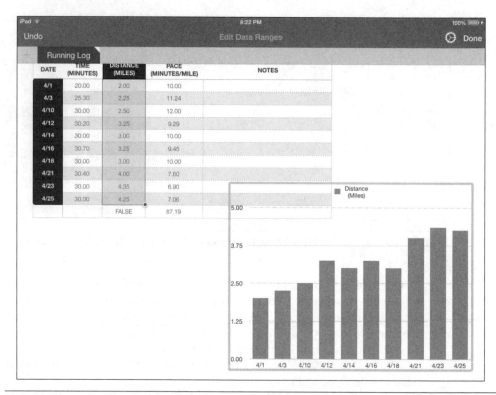

FIGURE 10-11 The chart is populated with the data I've selected in the table.

To create a chart using existing data:

1. Select the cells in the table that contain the data you want to populate your chart with.
2. Tap Create Chart in the menu. Tap 2D, 3D, or Interactive, and then tap a chart to add it to your spreadsheet. Swipe left or right to see more chart styles.
3. Drag the chart to the location you want it to occupy in the spreadsheet.
4. Tap the gear icon in the toolbar to change whether rows or columns are plotted as data series.
5. Tap the chart and tap Edit References if you need to change the data it uses (see Figure 10-12).
6. Tap Done in the toolbar when finished.

Adjusting a Chart's Appearance

Even the prettiest of charts may need to be changed to better suit the rest of the spreadsheet or other documents it may be presented with. Numbers for OS X and iOS are old hands at helping you easily make any adjustments necessary.

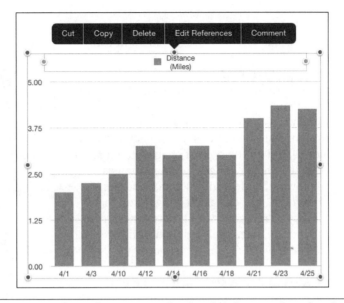

FIGURE 10-12   Tap Edit References to change the data used in the chart.

OS X

To make changes to charts using Numbers in OS X:

1. Select the chart to edit; this action opens the Charts Format bar.
2. Make changes to your chart using options in the tabs available (the options under each tab vary greatly depending on the type of chart you're using):
   - **Chart**   Make changes to items such as the overall style, fonts, colors, shadows, and the like. You can also change the type of chart you're using, which may render some of your changes null and void if they're not supported for the new chart type you select.
   - **Axis**   Change the type of scale for your axis, enable value labels, edit gridlines, and more.
   - **Series**   Edit the way your data series are displayed in the chart.
   - **Arrange**   Make targeted changes to your chart's location in the spreadsheet.

iOS

To make changes to charts using Numbers in iOS:

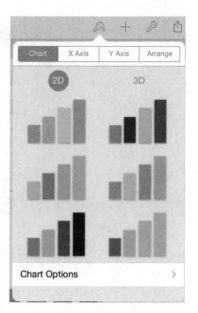

1. Select the chart to edit.
2. Tap the Format inspector icon (paintbrush) in the toolbar.
3. Make changes to your chart using options in the tabs available (the options under each tab vary widely based on the type of chart you're using):
   - **Chart** Make changes to items such as the overall style, fonts, colors, shadows, and more. You can also change the type of chart you're using, which may render some of your changes null and void if they're not supported for the new chart type you choose.
   - **X Axis and Y Axis** Change the type of scale for your axis, enable value labels, edit gridlines, and more.
   - **Series** Edit the way your data series are displayed in the chart.
   - **Arrange** Change the order of the chart in regard to other elements in your spreadsheet by moving it forward or backward, and determine how to wrap text around the chart.

Summary

Wow, that was a workout! Chapter 10 is full to the brim with info on filling tables and charts with data, formatting cells, getting familiar with functions and formulas, and removing the barnacles off your boat. Oops, that last one was edited out of the chapter due to length—sorry about that.

11

Looks Aren't Everything... But They Don't Hurt

HOW TO...

- Work with images and shapes in Numbers
- Add audio and video to a spreadsheet
- Layer and group spreadsheet objects
- Add text to a spreadsheet
- Perform basic editing and commenting

As the title of this chapter states, looks aren't everything, but they don't hurt (not that I would know...), and this can't be more true in the realm of office and personal documents than it is for the lowly spreadsheet. Poor spreadsheet: the best it could hope for, until Numbers, was perhaps multicolored rows and columns. Please don't misunderstand; I'm perfectly aware that you can add images and other objects to spreadsheets in Excel and other such apps, but let's face it—none can touch Numbers for the ease in which you can perform such a miracle. If you've worked with Pages and Keynote, you will easily understand that last statement, but if not, let's look at how simple sprucing up spreadsheets in the world of Numbers can be.

Putting Some Pizzazz in Spreadsheets

When I say "spruce up" your spreadsheets, I don't mean to turn them into coniferous trees, but to transform them into showpieces, rather than simply black and white rows and columns of data. Through the use of images, audio and video, and shapes, you can turn even the most mundane of information into a feast for the eyes, and Numbers is eager to play your willing assistant.

Using Images

Numbers is as adept at using, placing, and editing images as its word processing and presentation-creating iWork cousins. As with Pages and Keynote, Numbers also uses templates containing image placeholders as one way to work with images. These placeholders are simply suggested places within a spreadsheet that you can replace with your own images.

Let's check out how to place and work with images in each version of Numbers.

Adding Images to a Spreadsheet

Each version of Numbers (OS X, iOS, and iCloud) makes it easy to insert images into spreadsheets, with or without placeholders.

OS X   There are four über-easy ways you can get images into your spreadsheets when working in Numbers for OS X:

- Drag an image from the Finder into your spreadsheet and drop it into place.
- Click the Insert menu and select Choose, browse your Mac for the image you want, select it, and then click Insert.
- Click the image button in the lower right corner of an image placeholder (the button looks like an illustration of a mountain and the sun) and choose an image from your iPhoto or Aperture library.
- Click the Media button in the toolbar and choose an image from your iPhoto or Aperture library.

iOS Adding images to a spreadsheet using Numbers for iOS is simple:

1. Tap + in the toolbar and then tap the Media tab (its icon contains a musical note), or tap + in an image placeholder (lower right corner).
2. Tap an image to select it; Numbers only shows you images that are stored on your device.

iCloud Do one of the following to add an image to a spreadsheet in Numbers for iCloud:

- Drag an image from the Finder (or your PC's desktop) and drop it in the spreadsheet wherever you desire.
- Click the Image button in the toolbar, click the Choose Image button, browse your computer for the image you want, and then click Choose.

Masking (Cropping) an Image

To mask an image is to hide parts of it that you don't want to be seen in your spreadsheet, but all the while the actual image itself remains unchanged. It's kind of like cutting a hole in a piece of construction paper, and then placing the hole over the face of someone in a picture; the rest of the picture is unharmed, but all that is visible is the face in the hole. The task of masking is performed very similarly throughout each version of Numbers:

1. Double-click (or double-tap if in iOS) the image you want to mask to show the masking controls. The default mask is set to the original size of your image.
2. Use one of the following techniques to mask your image:
   - Drag the slider to resize the image.
   - Drag the image itself to reposition it within the mask window.
   - Move the mask by dragging its border.
   - Resize the mask by dragging its handles.

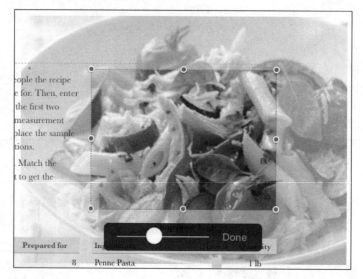

3. Click or tap Done when finished masking the image. You can also simply click or tap outside of the mask window.

Removing Parts of an Image

The Instant Alpha tool in Numbers for OS X or iOS (iCloud doesn't yet support this feature) allows you to hide parts of an image you don't want shown in your spreadsheet, while leaving the original image unchanged. Imagine making a copy of a picture and then cutting out the background, and you've got a rough idea of how Instant Alpha works.

OS X   To use Instant Alpha in Numbers for OS X:

1. Select the image you're working with.
2. Click the Instant Alpha button in the Image tab of the Format bar.
3. Use the targeting tool (looks like a square containing cross hairs) to find the color you want to remove from the image. The targeting tool is only visible when the pointer is over the selected image.
4. Click to begin removing the selected color from your image. Drag to remove more of the color (and those surrounding it). Hold down the OPTION key while dragging and all instances of the color will be removed from the image instantly. Hold the SHIFT key while dragging to add colors back to your image.
5. Click Done when your task is complete.

 Zoom into the image for more precise control of color removal.

iOS   To use Instant Alpha in Numbers for iOS:

1. Select the image.
2. Tap the Format inspector (paintbrush) icon in the toolbar.
3. Tap the Image tab, and then tap Instant Alpha.
4. Touch-and-drag your finger over the area (or color) that you want to remove in the image. The more you drag, the more of the color, and those surrounding it, is removed. As in OS X, zooming in on the image will give you greater control over what elements you remove.
5. Tap Done when finished.

Adjusting Color Levels in an Image

Sometimes colors within images can appear muted (especially in older ones) or can go to the opposite end of the spectrum and pop right off the screen (or page). Numbers for OS X allows you to adjust color levels in an image so that you can make corrections or add effects as suits your needs. iOS and iCloud versions of Numbers don't offer this handy feature, however.

To make color adjustments to an image in Numbers for OS X:

1. Click to select the image.
2. Click the Image tab in the Format bar.

3. Make basic adjustments with the Exposure and/or Saturation sliders. You can also click Enhance to let Numbers make automatic adjustments.
4. Click the slider button (located between the Enhance and Reset buttons) for more advanced color features. Clicking this button opens the Adjust Image window, which gives you 12 different options for making changes you like. You can also reset the image to its default color settings from this window.

Adding and Revising Shapes

Adding shapes (boxes, circles, lines, etc.) is another way in which you can introduce a little punch to an otherwise yawn-inducing spreadsheet. Numbers has a nice selection of shapes already built-in, but you can always draw your own as well (in OS X only).

Adding Shapes to Your Spreadsheets

While you can only use the OS X version of Numbers to draw your own shapes, all three versions of Numbers are capable of adding shapes to spreadsheets.

OS X To add a shape using Numbers for OS X:

1. Click the Shape button in the toolbar.
2. Choose a shape from the pop-up menu and click it. Use the gray dots at the bottom of the menu or the left and right arrows found on either side of the menu to scroll through the myriad of options.
3. Click-and-drag the shape to place it anywhere within your spreadsheet.
4. Adjust the shape's size by clicking-and-dragging its handles.

iOS   To add a shape using Numbers for iOS:

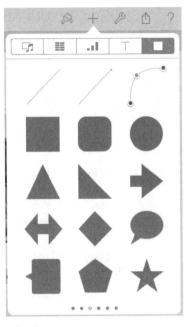

1. Tap the + button in the toolbar.
2. Tap the Shape tab (simply looks like a square). Swipe to the left or right to see more shapes in the menu.
3. Tap-and-drag a shape to the location you want to place it in your spreadsheet, and then remove your finger from the screen to drop it in.
4. Adjust the size of a shape by dragging its handles.

iCloud   To add a shape using Numbers for iCloud:

1. Click the Shape button in the toolbar.
2. Click the shape to place it in the spreadsheet.
3. Drag the shape to the location you prefer within your spreadsheet.
4. Use the options in the Shape tab of the format panel (right side of the window) to change the color and other attributes of the shape.

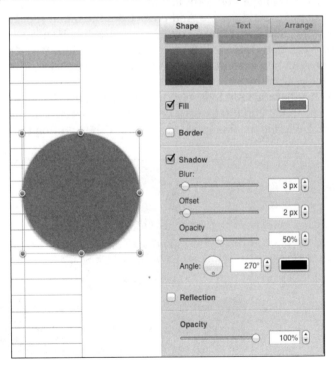

Adding Text to Shapes

Numbers for OS X and iOS allow you to add text inside of a shape (not so for the iCloud version), very similarly to adding text to a text box.

 Tip   You can change the format of text (font, color, etc.) within a shape just as you can within a text box.

To add text to a shape using Numbers for OS X or iOS:

1. Double-click (OS X) or double-tap (iOS) the shape.
2. Type your text once the cursor appears inside the shape. If the text doesn't fit within the shape, you can trim the text, change the font size, or resize the shape by dragging its selection handles until the text fits properly.

Editing a Shape's Curves

With Numbers for OS X (not iOS or iCloud), you can edit the curves of an image using sharp lines or curved lines. This is one way that you can create your own shapes, without having to start from scratch (which I'll show you how to do in a bit).

To edit the curves of a shape using Numbers for OS X:

1. Select the shape you want to edit.
2. Choose Format | Shapes And Lines from the menu (not the Format button in the toolbar) and select Make Editable from the list. Handles now appear on the edges of your shape (along with tips on how to use them), as shown in Figure 11-1.
3. Drag the handles to create new shapes. Double-click a handle to change the kind of line it produces:
   • A square handle tells you the handle creates sharp (straight) lines.
   • A circle handle tells you the handle creates curved lines.
4. Click outside the shape when you're finished editing the curves.

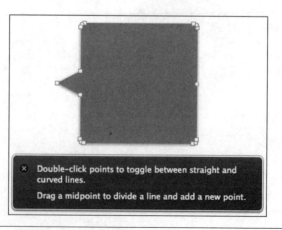

FIGURE 11-1   Drag the handles to modify a shape.

Move your mouse over the edges of the shape when editing curves to reveal the midpoint handles (they're hidden), which you can use to make even more changes.

Changing Attributes of Some Shapes

You can change certain attributes of some shapes within the OS X and iOS versions of Numbers. These shapes include the star, pentagon, arrows, speech balloons, and the rounded-corner square. Changing a shape's attributes would be something like adding more points to a star, making the stem of a speech balloon longer or shorter, and stuff like that.

To change a shape's attributes:

1. Select the shape.
2. When the handles appear, you'll notice that one or more of them are green. These green handles allow you to make the attribute changes.
3. Drag the green handles to discover how you can modify the shape.
4. Click (OS X) or tap (iOS) outside of a shape to stop modifying it.

Drawing Your Own Shapes

Numbers in OS X (only) allows you to draw your own shapes, using the high and mighty Pen tool. Be warned that using the Pen tool effectively can take time to master.

Here's how to use the Pen to create your own shapes:

1. Click the Shape button in the toolbar and click Draw With Pen at the bottom of the menu, as shown in Figure 11-2.
2. Click the area on the page where you want to begin your drawing. This action creates the first point on the screen, which is a red square.
3. Click another area on the screen to place the second point. This action will draw a straight line between the points. To create a curved line, click the area where the second point goes and begin dragging.
4. To finish creating your shape, click the first point made to close it, or press ESC to leave it open.

Including Video and Audio

Numbers for OS X and iOS make it really easy to add audio or video to your spreadsheets, which would most assuredly make yours stand out from the crowd during your office's next "meeting of the minds." Numbers for iCloud doesn't get to join in the multimedia fun, though.

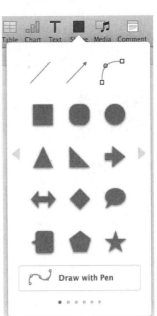

FIGURE 11-2 Click Draw With Pen to create your own shapes in Numbers for OS X.

OS X

Add audio or video to a spreadsheet using Numbers for OS X in one of two ways:

- Drag the audio or video file from the Finder and drop it into the spreadsheet.
- Click the Media button and choose a file from the Music tab or Movies tab.

Adjust audio or video playback options by selecting the audio or video in the spreadsheet and clicking the Audio tab or Movie tab in the Format bar. The following options are available for your tinkering pleasure:

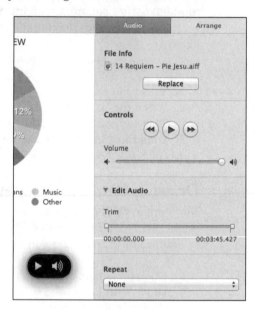

- **Controls**   Forward, Reverse, Play, and Volume are all available.
- **Edit Audio/Movie**   Trim the audio or movie to play only the parts you want. If you are using a movie, you will see a Poster Frame option, which allows you to select which frame of the video displays when the video isn't playing.
- **Repeat**   Select None to play the file only once, Loop to continuously play the file from beginning to end over and over, or Loop Back And Forth to have the file play forward and then backward over and over again.

 If you want your movies to play on an iPad or iPhone, you'll need to enable the option to Optimize Movies For iOS in the General tab of Numbers for OS X's Preferences (choose Numbers | Preferences from the menu to open them).

iOS

To add a video using Numbers for iOS:

1. Tap the + button in the upper right of the toolbar.
2. Tap the Media button (its icon contains a musical note).
3. Tap either Camera Roll or My Photo Stream and find the video you need.
4. Tap the video and then tap Use to place it in your spreadsheet.

Adjusting playback options is a simple enough task:

1. Tap the audio or video.
2. Tap the format inspector icon (paintbrush) and then tap the Movie tab.
3. Choose from these playback options: None, Loop, or Loop Back And Forth.

Changing the Appearance of Objects

After you've populated your spreadsheets with objects such as shapes and images, you may be wondering whether you can make changes to them after the fact. The answer is, of course, yes.

You can make many changes to objects, such as:

- Adding effects, such as shadows and reflections
- Changing or adding fills to text boxes and shapes
- Adding or editing borders around them
- Adjusting the opacity of images and shapes
- And more, depending on the type of object selected

To change the appearance of objects in spreadsheets using Numbers for OS X or iCloud:

1. Select the image, shape, or text box you want to adjust.
2. Click the Format button in the toolbar (OS X only).
3. Select the Style, Text, Arrange, Image, or other various tabs (depends on the type of object you select) to make changes to your spreadsheets objects.

To change the appearance of objects in spreadsheets using Numbers for iOS:

1. Tap to select the object you want to make changes to.
2. Tap the Format inspector icon (paintbrush) in the toolbar.
3. Tap the Style, Image, Arrange, Text, or other tabs (again, depending on the type of object selected) to make changes to the selected object.

Aligning, Moving, Resizing, and Rotating Objects

The position of an object within your spreadsheet is crucial to presenting information effectively. Placing your company logo over a critical chart probably won't score points with the boss. Finding the right spot in your spreadsheets for objects is simple, using any version of Numbers.

OS X

There are several ways to position objects in Numbers for OS X.

- Position objects based on page coordinates:
  1. Select the object you want to move.
  2. Click the Arrange tab in the Format bar.
  3. Enter x and y coordinates in the Position fields.

- Position objects on a vertical or horizontal axis:
  1. Select the object you want to move.
  2. Click the Arrange tab in the Format bar.
  3. Click the Align pop-up menu and choose an option.

- Position objects evenly:
  1. Select three or more objects you'd like to move.
  2. Click the Arrange tab in the Format bar.
  3. Select an option from the Distribute pop-up menu. The Evenly option places even spacing between all the objects vertically and horizontally. The Horizontally option only spaces them evenly on a horizontal axis, and the Vertically option spaces them evenly on a vertical axis.

- Position objects one or more points at a time:
  1. Select the object you need to move.
  2. Press an arrow key once to move one point at a time. Hold down the SHIFT key while pressing the arrow key to move ten points at a time.

iOS

Alignment guides show you how items line up together visually onscreen, making object arrangement so much simpler than not having guides at your disposal. The three types of alignment guides in Numbers for iOS are

- **Center**   Displays when the center of the selected object aligns with the center of another object or the center of the page.
- **Edge**   Displays when the edges of the selected object align with the edges of another object.
- **Spacing**   Displays when three or more items are spaced equally apart on a straight line.

Turn on alignment guides easily:

1. Tap the Tools icon and tap Settings.

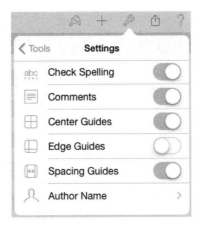

2. Toggle the switches next to the guide types you want to enable. A guide is enabled if its toggle switch is green.

You can also position objects by moving them one or more points at a time. Touch-and-hold an object with one finger, and then swipe anywhere else on the screen with another finger in the direction you want to move the object. You can even move the item several points at a time when swiping with two or more fingers:

- 2 fingers = 10 points
- 3 fingers = 20 points
- 4 fingers = 30 points
- 5 fingers = 40 points

iCloud

Alignment guides are employed in Numbers for iCloud, too, making it so much simpler to position objects in spreadsheets. The same three types of alignment guides are available as for Numbers in iOS:

- **Center**   Displays when the center of the selected object aligns with the center of another object or the center of the page.
- **Edge**   Displays when the edges of the selected object align with the edges of another object or the edges of the page.
- **Spacing**   Displays when three or more items are spaced equally apart on a straight line.

To enable alignment guides, click Tools in the toolbar, hold your pointer over Settings, and then click each guide type you want to use. A check mark will appear next to enabled guides.

You can also position objects based on page coordinates in iCloud:

1. Select the object.
2. Click the Arrange tab in the format panel.
3. Enter x and y coordinates in the Position fields.

Staying Close: Layering and Grouping Objects

Grouping objects allows you to move more than one object at once. This is convenient if you've got objects spaced just right and discover that you need to move all of them to a different location, but want to retain your spacing (without having to figure it out all over again).

Grouping objects in Numbers for OS X and iCloud is performed in similar fashion:

1. Select the objects you want to be grouped:
   - **OS X** Hold down the SHIFT key while clicking each object.
   - **iCloud** Hold down the ⌘ key (Mac) or CONTROL key (PC) while clicking objects.
2. Click the Arrange tab in the Format bar (OS X) or format panel (iCloud).
3. Click the Group button to group the objects (you can also click the Ungroup button to undo the grouping of objects).

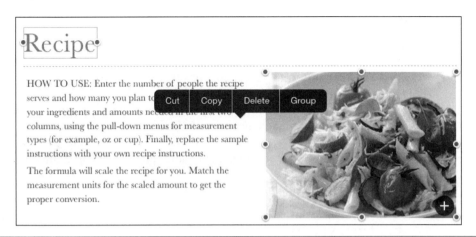

FIGURE 11-3   I'm grouping an image and a text box in this spreadsheet.

To group objects in Numbers for iOS:

1. Touch-and-hold the first item.
2. Tap other items while continuing to hold the first.
3. Lift both fingers from the screen.
4. Tap Group in the pop-up menu to group the items (tap Ungroup to undo the grouping), as shown in Figure 11-3.

Adding and Editing Text

You already know that you can add text to cells in your spreadsheets, but that's not what we're referring to in this chapter. Here, in this section of Chapter 11, we're focusing on adding blocks of text, such as descriptions for items in your spreadsheets, instructions on how to use the spreadsheet, information about the author, or anything else you can type (or tap) on a keyboard.

Texting It Up

When you create a new spreadsheet using the Template Chooser, you could select a template that contains text boxes already. If so, adding your own text is almost sinfully simple: click or tap a text box and start typing.

Yes, that's all there is to it.

"But, I want to add my own text boxes!," you shout. Well, here are the ABCs of doing so, using all three versions of Numbers.

OS X

To create a text box in OS X:

1. Click the Text button, whose icon looks like a T (not Mr. T, mind you), in the toolbar.
2. Choose the type of text box you want to use and drag-and-drop it from the Text window into your spreadsheet, or just click it and it will appear in the middle of the spreadsheet window.
3. If you want to move the text box, click-and-hold the text and drag the box to the position you'd like it be. Ta-da!

iOS

To create a text box in iOS:

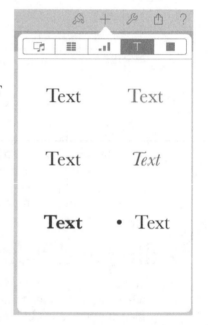

1. Tap + in the toolbar.
2. Tap the Text tab in the window; it looks like a T (again, no relation to "Mister").
3. Choose the kind of text box you want to add to the spreadsheet and tap it.
4. To move the text box, tap-and-hold the text and drag the box to its new position.

iCloud

To create a text box in iCloud:

1. Click the Text button in the toolbar; shockingly, it also looks like a T. The text box simply appears in the spreadsheet.
2. Format the text box using the Shape, Text, and Arrange tabs in the Format pane on the right side of the window.
3. To move the text box, simply click-and-hold the text and drag the box to where you'd like it to be.

Adjusting Formatting and Appearance of Text

Properly formatting text is extremely important to conveying the information in your spreadsheet in an appropriate manner. For example, you probably won't want to use the Comic Sans MS font for showing your company's quarterly profits. **Just sayin'.**

OS X

As when working with objects in your spreadsheets, all the text formatting action takes place in the Format bar in Numbers for OS X. The text options are on the right side of the spreadsheet window whenever you select text in the spreadsheet (the Format inspector should be selected in the toolbar, of course, or you won't see them at all).

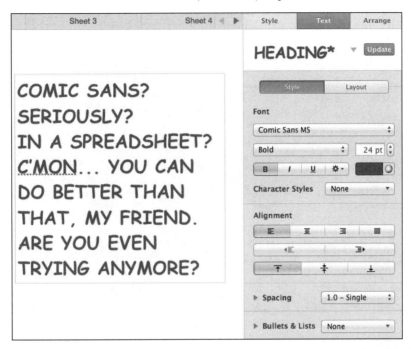

The Style tab lets you make formatting selections for the actual text box. You can add and change elements such as borders, fills, shadows, and the like.

To choose a font for your text, click the Font pop-up menu in the Text tab (click the Style button if it's not selected) of the Format bar and select one from the list (scroll up and down to see all the available fonts). Adjust the font's appearance by changing its typeface, size, color, and so on from within the Text tab. There are more options in the Layout section of the Text tab, as well, which you can use to set up indents, tabs, columns, and such.

 Click the gear icon (to the right of the Underline button) in the Style section of the Text tab to access advanced options like baseline, ligatures, strikethrough, and more.

The Arrange tab of the Format bar helps you to align the text to the left side, center, or right side, as well as justify the text (aligning it to both the left and right margins).

iOS

You can make adjustments to text formatting in Numbers for iOS in a couple of different ways: by making changes to the entire text box at once or by manually changing the text itself.

To make changes to the entire text box at once:

1. Tap the text box to select it.
2. Tap the Format icon (the paintbrush) in the toolbar.
3. Use the options within the Style, Text, and Arrange tabs to format the text.

To make manual changes directly within the text:

1. Tap the text inside the box to select it.
2. Tap the Format icon (paintbrush) in the toolbar.
3. Use the options within the Style, List, and Layout tabs to format the text.

iCloud

To change the appearance of text in Numbers for iCloud:

1. Select text in the spreadsheet to open the format panel. To make changes to the entire text box at once, just select the box and not the text within it.
2. Use the options in the Text tab to make adjustments to your text.

Check Yur Spelling

I've personally nevver misspelled a werd in my life, but sum of you reeders probabley hav. Thankfully, for you chronick misspelllers, Numbers can automatically chek for spelleng errors and replase them for you. Numbers is also really big helpful with us grammar too I bet that's a relief to you bad grammar people.

(Sincere apologies to my editors for the preceding paragraph!)

OS X

The OS X version of Numbers is on patrol for spelling errors and makes corrections by default. Numbers displays misspelled words with a red-dotted underline. If you type a misspelled word and Numbers catches it, the misspelling is automatically corrected and temporarily underlined with a blue-dotted line. You can also correct a misspelled word yourself by CONTROL-clicking (or right-clicking) it and choosing the correct spelling from the pop-up menu.

Spell-checking options can be found by choosing Edit | Spelling & Grammar. Your options are as follows:

- Show Spelling and Grammar opens the Spelling and Grammar window, which is discussed following this list.
- Check Document Now forces Numbers to check spelling immediately.
- Check Spelling While Typing is enabled by default and the aforementioned red-dotted line underlines misspelled words.
- Check Grammar With Spelling causes possible grammatical errors to be underlined with a green-dotted line, and misspelled words are still displayed with the familiar red-dotted underline.

The Spelling and Grammar window in Numbers for OS X contains some options not available in the iOS and iCloud versions:

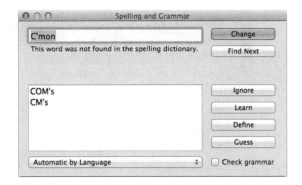

- Misspelled words are displayed in the top field and possible corrections are shown in the lower field. Click the Find Next button to move to the next misspelled word in the spreadsheet.
- Select a word in the list of possible corrections and click Change to use it.
- Click Ignore to force Numbers to skip the word.
- Click the Learn button to add the word to Numbers' dictionary (if Numbers doesn't have a word in its dictionary, it will think it's misspelled).
- Click Define to have Numbers look up the meaning of the word in a dictionary.
- Click Guess to have Numbers make spelling suggestions to you.
- Check the Check Grammar box to enable this feature.
- Force Numbers to automatically correct misspelled words based on a particular language set.

iOS

Spell checking is an easy task in Numbers for iOS:

1. Tap the Tools icon (wrench) in the toolbar.
2. Tap Settings.
3. Toggle the Check Spelling switch on (green) or off (white). Misspelled words are displayed with a red-dotted underline when this feature is enabled.
4. Tap a misspelled word and then tap one of the suggested corrections. If no suggestions are offered, tap the right arrow, tap Replace, and then tap the correct word spelling from the offerings.

iCloud

Checking spelling within Numbers for iCloud is just as effective and easy:

1. To turn spell checking on or off, click Tools in the toolbar, choose Settings, and then click Check Spelling. Numbers is on spelling patrol when a check mark is displayed next to the option. Misspelled words are displayed with our friend, the red-dotted underline.
2. Click a misspelled word and then do one of the following:
   - Select the correct spelling from the list.
   - Type the correct spelling.

Summary

At last, we've traversed the landscape of Numbers! You now have the tools at your disposal to deliver spreadsheets that would make even the most stalwart and focused of accountants reach for the tissues. That well-deserved raise is on the horizon, my friend!

A

Keyboard Shortcuts

Pages, Keynote, and Numbers are already fairly straightforward in their approaches to working (and/or playing), but there's another little trick up their sleeves: the venerable keyboard shortcut! Keyboard shortcuts are used almost universally when it comes to apps, especially for common tasks such as printing, copying, pasting, and the like. However, we're mainly concerned here with identifying the keyboard shortcuts that are germane to the iWork apps themselves (although I'll certainly list some of the common ones as well, since many of you may still be fairly new to the Mac).

There are dozens of keyboard shortcuts available within iWork. We'll cover the most important and frequently used shortcuts here, but you can access the full list for each app in its own Help, accessed by the following URLs in your favorite web browser (Safari, anyone?):

Pages for OS X	http://help.apple.com/pages/mac/5.1/#/tan014c3bd19
Keynote for OS X	http://help.apple.com/keynote/mac/6.1/#/tan951def1c9
Numbers for OS X	http://help.apple.com/numbers/mac/3.1/#/tan6f3e4ba25
Pages for iCloud	http://help.apple.com/pages/icloud/1/#/gil27154d872
Keynote for iCloud	http://help.apple.com/keynote/icloud/1/#/gilf0fb207d1
Numbers for iCloud	http://help.apple.com/numbers/icloud/1/#/gil466289a0b

As you've probably guessed, these keyboard shortcuts are used only by the OS X and/or iCloud versions of the iWork apps, since the iOS versions don't rely on a physical keyboard for input.

Happy shortcutting!

Universal Shortcuts

Action	Shortcut	OS X	iCloud
Open an existing document	⌘-O	Yes	No
Open a new document	⌘-N	Yes	No
Close the Template Chooser	ESC	Yes	No
Save	⌘-S	Yes	No
Save as	⌘-S-OPTION-SHIFT	Yes	No
Duplicate	⌘-S-SHIFT	Yes	No
Close current window	⌘-W	Yes	No
Close all windows	⌘-W-OPTION	Yes	No
Bold text	⌘-B	Yes	Yes
Italic text	⌘-I	Yes	Yes
Underline text	⌘-U	Yes	Yes
Increase indent	TAB	Yes	Yes
Decrease indent	TAB-SHIFT	Yes	Yes
Add a line break	SHIFT-RETURN	Yes	Yes
Add a paragraph break	RETURN	Yes	Yes
Cut selected items	⌘-X	Yes	Yes
Copy selected items	⌘-C	Yes	Yes
Paste copied or cut items	⌘-V	Yes	Yes
Find	⌘-F	Yes	Yes
Find next	⌘-G	Yes	Yes
Find previous	⌘-G-SHIFT	Yes	Yes
Group selected items	⌘-G-OPTION	Yes	Yes
Ungroup selected items	⌘-G-OPTION-SHIFT	Yes	Yes
Lock selected items	⌘-L	Yes	No

Action	Shortcut	OS X	iCloud
Unlock selected items	⌘-L-OPTION	Yes	No
Add a hyperlink to selected text	⌘-K	Yes	No
Undo an action	⌘-Z	Yes	Yes
Redo an undone action	⌘-Z-SHIFT	Yes	Yes
Print	⌘-P	Yes	Yes
Select all	⌘-A	Yes	Yes
Deselect all	⌘-A-SHIFT	Yes	Yes
Select a word	Double-click the word	Yes	Yes
Select a paragraph	Triple-click the paragraph	Yes	Yes
Minimize the current window	⌘-M	Yes	No
Quit the app	⌘-Q	Yes	No
Open app preferences	⌘-,	Yes	No
Hide app	⌘-H	Yes	No
Show rulers	⌘-R	Yes	No
Jump to the next selection	⌘-J	Yes	Yes
Open Fonts window	⌘-T	Yes	No
Open Colors window	⌘-C-SHIFT	Yes	No

Pages-Specific Shortcuts

Action	Shortcut	OS X	iCloud
Open a new document in the Template Chooser	⌘-N-OPTION	Yes	No
Open a new document in the Template Chooser	Select the template and press RETURN	No	Yes

Keynote-Specific Shortcuts

Shortcuts Used While Playing a Presentation

Action	Shortcut	OS X	iCloud
Play open presentation	⌘-P-OPTION	Yes	No
Next slide	RIGHT or DOWN ARROW	Yes	No
Previous slide	LEFT or UP ARROW	Yes	No
Pause	F	Yes	No
Pause and show black screen	B	Yes	No
Pause and show white screen	W	Yes	No
Show slide number	S	Yes	No
Show pointer	C	Yes	No
Reset timer	R	Yes	No
Scroll presenter notes up	U	Yes	No
Scroll presenter notes down	D	Yes	No

Playing Movies in Presentations

Action	Shortcut	OS X	iCloud
Pause/play	K	Yes	No
Jump to beginning	L	Yes	No
Jump to end	O	Yes	No
Rewind (if paused)	J	Yes	No
Fast forward (if paused)	L	Yes	No

Note There are no Numbers-specific shortcuts, so please don't think that section was mysteriously missing from your copy of the book. Sorry, but they're all like this.

Glossary

alignment guides   When enabled, appear as you move an object to help you align it properly with other objects.

Apple ID   An account you can set up for free with Apple that allows you to access multiple services offered by everyone's favorite fruit-named company.

bidirectional text   Text that doesn't know whether it's coming or going. Just kidding. Some languages, such as Hebrew and Arabic, are written from right to left, while others (English, for instance) are written from left to right. iWork supports the use of both kinds of text.

cell   A single block in a table or spreadsheet in which you can add content.

column break   Starts a new line at the top of the next column.

cursor   Displays where you are currently working in the document. Also known as the insertion point.

Dictionary   OS X's built-in dictionary and thesaurus app.

formula   Mathematical equations placed in cells to automatically calculate data from other cells in a document.

hyperlink   A website link applied to text that sends those who click it to the associated website.

iCloud   Apple's web-based service that allows you to save documents, music, and other data for access across all of your devices, such as your Mac, iPad, iPhone, and even Windows-based computers.

iCloud.com   Website that allows you to log in using your Apple ID and access the web versions of Pages, Keynote, Numbers, and a host of other online apps (such as Mail).

iOS   The operating system that runs every iPad, iPhone, and iPod touch on the planet (and perhaps other planets as well, but I've not been able to confirm that as of this writing).

insertion point   Displays where you are currently working in the document. Also known as the cursor.

Instant Alpha tool   Used to make some areas of an image transparent.

invisible   A hidden character that denotes where special formatting, such as a line break or page break, has been applied.

iTunes   Apple's multimedia "Swiss Army knife" of an app that can be used to listen to and purchase music, watch and purchase movies and television shows, sync iOS devices with your computer, and much more. In iWork's case, iTunes can help move documents to and from said iOS devices.

Keynote   iWork app that handles creation, management, and display of presentations.

line break   Starts a new line but not a new paragraph.

masking   Hiding portions of an image.

master objects   Objects that appear in the same place and in the same format in the background of every page in a document.

Numbers   Part of the iWork suite of apps, enables the user to easily build spreadsheets and present data through charts and tables.

object   Literally anything you can place within a document (text, shapes, images, etc.).

object style   A collection of preset characteristics (border, shadow, color, etc.) that can be applied to an object to quickly format it.

OS X   The operating system that ships with every Apple computer.

page break   Starts a new line at the top of the next page.

page layout document   Basically, a totally blank canvas ready for you to add anything you like to it.

Pages   iWork's word processing and page layout app.

Pages EndNote plug-in   A plug-in that you can download from Apple's App Store to allow you to use the third-party bibliography and citation app, EndNote, with Pages.

paragraph style   A collection of preset text characteristics (font, color, size, etc.) that can be applied to a paragraph to quickly format it.

phonetic guide   When enabled, appears with words that are written in the supported Chinese, Japanese, or Korean languages to help English speakers pronounce them correctly.

placeholder   Text or images in a template that you can replace with your own while retaining its formatting.

QuickTime Player   Apple's default media player. All audio and video files used in iWork documents must be supported by QuickTime. Go to http://support.apple.com/kb/ht3775 to see a list of supported file formats.

section   An area of a document that contains its own unique formatting, such as headers, footers, page numbers, and so on. A document can contain multiple sections.

selection handles   Small markers that denote the corners and edges of selected objects. Can be clicked-and-dragged or tapped-and-dragged to reshape or resize an object.

Smart Quotes   When enabled, automatically turns quotation marks into curly quotation marks.

template   A collection of document, presentation, or spreadsheet elements that contains predefined font settings, text and graphical layouts, and the like. A template can be modified to fit whatever the user's needs may be without tampering with the original template.

Template Chooser   Contains a list of templates available for the user to help them create new documents.

toolbar   Located at the top of every open document, provides quick access to many of the most commonly used tools via distinct buttons.

word processing document   A document that contains a body text area and contains mostly text.

Index